The Hidden
Pierre Elliott Trudeau

The Hidden
Pierre Elliott Trudeau
The Faith Behind the Politics

Edited by:
John English
Richard Gwyn
P. Whitney Lackenbauer

© 2004 Novalis, Saint Paul University, Ottawa, Canada

Cover design: Christiane Lemire
Cover photograph: Jean-Marc Carisse / www.carisse.org
Layout: Richard Proulx

Business Office:
Novalis
49 Front Street East, 2nd Floor
Toronto, Ontario, Canada
M5E 1B3

Phone: 1-877-702-7773 or (416) 363-3303
Fax: 1-877-702-7775 or (416) 363-9409
E-mail: cservice@novalis-inc.com
www.novalis.ca

Library and Archives Canada Cataloguing in Publication

The hidden Pierre Elliott Trudeau : the faith behind the
politics / edited by Richard Gwyn, John English, P. Whitney Lackenbauer.
——

Papers from a conference held at St. Jerome's University, Waterloo, Ont., May 9-10, 2003.
Includes bibliographical references.
ISBN 2-89507-550-6

1. Trudeau, Pierre Elliott, 1919–2000–Religion. I. Gwyn, Richard, 1934–
II. English, John, 1945– III. Lackenbauer, P. Whitney

FC626.T7H52 2004   971.064'4'092   C2004-904381-1

We acknowledge the financial support of the Government of Canada through the Book Publishing Industry Development Program (BPIDP) for our publishing activities.

5 4 3 2 1   08 07 06 05 04

"...I naturally asked myself questions about the truth of all this, and about the meaning of freedom, predestination, and liberty of choice and so on. But to have asked questions of yourself about it, I think is not too important. Let's say that I remained – I remain – a believer."

Pierre Elliott Trudeau, *Against the Current*

Table of Contents

Prologue

To start by committing the single literary crime for which no forgiveness is attainable, namely that of quoting myself, I wrote this about Pierre Trudeau and religion in my biography, *The Northern Magus*, now almost a quarter-century ago:

> Brebeuf [College] anchored him for life to the Catholic Church. He isn't entirely a conventional Catholic and doesn't accept all its dogmas. "I believe in the Protestant rule of conscience and that you must not deliberately hurt others." But the church, as an institution, he accepts totally. He rarely misses Sunday mass; through his twenties he went to mass daily with his mother. (Twice as Prime Minister, when Margaret demurred, he went to Christmas Eve midnight mass with John and Geills Turner.) After his audience with the Pope in 1969, an aide remembers that on the overnight flight home, "he stayed wide awake all night, his eyes open, and shining."

That was it. A half-paragraph, with no analysis and a couple of anecdotes deployed to fatten out the chronicle. By comparison, there were pages and pages on Brébeuf and on the Jesuit mystique, with loving references to the legacies, the pursuit of excellence, the supremacy of mind over matter, the Zen-like technique of winning arguments by extending an opponent's proposition to its illogical, logical absurdity, that the Jesuits had imprinted onto Trudeau.

There was nothing exceptional about this minimalism. No reviewer remarked on or criticized the neglect of this aspect of Trudeau's formation and personality. (As a comparison, imagine any chronicler of Trudeau failing to discuss the influence upon him of the fact that he was Québécois, or that he was rich.) Neither, more strikingly, did any of Trudeau's friends or cabinet ministers or aides comment in public or in private about the absence of any discussion of Trudeau's faith, even though many were well aware of its importance to him, or actively shared his interest and commitment, or just knew that it mattered to him because they had had to arrange – while on trips abroad or during election campaigns, and always in a way that would not attract the attention of accompanying reporters – for him to attend Sunday mass at some suitable church or chapel. Except for the extended exposition given by Stephen Clarkson and Christina McCall to Trudeau's interest in the 1930s Catholic doctrine of Personalism and of his familiarity with the writings of Emmanuel Mounier in their two-volume biography of him, this lack of attention to or comment about Trudeau's faith persisted throughout his life.

There was of course Trudeau's famously fiercely guarded sense of privacy, that *noli me tangere* quality that kept almost everyone at their distance except a few intimate friends such as Gerard Pelletier. About religion, his reticence was especially protective. He wrote voluminously about all manner of topics, from the law and the constitution to political science, philosophy, economics. His own published references to religion were all fleeting. In *Against the Current* he wrote: "I naturally asked myself questions about the truth of all this, and about the meaning of freedom, predestination, and liberty of choice and so on. But to have asked questions of yourself about it, I think is not too important. Let's say that I remained – I remain – a believer." In his *Memoirs* he wrote briefly about Personalism. It was "[a philosophy] that reconciles the individual and society.... It was thus that the fundamental notion of justice comes to stand alongside that of freedom in my political thought." And he gave an interview on the topic to the *United Church Observer* in 1971. In it, he declared as his creed, and as a summary of the *credo* that all Catholics believe in or they are not Catholics, "I believe in life after death, I believe in God, and I am a Christian." That was extraordinarily little for someone who practised his faith his entire life, who never missed Sunday mass, who went often on spiritual retreats that extended over days and on occasions over weeks, who read and reread the Gospels and the Bible, who read omnivorously philosophy and church history and doctrine, and who was fascinated by all expressions of spirituality, perhaps most particularly by Buddhism, and who discussed philosophy at length and with intense rigour with friends. Someone, finally, who went through a crisis of faith after the tragic death of his son Michel, and who found the cause, and the courage, to return to his faith before his death.

The times made a considerable difference. Today, it has become a cliché to remark that a critical difference between the U.S. and Canada is that Americans are far more religious than Canadians. This cross-border disparity has always applied. Except that it used to be the other way around. Until the mid-1960s, two-thirds of Canadians regularly attended church on Sundays while only four in ten Americans did. Then Canadians converted to secularism. The most dramatic change was in Quebec, where nationalism displaced the Church as society's organizing principle. At the same time, right across the country people turned away from the established churches and embraced liberalism and non-judgmental tolerance and moral relativism. (Why it is that Americans should have become increasingly religious over time is another story.) Trudeau appeared in the public's view at exactly the moment when Canadians were turning away from religion. He not only mirrored the prevailing liberalism of Canadians, he personified it and magnified it. Trudeau first impressed himself upon Canadians' consciousness when, as justice minister in 1967, he brought down a package of reforms to the Criminal Code. His descriptive phrase, "The state has no place in the bedrooms of the nation," entered the national vocabulary. The point here is that Trudeau's mid-1960s changes in the laws concerning divorce and about the de-criminalization of homosexuality and of abortion contradicted the teachings of his Church. He was performing, this is to say, as a prototypical, secular liberal leader. So Canadians, a great many of them, assumed then and for decades afterwards that he himself was, like most of them, a secular liberal.

It was only when he died that most Canadians realized Trudeau had lived his life as a deeply believing and a scrupulously practising Catholic. His funeral service in the Cathedral of Notre Dame in Montreal, the languages used alternating between French, English, and Latin, was most striking in its naturalness. The service was grand and sonorous, at times theatrical, at other times achingly tender. But despite its grandeur it was above all an intimate, a family, affair in which all in the congregation, whether or not they themselves were Catholic, understood and accepted fully the centrality to Trudeau of his faith. From the later commentary on hot-line shows and letters to the editor, it was clear that a great many Canadians were surprised and intrigued to learn that someone so liberal and individualistic, so rational and so intimidatingly intelligent, should have been all his life a faithful member of a creed that they viewed, to the extent they knew or cared to know anything about it at all, as authoritarian and obscurantist.

"He haunts us still," Clarkson and McCall wrote in a memorable epitaph about Trudeau. His last haunting legacy to Canadians was, perhaps, to have sent out to them the message that the pursuit of excellence that he strived for his entire life encompassed not only the intellectual and the physical – the perfect canoe stroke, the books read from cover to cover without a single word skipped – but, every bit as much, the spiritual, the doctrinal, the philosophic, the religious. And for him to have done this in the manner of a true educator, without having said anything about it at all, let alone to have preached about it.

* * *

The conference of which this volume contains the presentations and discussions, as well as this commentary and the concluding one by co-chair John English, came about in part because of a healthy coincidence of self-interests. As chancellor of St. Jerome's University in the University of Waterloo, I was glad to have a chance to showcase some of the considerable talents of this 140-year-old Catholic institution of higher learning. For his part, John English, then at work on a three-volume authorized biography of Pierre Trudeau, was glad to have the chance to assemble many of those best informed about Trudeau's spirituality. Getting enthusiastic approval and wholehearted support for the proposed seminar, *The Hidden Pierre Trudeau: His Spirituality, His Faith, His Life, His Times,* from St. Jerome's President Michael Higgins took, almost literally, less than a minute.

There was a fair bit more to it than just this. As an inquiry into the religious life and thoughts of a well-known public figure, the seminar, insofar as those who organized it could determine, was the first of its kind in Canada and was most unusual in any country. Novelty is not in itself of any great consequence. But it is relevant to the nature of the undertaking.

Most probably it could not have been staged at all, nor could it have attracted so easily so many knowledgeable speakers and participants, had it been held much earlier than its actual dates of May 9–10, 2003. In previous times, many would have found the project odd, or embarrassing, or presumptuous, or, the most damaging reaction of all, irrelevant. Some time in the 1970s, religion became privatized in Canada. This is a condition well beyond the firmly established one of the separation of church and state. Religion became something that individuals did or, much more often, did not do, entirely by themselves, like a private passion for orchids or for old maps. In public discourse, it became virtually an irrelevancy. Occasionally, a particular established church would be criticized severely, as often as not justifiably, over specific transgressions such as the manner of the operation of residential schools for Native peoples, or over sexual scandals. But religion's intellectual and moral contributions to the collectivity shrank to the marginal, and to the near-invisible.

It would be a gross exaggeration to say that religion, at the start of the twenty-first century, again plays a significant role in Canadian life and thought. Rather, if hardly reborn, religion is no longer in retreat.

The evidence is suggestive rather than conclusive. The most recent of the regular surveys of Canadians' attitudes towards religion by University of Lethbridge sociologist Reginald Bibby shows a definite uptick in interest. At St. Jerome's University itself, there has been a noticeable increase in the number of students explaining that what attracted them to the institution was that it is, unapologetically, an institution of faith. The extraordinary appeal of Mel Gibson's *The Passion of the Christ* – if appeal is the right word to apply to so brutal an epic – surely reveals an underlying and seldom expressed wonder about and a searching for religion. Even the incredible sales (seven million copies in print) of the savagely anti-Catholic novel *The Da Vinci Code* constitutes a back-handed recognition of the enduring attraction of the religious narrative. Most recently, the annual Couchiching Conference, that quintessential expression of the deep Canadian faith in talking about all problems from all points of view, chose in 2004, and for the first time in its long history, to debate faith (or aspects of it) under the title *Religion, Pluralism and the Secular Society*. It does seem pretty clear that there is out there an unsatiated hunger for something more than the material and the comfortable.

Anyone's guess why this should be so is as good as the next person's. In the kind of consumption-obsessed society that we have become, whenever any commodity becomes scarce, it gains in value. Maybe the very fact that so many now come of age with almost no experience of or knowledge about religion and its mysteries and its ceremonies has served to motivate some young people to search out what it was that once inspired their parents, or, more commonly, their grandparents.

Even without searching for it, people today hear the word "religion" far more than they did a few years ago. It is cited, of course, in any discussions about the causes of global terrorism. Less dramatically, but as substantially, religious precepts and ethical values get cited in the debates now underway about how society should deal with issues such as genetic engineering. Once, human beings were assumed to be distinct because they were made in the image of God. Now that they can be made in their own image, the very meaning of humanity is called into question, which rather leaves secularism at a dead end. In this country, as well as in some other industrial nations, religion has become part of the regular political discourse; as a result of multiculturalism and immigration, issues such as public funding of religious schools, the establishment of *sharia* courts, the validity of distinguishing religious apparel such as turbans and head scarves, and the need for the inclusion into labour contracts of multiple religious holidays now have to be debated. The religious convictions of such world leaders as U.S. President George W. Bush and British Prime Minister Tony Blair are well known. In Canada, some members of the public have taken note of and have been intrigued by the fact that, but for the brief intermission of Kim Campbell, all of Canada's prime ministers have been Catholics (and in most instances practising Catholics) back to Trudeau in 1968, or now for almost forty continuous years. It is not a conspiracy, but it has to be more than coincidence, and has something to say about religion's role in infusing an individual with a sense of public duty.

To put it simply, religion today is more relevant than it has been in a long time, if undoubtedly as deserving as ever of criticism. It was not only because of politeness, therefore, that no commentator questioned the holding of a seminar on Trudeau's spirituality as being in any way odd, embarrassing, presumptuous, or irrelevant.

One commentator who would have reacted in the same accepting way would surely have been Trudeau himself. Had he been alive, he would of course have detested people discussing so private a part of himself. But he would also have wondered why it took them so long to get around to it, after having for so many years so thoroughly deconstructed everything else about him. In his presentation to the seminar, the writer Bruce Powe recalled that in 1998 he talked with Trudeau about a conference to be held later that year in order to review and debate every aspect of his life and doings, from politics to economics to the constitution to foreign policy. Included in this list, reported Powe, was to be a paper about Trudeau and religion by Michael Higgins, then newly appointed as president of St. Jerome's. Trudeau's response was: "At last." The deed has at last now been done fully. Whether it was done well is for the reader to judge.

Richard Gwyn

Editor's Note

In his 1978 biography, *Trudeau*, George Radwanski quoted a Liberal insider who predicted, "Somebody is going to say some day, 'Will the real Mr. Trudeau please stand up,' and about fifty-eight people will rise."[1] Restated in a more constructivist way, perhaps each of fifty-eight people will have something different to say about the Pierre Trudeau they knew. Claire Hoy captured the competing and contradictory images associated with Trudeau's public portrait when he described him as "the most maddening, pleasing, perplexing, loved, hated, worshipped, vilified, vulgar, sophisticated, stubborn, passionate, obnoxious, arrogant, frivolous, brilliant politician this country has ever produced."[2] The myriad opinions reflect his own complexity and his profound influence on Canadians' lives. For decades, commentators have sought to explain the influences on his life – his formative years in Quebec, his political philosophy, the principles guiding his actions – and the enigma that he remains. Even after his passing, much remains hidden about a man whose intensity in public dialogue and debate was matched by an intense silence on private matters.

This book is based upon the conference *The Hidden Pierre Trudeau: His Spirituality, His Faith, His Life, His Times*, held at the University of Waterloo and St. Jerome's University, Waterloo, Ontario, in May 2003. Prime Minister Jean Chrétien's opening message to the conference set its context, and indicated its importance:

> Pierre Trudeau's convictions and his dream for a modern Canada set in motion forces of change that are still shaping the soul of our people and our nation. His motto was: *"Reason over Passion."* Yet it was his passion for Canada that defined him. Indeed, it was his vision of a just society that captured the imagination of the country, and forever changed an entire generation of Canadians.

His intellect, achievements and individual style have sparked intense study and debate. However, I am very pleased that this conference is devoted to studying qualities of perhaps lesser public focus but, no doubt, of equal importance: the faith and spirituality that shaped his character and his leadership. A faith from which I know he derived great private sustenance through the many challenges he faced over the remarkable journey of his life.

This book makes available for present and future generations the reflections of Trudeau's friends and political contemporaries, biographers, journalists, and scholars. Their presentations provide insight into, and will stimulate continued debate about, the spirituality, faith, life, and times of one of Canada's best-known public figures.

Most of the contributions to this collection are transcripts of oral presentations at the conference, edited for clarity and readability rather than content. There has been no attempt to impose a standard voice or style on the contributions. Instead, the editor has tried to retain the language and tone of the speakers. Several scholarly papers, which allowed various speakers to expand upon their arguments and to include references to source materials, have also been included. Presentations that reflected on faith and public life but did not deal with Trudeau and his times have not been included in this book.

In addition to the individual presentations, the symposium also featured interesting exchanges of ideas amongst the panellists and the audience. Several excerpts from these discussions are included herein. The discussion on "Trudeau's Spiritual Pilgrimage" contains excerpts from the discussion panel on that theme, as well as an exchange from that on "Faith and Personal Experience." The discussion in Part IV comprises excerpts from two separate discussions. Given the overlap of themes, I chose to group the comments together. The discussions found in Part V and Part II followed presentations on "Faith, Politics and Personal Experience" and "Religion and Politics in Quebec" respectively.

For those readers who wish to explore experiences and themes dealt with in the various presentations, I have provided a selected list of further readings related to Pierre Trudeau, his times, and the Catholic Church in Canada.

The conference from which these papers are derived would not have been possible without the generous support of various organizations and individuals. Conference sponsors – Canadian Heritage/Patrimoine canadien, the *Catholic Register*, the Donner Canada Foundation, Dr. Desta

Leavine, R-B-J Schlegel Holdings Inc., St. Jerome's University, and the University of Waterloo – made the gathering possible. The important keynote addresses by the Rt. Hon. John Turner and the Hon. Allan MacEachen are included in the pages that follow; the superb presentations and the frankness of plenary discussions attest to the qualities of the speakers who participated. The session chairs and commentators – Richard Alway, Stephen Clarkson, James Coutts, John Fraser, Allan Gotlieb, Richard Gwyn, Patrick Harrigan, David Johnston, Hon. Otto Lang, Ken McLaughlin, Walter McLean, and Joseph Sinasac – provided order and shared their own insightful reflections.

Special thanks to Jennifer Beckerman, Darren Becks, Carol Cooper, Joan Euler, Harry Froklage, David Seljak, Joseph Sinasac, and Lena Yost, who served on the organizing committee. David Black and Marc Nadeau translated promotional materials and correspondence, and Cris Hawkins and Becky Thompson provided vital assistance. Michael Higgins, the president and vice-chancellor of St. Jerome's University, shared his vision and was instrumental in making the conference a reality. Kevin Burns, commissioning editor at Novalis, greatly facilitated getting this book to press with the utmost efficiency and professionalism. Finally, the conference and this book would not have existed without the vision and indefatigable effort of organizing committee chairs John English and Richard Gwyn, both co-editors of this book.

P. Whitney Lackenbauer

I

Trudeau's Spiritual Pilgrimage

Defined by Spirituality?

Michael W. Higgins

Before we set out on our journey to discover something about the spiritual pilgrimage of Pierre Elliott Trudeau, it is helpful to set the context. In Canada, unlike the United States and the United Kingdom, we do not like to talk about religion and public life. It makes us uncomfortable. A perfect illustration of this unhappy truism can be seen in the recent portrait that appeared in *The Globe and Mail* by Doug Saunders on the life and leadership of Prime Minister Tony Blair.[1] In this otherwise informative and insightful piece on Prime Minister Blair, Mr. Saunders manages to avoid any – partial, allusive, or even exotic – reference to the quite considerable role that religious conviction plays in the life of England's current prime minister. In an interesting piece in the June 2003 issue of *Vanity Fair* entitled "Blair's Big Gamble," David Margolick provides an illuminating profile of Blair and his relationship with President George W. Bush that pays considerable attention to the role of religion in the makeup of both these influential politicians.

Canadian skittishness – at least that of the media – on raising issues of faith, spirituality, religious conviction, and philosophical tenets in relation to public leadership stands in sharp contrast to the open season religion provides U.S. and British journalists. Jim Wallis, an American activist and writer, puts the case very well in his "Should Joe Lieberman Keep His Faith to Himself?":

> Secular fundamentalists make a fundamental mistake. They believe that the separation of church and state ought to mean the separation of faith from politics. While it is true that some conservative religionists might want to blur the boundaries between

church and state, most advocates of religious values in the public square, like Lieberman, do not. Most of us don't support state- or school-sanctioned prayer in public schools, nor officially backed prayers at high school football games in Texas.

Yet open talk of how a candidate's faith shapes his or her political values should be viewed as a positive thing – it is as relevant and appropriate as many other facts about a politician's background, convictions, and experience for public office. The more talk about values the better in political campaigns and, as Joe Lieberman has pointed out, religion is a primary source of values for many Americans. Clearly, minority religions and non-religious people must always be respected and protected in our nation. But the core commitments of religious liberty need not be compromised by an open discussion of faith in public life. Indeed, the kind of talk about religion and politics Lieberman has sparked in this election campaign represents, according to columnist E. J. Dionne, "not a threat to religious liberty but its triumph."[2]

What is true for Americans in this regard is also true for Canadians. Talk about religion and politics in the public forum is neither sectarian nor partisan nor a source of intolerance and root cause for persecution. It is a guarantor of liberty for all our citizens. The role, then, of spirituality and faith in the making of Pierre Elliott Trudeau is entirely appropriate for public consideration and digestion. Why should it be otherwise? In my view, Pierre Elliott Trudeau was a man of intense, intelligent, and reflective faith, and this critical dimension of the man needs to be rightly considered when assessing his role and impact on Canadian society.

His funeral liturgy was conducted with great grace by all the principal players and presided over by Jean-Claude Cardinal Turcotte, the cardinal archbishop of Montreal, with sensitivity and dignity. The homilist, Father Jean-Guy Dubuc, carefully composed and delivered his homily with genuine feeling. The readings were judiciously chosen, the choir in fine form, and the artful alternation between post–Second Vatican Council liturgical practice and form with pre–Second Vatican Council hymnody and chant provided an exquisite portrait of Trudeau's aesthetic and spiritual leanings.

Ontario critic and television personality Ian Brown, however, observed that the "service droned on. That's how the Catholic fathers do it; they prevent you from feeling any grief by boring you unconscious." Ouch! This is altogether rather precious when you consider that it emanates from one inclined to sermonize at will.

But more serious still was a column by that otherwise reliably informed and intelligent critic of national and personal quirks and quandaries, Margaret Wente of *The Globe and Mail*. Her "Counterpoint" column about Trudeau the father and lover was insightful and well-crafted, but her subsequent column on the memorial celebrations and funeral mass amounted to a shocking disclosure of ignorance. In one instance she remarked that "in the days after Mr. Trudeau's death, he surprised us all over again with what we hadn't known about him. He surprised us with his bottomless tenderness toward his children and with his religiosity." Religiosity means excessively or sentimentally religious. Pierre Trudeau "sentimentally religious"? The Jesuit child with an intellectual taste for the rigours of Aristotle and Thomas Aquinas sentimental?

Wente writes that "it's unnerving, that faith. It came from a tradition of high-church intellectualism that has almost died out and is almost incomprehensible to worldly children of a secular age like us." What, pray tell, is "high-church intellectualism"? Is this a new epiphenomenon to be observed in the Catholic world that has succeeded so far in evading the careful scrutiny of Catholic scholars? Or is it, yet once again, a depressing instance of sloppy writing and imperfect understanding of the subject matter?

The intellectual and spiritual tradition of which Trudeau was a superb part is a tradition that embraces a goodly number of the political leaders of our country, admitting the wide range of variations and permutations due to intellect, character, and level of spiritual maturity. Brian Mulroney, Joe Clark, John Turner, Marc Lalonde, and Jean Chrétien are just a few of the political notables of the tradition Wente terms "incomprehensible to worldly children of a secular age like us."

To be a religious thinker does not mean that one is inclined to religiosity. Quite the contrary. To be a man or woman of faith in a secular age may well be far less the minority experience that dogmatic secularists believe it to be. The faith of Pierre Elliott Trudeau was constitutive of his very self-definition, of his very meaning as a human being, of his vocation as a father and national leader. The faith of Pierre Elliott Trudeau was private in its intensity but public in its expression. The final mass was not a convention for him, not an aesthetic experiment, a churchly tradition required by protocol. It was at the core of the man, and he applied to his faith that same level of passion and logic that so many of us have come to admire in other spheres of his public life.

Trudeau's spirituality was as much a part of the legacy as all his other accomplishments; to miss that simple point is to diminish him and ourselves.

In a recent article by Vancouver reporter Rod Mickleburgh on the recovery of Mike Harcourt, the former B.C. premier whose near-fatal fall at his beach cottage left him potentially paralyzed for life, Mickleburgh writes: "The ordeal, and the flood of prayers that were said on his behalf, have strengthened a part of Mr. Harcourt that he rarely talks about – spirituality. 'I'm not a great supporter of organized religion because, too often, people don't practise what they preach,' he said. 'But I've always been spiritual.'"[3]

This dichotomy – religion vs. spirituality – is, in my view, a false one. There is no surprise in Mike Harcourt's reflections; they are undoubtedly sincere and speak authentically of his own experience. What is a surprise is that he would use such terms at all, that a national newspaper known during the William Thorsell years as either hostile or indifferent to religion, and that a topic traditionally viewed as *verboten* in journalistic and political circles in the country, has now become, if not common-place, certainly acceptable.

And so it has become acceptable to have not just an allusion, an utterance, a sound bite, or a talk on Trudeau and spirituality, but indeed a whole conference. Historians, religious studies scholars, political scientists, sociologists, and theologians will have much to chew on as they try and figure out why Canada is doing what has long been acceptable in the U.K., the U.S., and Australia: examine in the media the faith convictions, traditions, and spirituality of public figures.

Trudeau and his contemporaries were "puck shy" when it came to religion and public life. Religion is private property only. Beware! Something of a rationale for that position can be gleaned from Edith Iglauer's 1969 *New Yorker* profile of the new prime minister when she quotes Trudeau's Jesuit mentor Robert Bernier:

Even as a boy, Pierre needed a sense of dedication. To swallow the world takes a long time, and he started by getting an international background – preparing himself for anything and waiting to see where he could best go. I think he really committed himself to Canada with the magazine *Cité Libre*. We had the Duplessis government in Quebec, and the occasion was right. The domination of the clergy over political matters at that time in Quebec was detestable. They had been the most learned men for a couple of hundred years, and everyone had consulted them, but then they became detrimental to liberty and it was time for them to step back into the religious life. Pierre thinks, as a political man should, about the order in this world. Religion is something else; it's what to do to get into the other world.[4]

Not quite the enlightened post–Second Vatican Council thinking that you find in Trudeau's contemporary, fellow religionist, and occasional political opponent, [the late] Claude Ryan:

Far from being marginal, religious faith can and should play a central role in the conduct of the Christian who is actively engaged in public life. I believe that our politicians should more and more accept to be transparent with the population as regards their religious opinions.... I do not question the sincerity of a politician who prefers to keep his religious opinions to himself. I do not doubt either that some politicians may have excellent personal reasons to do so. But Christian faith is not a faith that must remain exclusively private. I believe, as Newman did, that I owe it to my friends to let them know exactly who I am and what I think.[5]

Ryan's Catholicism was activist, engaged, Liberationist, and deeply rooted in the social teachings of the Church, whereas Trudeau's was philosophical, detached, classical, and insular. Trudeau had no stomach for the social initiatives of the Canadian episcopate – particularly as they involved a sharp critique of his own government's fiscal policies – and when his friend Gerald Emmett Cardinal Carter of Toronto publicly distanced himself from the Canadian bishops' 1983 "Ethical Reflections on the Economic Crisis," Trudeau mused aloud and for the clear benefit of the media: "The fox is now among the chickens." Trudeau much preferred the company of French Dominican intellectuals to Pedro Arrupe's Jesuits.

If Trudeau had little taste for applied theology, he had a clear predilection for ecclesiological and epistemological investigations. If he was not fond of chatting with the likes of Dr. Tony Clarke and Bishop Remi De Roo, he was quite taken with the idea of a stimulating colloquy with the likes of Père Yves Congar and Père Marie-Dominique Chenu. In short, Trudeau delighted in the cut and thrust of Catholic intellectual life. After all, the Jesuit child knew the value of first sources, the importance of languages, the Jesuit love of the syllogism, the centrality of *eloquentia perfecta* in the making of a Christian gentleman, and the intellectual allure of the Jesuit motto to do all things, explore all things, for the greater glory of God – *ad majoram Dei gloriam*. In addition, of course, there is that wellspring of French Catholic intellectual life – the Personalist School – with philosophers Emmanuel Mounier, Gabriel Marcel, and the non-Gallic Lublin School of Philosophy. This is Trudeau the Catholic thinker.

His spirituality, although undoubtedly intellectualist in part, was a genuine spirituality of resistance, grounded in a love both for justice and for the contemplative dimension. He had little time for the easy spiritualities that are so effortlessly marketed in Western culture as the next phase in human self-fulfillment. The *Chicken Soup for the Soul* school of spirituality espouses a strategy of self-enhancement techniques, a feel-good process of self-affirmation, that appeals to those hungry for spiritual fulfillment but disinclined to struggle for spiritual enlightenment. Trudeau would never have opted for the easy way out in matters of the spirit any more than he would have in matters of the mind or body. His native temperament, Jesuit formation, stoical bearing, and competitive nature would have resisted the insubstantial nutrition proffered by *Chicken Soup* of any persuasion. Scrupulous, skeptical, and subversive, Trudeau's Jesuit or Ignatian spirituality is one of right-knowing and of making things just. It is a spirituality that does not so much proscribe experience as much as it invites one to sift and gauge its true measure. Found in an enchiridion or handbook, it is not a spirituality of the handbook. It is to be lived in its fullness in the present.

What, then, of Trudeau the Jesuit child?

Certainly there are numerous references to Trudeau's Jesuit training, to the Jesuit influences on his life, his Jesuit formation, as a cursory read of Andrew Cohen and J.L. Granatstein's *Trudeau's Shadow: The Life and Legacy of Pierre Elliott Trudeau* (1998) will bear ample witness. Journalists, biographers, political scientists, historians, and international commentators have written, sometimes with tiresome regularity, about the Jesuit-like qualities of temperament, intellect, and style of Pierre Elliott Trudeau. But what, precisely, in the context of the pre–Thirty-second General Congregation of the Society of Jesus (pre-1975) era, does this actually mean? For example, the education that Pierre Elliott Trudeau received as a Jesuit child would have been comparable to that which stamped the estimable Richard Gwyn of *The Toronto Star* when he was moulded by the Company of Loyola at Stonyhurst, the great Catholic public school in England. But it clearly would not have been the same kind of Jesuit stamp felt by the media philosopher Mark Kingwell when he received his moulding at St. Paul's College in Winnipeg in the 1970s. Why?

Let me provide you with a very brief history of Jesuit education. Their first university – a *studium generale* – was established in 1547 at Gandia and their first classical college at Messina one year later. By the time of their suppression as an Order in 1773 they had 800 colleges and seminaries and 15,000 teachers to be found chiefly in Europe, the Americas, and India. The Jesuits are responsible for instituting the first organized system of education in the Western world with its definable time structure and curriculum, and with the progression in an orderly and intelligible form from the lowest class to the highest. In 1599 the *Ratio Atque Institutio Studiorum Iesu* was codified and formulated under the fifth general of the Society of Jesus, the Italian aristocrat Claudio Aquaviva.

Diego Ledesma, one of the greatest of all Jesuit educators, advanced four reasons for a Jesuit education:

i.   the cultivation of languages

ii. *eloquentia perfecta*

iii. logic

iv. the perfecting of Ciceronian and Scholastic splendour and rational refinement (an example of Trudeau's own famed "intellectual pugilism").

The education that Trudeau received at the Collège Jean-de-Brébeuf (the Lower Canadian Province of the Society of Jesus) was a formation secured by centuries. Although the great compendium of Jesuit public education, the *Ratio*, was very differently applied during the post-Suppression period (the Jesuits were reactivated following the formal reinstatement of the Society of Jesus in 1814), there are continuities of influence, style, and emphasis dating back to the sixteenth-century foundation. This was changed in great measure in the mid-1970s, but by that time Mr. Trudeau had long since graduated from Brébeuf.

The influence on Trudeau by individual Jesuits is critical, but it is also rather different from the "shaping strategy" to be found within the institution itself quite independent of any personality. Bob Rae, the former premier of the province of Ontario, in his article "Hedgehog or Fox?"[6] provides informed commentary, although quite obliquely, on the Jesuit style, highlighting with grudging respect Trudeau's predilection for the subtle manoeuvre, clever repartee, and sophisticated argument. These are undoubtedly Jesuit qualities of mind, although Rae does not identify them as such. Still, they are very different in kind from the jesuitical or sophistical skills that one finds ably exercised by Trudeau's later contemporary President Bill Clinton.

In the end, however, if one is to discover the genuine and enduring influence of the Jesuits in their education formation, it must be found at the source of all Jesuit educational theory: the *Spiritual Exercises* of St. Ignatius of Loyola. As law professor and author Robert Drinan observes of his life as a Jesuit,

It is remarkable that they – the *Spiritual Exercises* – have the power to guide you, almost like *The Imitation of Christ*. You pick it up at any point and you find out what you need to know at that very moment. The *Spiritual Exercises* gives you the foundation, but I think that, like St. Ignatius himself, we need to move beyond the basics. He was a mystic for most of his life, his spirituality deepened as he matured, and I think that you can say that for most Jesuits. They deepened their own spiritual lives by going back to the things of Ignatius, to the first 30-day retreat, and then to the second 30-day retreat that we do during our tertianship. The concepts of the *Spiritual Exercises* have a way of getting into your soul in such a manner that you may not be able to articulate them, but they are there – real, pervasive and determinative.[7]

There is little textual or oral evidence that Mr. Trudeau read the *Exercises* or had seen them as a guide in his personal life, but it is safe to conclude that the shaping that his own masters had in the tradition of the *Exercises* helped to cultivate in their charge an intellectual and spiritual disposition that would last for his whole life.

But the Jesuit makeup of Trudeau is only part of the pilgrimage. For most of his life, Trudeau sought out confessors, confidants, interlocutors, and intellectuals from within the Order of Preachers – the "*domini canes*," the Dogs of the Lord, the Dominicans. Louis-Marie Regis, Benoit Lacroix, and Gilles-Dominique Mailhot were just a few of the Canadian Dominicans who were close to him. Michel Gourgues, Rector of the Collège Dominicain philosophie et théologie, has observed:

Trudeau's ties with the Order flourished throughout the years. Indeed he considered himself a lay Dominican, having taken philosophy courses in his youth and afterwards staying in contact with one of his teachers, Father Louis-Marie Regis, whom he thought of as his spiritual director and as a friend. In fact, he asked Père Regis, among others, to bless his marriage and he attended his funeral mass in 1998. While he was Prime Minister, he would regularly but at unexpected times visit Père Regis's priory. When Yves Congar came to teach for a term at the Collège Dominicain in Ottawa, Trudeau was anxious to meet him and invited Père Congar to Sussex Drive for a meal. Congar was quite struck by Trudeau's familiarity with his work, including his magisterial and seminal work, *Towards a Lay Theology*.[8]

Very possibly, what Trudeau found compatible in Dominican spirituality is the Order's commitment to truth (their motto is *"veritas"*), a truth that is not simply intellectualist (a "what") but relational (a "who") – an understanding of truth that emerges out of the dynamic of contemplation and action, out of the tensions of the thinker and the lover.

This assiduous pursuit of truth, centered in liturgy and common life, nurtured by friendship and prayer, is the hallmark of all the luminaries of the Order. If the focus has been on the Middle Ages [remember Trudeau's many conversations and seminars on medieval thought and dialectic at Université de Montréal, a point highlighted by Dominican scholar and activist Philippe Leblanc], it is because the renewal of Dominican life in the 20th century has been achieved by returning to its authentic roots, its post-conciliar *ressourcement*. The great Dominicans of the 20th century – Sertillanges, Lagrange, Chenu [Trudeau visited him almost every time he was in Paris], Congar, and Schillebeeckx – have all lived lives of intense activity marked by scholarship and a lively interest in their neighbours' good.[9]

One of the attributes of the Dominican charism appears, according to former Master General Timothy Radcliffe (scion of a venerable Recusant family, Ampleforth-educated, and past Oxford professor), to be freedom: the freedom of the poor itinerant preacher, the freedom to scatter, "the freedom of the compassionate person, who dared to see and to respond." And, in the end, the freedom from a government that involves limiting the freedom of the individual to a government that "enables us to share a common responsibility for our life and mission."[10]

The intellectual appeal of the Dominicans and the methodological rigour of the Jesuits needed some counterbalancing, and I believe that could be found in the Benedictine tradition, with its sweet savouring of the word and mystery in *lectio divina* and its plenitude of graces, its natural rhythms of mind, body, and spirit. Dom Laurence Freeman, onetime prior of the Benedictine Priory of Montreal who would have had regular congress with Trudeau during the years that the Christian Meditation Community flourished on Pine, succinctly identifies the features of Benedictine spirituality:

The Benedictine tradition continues to inspire me because of its vision of the possibility of an integration of the different activities and constituents of life. St. Benedict sees the monastic life as a harmony of prayer, work, manual work, creative work, and study, a harmony that is held together centred in a spirit of charity and a love of God and of neighbour.... I think the essence of the Benedictine approach has always been hospitality, openness and flexibility, and the willingness to allow people to share life and the experience of the community according to their own capacity and according to their own calling.... it strikes me as a being broad-minded, healthy, normal and human way of living the search for God.[11]

Trudeau frequently chose Saint Benôit-du-Lac – a community of the Solesmes tradition – for his retreats, as well as meditating and attending the Hours and the Eucharist at Montreal's Benedictine Community with some regularity. I saw him there once at the Office of Sext, seated on the floor, meditating, emptying his mind, his personal mantra methodically recited, his visage serene, posture perfect, surrounded by young McGill students and fellow intellectuals such as Charles Taylor. I do not know if he ever met the founder and *eminence grise* of the Christian Meditation Movement, the former professor of international jurisprudence at Trinity College, Dublin, Dom John Main. It is Main's conviction of the centrality of meditation to the fully-lived and examined life that struck a chord with Trudeau. Experience is not eschewed, the inner journey reduced to easy formulae, the intellect disparaged and feared, stillness and silence rendered suspect, rubric and ritual displacing hard and honest inquiry. For Main, as for Trudeau, "we have to make contact with the ground of our being. And unless that process is underway, all our experience will leave us in the shallows.... More and more men and women in our society are beginning to understand that our personal problems and the problems that we face as a society are basically spiritual problems."[12]

In the end, Trudeau was a spiritual hybrid: a disciplinarian (the Jesuit), a philosopher (the Dominican), and a contemplative (the Benedictine). Never overtly or publicly "theological" in the way of a Baroness Thatcher or Tony Blair, or of compatriots Claude Ryan or Gérard Pelletier, never fervent and evangelical in the way of a George W. Bush or Jimmy Carter, ever suspicious of ecclesial and state commingling, yet nonetheless comfortable in the presence of senior Catholic ecclesiastics such as Gerald Emmett Carter, Trudeau's maturing (and occasionally mutating) spirituality suffused, anchored, and directed his inner life. In no small part, it defined him.

An Explicit Destination?

Stephen Clarkson

If you think about a political figure now, when religion's shaking impact on the world has clearly defied the "end of history" analysts of globalization, it is particularly appropriate to start with the serious understanding that men and women's constructions of God have powerful impacts on our world. George W. Bush in the White House, and Osama Bin Laden in his dark house (wherever that may be), represent two civilizations in which God or Allah is invoked as justification for wanting to destroy the other, identified as Satan or the Devil. It just reminds us that the role of religion is something that the academic community should take seriously. Positivist social scientists, who have dominated academic spaces on both sides of the Atlantic for over a hundred years, have failed quite notably in coming to grips with the role of religion in the life of the individual.

The role of religion has been addressed with difficulty. It has been perhaps better handled in the analysis of movements that are obviously religious in their essence, but less well handled in considering the role of what social scientists like to call "human agency," which, translated for us lesser mortals, means the "individual in politics." Just to raise the question of the collective in the social movements and the individual actor is to come to the heart of what political scientists and political economists have a lot of trouble dealing with: the role of the individual. We like to analyze things in terms of movements or forces or trends. To come to the role of the individual, and particularly the role of religion in that individual's life, is an important issue to have on our intellectual agenda. I think to understand an individual, any individual – and in this case one of the great leaders of this country in the twentieth century – one needs to see not only the collective as distinct from the individual, but to see the relationship between the two as a dialectic. This somewhat Zen-like contradiction – a genuflection towards Pierre Trudeau – is "the fish is in the water and the water is in the fish."

The individual fish swims in his or her social environment – community – but the individual also has an impact on the water in which he or she is swimming. If you think of the fish in the water, what was the water from which Pierre Trudeau was launched? What was the water in which his parents gave him birth? Large movements, driven by faith in the 1920s on both sides of the Atlantic, were powerful and emerged through the 1930s as players in a gigantic struggle: on the right, fascism; on the left, communism (both nationalist); and in the middle, somewhere, some kind of liberalism. In none of these movements was God central. But they were faiths nonetheless, and Michael Higgins has referred to those people driven not by a notion of God but by a faith. Thinking more specifically of Canada during the 1920s and 1930s, I would say that the role of God was prominent – but more figuratively in English Canada, and more literally in French Canada.

In English Canada, there was of course William Lyon Mackenzie King. We know that the crystal ball and the Ouija board eventually became important factors in his life. But his early years were intensely driven by religious notions, and he came out of the social gospel movement, which was a powerful force. You could see it in English Canada in terms of some of the civil society organizations, such as the Student Christian Movement and the Young Men's Christian Association, whose buildings still dot the country. You could this see politically on the right, with William "Bible Bill" Aberhart emerging from a network of Bible study groups, and seeming to dominate Alberta politics almost overnight in 1935. You could see it on the political left with the Co-operative Commonwealth Federation (CCF), organizing also in the 1930s out of a "Ginger Group" in the House of Commons led by the Reverend J.S. Woodsworth. You could also see it in the centre with Liberalism, which morphed throughout that period from its negative *laissez-faire* small-state notion of government to the positive social-welfare, generous-state development of Liberalism that took place under Mackenzie King. Reluctant and slow as this change may have been, it had as its subtext the social gospel. So I think one can see that the water on the English side of Pierre Trudeau's life was profoundly influenced by the heritage of a Protestant ethic that was translated at the turn of the twentieth century into strong political and social-justice ideas.

In French Canada (obviously closer to the real water from which Trudeau was launched), the presence of God in society was almost literally visible in the skyscape. Every major building in every town had a cross on it. The Mount of Montreal had a huge cross on it. The Church was visible everywhere, as was appropriate in a society in which the Church had been the prime social institution assuring the *survivance* of a beleaguered minority of French speakers in the ocean of English-speaking North America. When the young Pierre got to high school he was appropriately launched into a Catholic atmosphere.

The Catholic atmosphere at Collège Jean-de-Brébeuf was explicitly elitist, because Brébeuf was training the élites of Quebec. It was critical to the young Pierre. If I can switch from the fish in the water to the water in the fish, it was this water that was in the young Pierre when he was an adolescent growing up. He was profoundly marked by the teaching he was getting at school. To Michael Higgins' analysis I would like to add the difficult problem of how to understand Trudeau's psychological evolution. This is, of course, difficult to do as an outsider looking at someone else – and particularly at a major figure. Nevertheless, it seems clear from his friends, from his teachers, from people that we interviewed, that the death of his father when Pierre was fifteen had a profound effect on this young, somewhat puny adolescent. He had been struggling to affirm himself against a very powerful and overbearing father, who perhaps was violent towards his mother. This powerful force, not necessarily always positive in the family, disappeared from Pierre's life almost overnight. He could not even be in his father's presence at the end, because Charlie Trudeau was at training camp with his baseball team when it happened. It is as though Pierre was learning to affirm himself, pushing against this powerful presence in the household. He almost lost his balance when his father suddenly vanished. What was the impact on Trudeau's religious life?

The positive element of this impact came in the very intense relationship Trudeau had with his mother. As a result of his father's death, he went to mass regularly (whether daily or weekly) with his mother. It seems clear that he ingested a spirituality that he kept for his life, one that was intense and real, but that was also balanced or even contradicted by quite critical notions of, and even hostility toward, the church – as you can read in his writings about the negative role of the church in society.

There are quite critical notions of priests; none of whom, as far as I know, became friends. I think it is important to add to Higgins' analysis a sense that religious sensibility came early and intensely with what a Jungian would call a "mother complected" young man who was so closely involved with his mother that he did not actually leave home until he was forty, and he did not marry until his mother was almost dead. It can be added and connected with what Marc Nadeau says about the powerful role of *Jeunesse Étudiante Catholique* (see Part II of this book), but which was not a movement with which Trudeau himself was involved. His own Catholic political ideas, I think, come much more strongly from his personal encounters with Emmanuel Mounier in Paris, when he was briefly a student there after the war. Mounier's ideas were attractive because they were critical of the bourgeois Catholic Church: being religious was not just about going to mass and being smug and self-satisfied. Mounier's ideas considered the worker priest and the Catholic who is engaged as a Christian in society trying to change the miserable lot of the proletariat. When brought back to French Canada, these ideas provided a rationale and a mission – Mounier's journal, after all, was called *Esprit,* "Spirit" – a mission to those people like Pierre Juneau and Pelletier to stay home and change the place.

These double notions – needing to understand both the collective and the individual – bring me to the theme of "Trudeau's Spiritual Pilgrimage." I would like to end on this. The *Oxford Canadian Dictionary* defines "pilgrimage" in three ways. The first is a journey to a sacred place, the literal religious pilgrimage – a definition which it is a stretch to apply to Pierre Trudeau. The second is that of a sentimental, nostalgic journey to one's home or to one's birthplace. That, too, is certainly inappropriate, because if Pierre Trudeau was anything he was not nostalgic. He did not have much sense of his own past, nor did he like to talk about it. Nor was he sentimental – he was the least sentimental of men. The third definition is basically a life journey, and one can think of one's life as a pilgrimage. I think that is very appropriate for Trudeau because he lived a conscious life. It was a thoughtful life, lived through the mind.

I also looked up "spiritual" in the dictionary and found three definitions. The first two were centred on the sacred or holy, and it struck me that these were inappropriate when talking about Trudeau, because his own religious life was lived very privately. But the third definition was appropriate – it was a spirituality of the mind as opposed to of material things. So someone who is spiritual is a woman or a man for whom issues of the mind and not material possessions are the object. And I think that kind of spiritual pilgrimage is appropriate for Trudeau. He did live a life's journey and he did have a destination – whether you think of this as crushing Quebec separatism or creating a Charter of Rights.

He was in that sense a man going on a journey with an explicit destination, but he did it as a person of sensibility, a person of cultural refinement, a person of intellectual rigour. This is important to affirm, not just to try to understand this man in our political history, but to try to understand the present. The trend in one country is for politicians to wear their religion not only on their sleeve but on their chest, and at every speech to evoke their version of God, quite often with a Texas accent. The danger and destructive potential of politicians justifying what they are doing in the name of God, whose message they claim to understand, can be contrasted with a different model that Pierre Trudeau left us. His is that of a politician who has his own religion, who keeps that very much his own business, but has his cause defined in lay terms that he feels can be justified by reason over passion.

Discussion

Unknown Speaker: You spoke about Trudeau's relations with the Dominicans and Jesuits. I know less about his relations to the Catholic Church after the Second Vatican Council. Jeanne Sauvé, one-time Governor General of Canada, addressed some very hard critiques to the pope when she met him in Rome; she did not agree with some politics of the Catholic Church. Did Trudeau directly address some of his criticisms to the Catholic magisterium, like some theologians he knew?

Michael Higgins: That is a good question and I thought about that a lot, because there are aspects to his theological reflection that cannot be divorced from his own spiritual formation. That suggests a certain disembodied approach to a much more organic Catholic conception of the relationship of theology and spirituality to the making of a just community. I did not wish to sound glib when I said that he would not find a great deal of happy company with the Pedro Arrupe Jesuits. I mean that the social activist/liberationist strains that you begin to see emerging in global Catholicism at the end of the 1960s, and you see running through the 1970s, were not particularly congruent with Trudeau's own spiritual perspective or indeed with his temperament. I think that in a real sense he become isolated within progressive Catholic circles in Quebec and indeed elsewhere.

When I tried to mine as many sources as I could on this subject – because he was quite elusive about these things – I found that the company with whom he liked to consort, the kind of issues he liked to debate, were invariably of this intellectualist form. An easy example of this is his regular conversations with the Dominican scholars about matters that sometimes are really quite arcane: about medieval thought and its particular Aristotelian roots, or ecclesiological issues that he would have discussed with Congar. He quite enjoyed *Toward a Lay Theology*, but that is a very early work published in the early 1950s, and

I have a real sense that the post–Vatican II world – with its strong interest in social issues – challenged a prime minister who was, in many ways, criticized for his obsessive concern with the role of the individual as opposed to the corporate community.

His involvement with the Charter and his indifference to some ethical and moral issues thus seem strange, but if you look at his personality, or the consistency of his interests, perhaps they are not so strange in the end. The reference I made to Cardinal Carter is a wonderful, brief cameo illustration of the fact that he liked bishops to do their episcopal thing. But he did not like it when they were critical of his economic policies or directions. There are aspects to Trudeau's Catholicism and Catholic thinking that seem to me the reflection of someone who enjoys the repartee of the salon rather than the streets. Stephen Clarkson talked about the spirit of the pilgrimage and the movements that were developing in the 1920s and 1930s. Of course, Trudeau would have been opposed to such explicitly Catholic movements, with their fascist underpinnings, such as the *Action Française*, and Charles Maurras. He would have been like Mounier, emphasizing the strong Personalist approach. But I always have the sense that this was shifted through the prism of his intellectual approach to Catholic teaching. That is why I wanted to talk more specifically about the spirituality. Not that they should be divorced – they should not be – but it goes some way to help us better understand the contradictions and complexities of the man. I do not wish to suggest in any way that he was the ideal Catholic intellectual. He represented in many ways a certain kind of continental Catholic intellectual, more comfortable before the Second Vatican Council than after. That is my sense of Trudeau.

Stephen Clarkson: I am really interested in what Michael has added in his presentation because my sense of Trudeau intellectually was that he did not do much new reading or thinking after he went into politics. I am learning something new, that he was engaged with Catholic theologians; my sense was that he had packed his intellectual baggage by the age of forty or forty-five, when he went into politics, and that was it – he had enough self-confidence that he did not think he needed to hear from anyone else, that he had all the ideas he needed and he went through his life with them. Another question in my mind was about the post-political Trudeau. From my brief dealings with him, I sensed that he reverted to his way of being as a younger man, more progressive politically. He may well have become more religious, or more explicit in his personal practice, going to retreats, as you note. The older Trudeau, who was not part of our analysis for the biography I wrote with Christina McCall, may have indeed become more theologically conscious. This is a question John English may be able to answer in his official biography.

Max Nemni (professor of political science at Laval University, co-editor of *Cité libre*): One thing that is extremely striking about Trudeau is how deeply religious he was, how deeply Catholic he was – not just in the end but throughout his life of devout faith. He would go to mass, would pray every day, and so forth. It seems to me that such a man would profoundly know that what he was doing was against Catholic teaching – accepting abortion, accepting homosexuality, making his famous "the state has no place in the bedrooms of the nation" statement. This to me is at the heart of how he could maintain his faith out of his political life, which is not something for which I reproach him. On the contrary; I greatly admire him for doing so. But is this not something to address?

Stephen Clarkson: What comes to mind is one thing that he said to a school comrade in his adolescence: if we have to go to confession every week, does that not mean that we have to sin in order to have something to confess? So perhaps Michael might address the more serious issue with that in mind. Pierre Trudeau was a deep believer in individual liberty, and if many of us criticize him for various aspects of his politics, it had to do in part with his defiant nineteenth-century liberalism. An understanding about his notions on abortion or adultery, those issues of family values, has to come from his powerful liberalism, where every man and woman has his and her own dignity and should have power over his or her own life.

Michael Higgins: Some of the issues that arose over his legislative initiatives, of his approach, have to be seen in the context of larger global Catholic leadership as well. What happens when you become the leader of a democratic state and you have responsibilities? John Kennedy, Charles De Gaulle, and Georges Pompidou were all Catholic heads of state who faced huge difficulties when it came to democratic decision-making, and policies with an ethical or moral aspect. How did their responsibilities as democratic leaders conflict with their relationship with their Church or with their communion? I do not want to make light of the matter because I think that is quite true, but Trudeau has to be placed in the context of a larger reality.

He is not unique in that respect. I think that he has become a bit of a lightning rod for people because of the accelerated nature of some of the introductions and changes that occurred within the Canadian political and social landscape from the 1960s on. But one has to remember that several distinguished former cabinet ministers giving presentations at this conference are much better at reflecting publicly on the inner anguish, the debates that went on in the cabinet sessions. Allan MacEachen, Otto Lang, and others have a real sense of that dynamic, that struggle that must have gone on at certain points in terms of his relationship to his own confessor. Of course, we don't know how he evaluated intellectually his political responsibilities as opposed to his responsibilities as a Christian. I imagine, given the kind of person that he was, that he wrestled with these questions. He was neither categorical nor dismissive, and I suspect that he put it within the context of the role, rights, and obligations of the individual. It is the individual in the end who does the damning, and the individual in the end who must account to God. Trudeau would have been aware of the importance of Catholic teaching in this matter, of the priority of conscience. In fact, it was not the Second Vatican Council but a council in the second decade of the thirteenth century that decreed that anything that goes against conscience paves towards hell. The role of conscience and decision-making in relation to an individual Catholic's moral responsibility is not a recent development.

It is possible that he had sufficient familiarity, or was sufficiently conversant, with Catholic Church history to know some of these things. Certainly in his conversations with Congar and others he would have been aware of them. I think it is too suggestive to assume he was merely responding to populist urges and, at the same time, that some of the changes he made with their ethical implications would not have reflected a conflicted politician in a leadership role. This is not to suggest that one should have expected the Roman Catholic Church to say suddenly that this was great and we agree with that mentality – of course not. The Church has to be faithful to its own tradition, to its understanding of that tradition, to how it mediates that tradition, to the changes and reforms inherent in the conflicts of its own schools. This is, of course, an important part of Catholic Church history.

Ron Graham: Trudeau always had a very clear and simple answer to Max Nemni's question. It came partially, as you said, from his individuality; but even more so it stemmed from his deep faith and belief in democratic pluralism and from the notion of Canada as a multicultural society – as a role model for the whole world in a sense that included religion. So he used to argue very clearly and very simply, in answer to exactly that question, that it was not his role to take his personal beliefs, no matter how strongly he might have held them, and to impose them on his fellow citizens who may be holding other beliefs (including non-beliefs). So his answer would have been, "I understand your concerns, and I may even share them personally, but it is not my role as a political leader to impose those on other cultures, including other religions and other beliefs within our society. That is not my role as a politician in a pluralistic society."

Unknown Speaker: I understand that he made several trips to the Middle East, literal pilgrimages, during his youth. Do you think these trips influenced his appreciation of democratic pluralism? Can you describe the effects of these pilgrimages?

Stephen Clarkson: They bring to mind Ronald Reagan's visit to Ottawa in 1981. Just after Reagan had ridden into the White House with his California cowboys, he came up to Ottawa. There was a lot of apprehension because Reagan had just withdrawn the East Coast Fish Treaty from the Senate, and in the icebreaking of their first encounter it came up that Trudeau had just come back from the Middle East and that he had been dancing with sheiks. Reagan said, "Well, you know the Jews believe in God, the Arabs believe in God, we believe in God. Why can't we all get together and fight the Soviets?" Apparently Trudeau just did not know what to make of this. This man – for whom the spiritual included a great sensitivity to other cultures, and who took enormous pleasure in travelling the world as prime minister the way he had as a young man – brought his multiculturalism to his politics at home, as Ron Graham just said. This was an important, if secondary, aspect of his bilingualism. That is not a very direct answer to your question, but I think Trudeau, of all Canadian prime ministers, had the greatest sensitivity to cultures around the world and therefore to Canada, which he could see as having a model role even if the rest of the world was ignorant about it.

I think his travels in the Middle East were just part of his world travels, so when you think about the impact on his politics, you would have to include his travels in China or Japan or Africa, and especially Europe. He was conscious of other religions, and when Michael Higgins mentions his capacity to meditate it makes me think of what he apparently learned as a very young man in Japan, when he spent time in a Buddhist monastery. I think you could see a lot of his meditative capacity in federal-provincial conferences, in the calm that radiated around his chair while the premiers were yelling and screaming at him. I think his religious sensibility cannot be understood just in terms of Catholic teaching and faith and doctrine, but in terms of his having tried to understand and experience and ingest other religious traditions. I think he was, in a way, a model multicultural person in his own spirituality.

Basheer Habib: It is interesting that Mr. Trudeau had a tremendous following from people of different traditions. Although we are talking about Mr. Trudeau from his religious extraction, I really think he was a monotheist in the truest sense of the word. Having said that, I wonder what his reaction to the current paranoia on the "Clash of Civilizations" concept would have been?[1]

B.W. Powe: First, I think it was said very well earlier that Pierre swam in the great ocean. He was keenly aware of the complexity of the world, of different kinds of cultures and values, and his sensitivity and perception made him a highly respected world statesman. As for how he would have responded to the Bush administration's unilateral action in Iraq, I have no idea. I think perhaps he would have sided with the multilateralism of the United Nations, as consistent with many of his stands over the years. But being the rigorous intellect that he was, he surely would have seen how contradictory – if not hypocritical – were some of the United Nations stands on things. Where were they on Rwanda, for example?

Tom Axworthy: And we have his views on terrorism.

B.W. Powe: Yes, which we know were very strong. Twenty-four Canadians were killed in the World Trade Center; only three were kidnapped during the October Crisis, and we know that he acted with great decisiveness and severity. I think Tom's point, if I can make it for him, is that Trudeau's record on terrorism was known to be very strong, decisive, and courageous.

Tom Axworthy: On the clash-of-civilizations concept, I was present at one debate where Trudeau did talk about this quite a bit. In his retirement, he was very active in a council that had been created by former German chancellor Helmut Schmidt and Japanese Prime Minister Pokuda. They would come together two or three times a year to discuss major subjects, and always in an exotic locale, which was part of the attraction that the international council held for him. In the mid-1990s, just as Sam Huntington came out with his article on the clash of civilizations, Schmidt convened a meeting on that theme. It turned into a fascinating set of discussions, because the group of retired leaders came out with an approach that I think was sensible, but also showed their quality. Their approach was based on the idea that we can point to many differences in our interpretation of the divine, but ethics are inherent in all faiths, and by and large there is a tremendous overlapping of morality in most religions. That is why religion is important. Religion is not the exclusive source of our sense of morality, but it is by far the most predominant and important voice in that area. Therefore, an approach predominant and important voice in that area. Therefore, an approach that looked at what is common in Islam, in the Confucian tradition, in Hinduism, and so on, was an important element to get away from the "clash." This was one of those discussions at its best. I am hard pressed to think of a group of leaders today who could so easily reach back to a whole host of literatures, know them so well, and make those sorts of connections. Trudeau signed his name, then, to a manifesto of the Interaction Council before 9/11 stating that to avert the clash of civilizations – you have all heard this before in interfaith dialogue – there should be a renewed emphasis on learning about each others' religious base. People around the world should be taught about comparative religions and ethics, the United Nations University should begin a whole series of courses on this, and school systems should try to avert the stereotyping that is so much behind the clash-of-civilizations mentality. So Trudeau's response was to learn about each other's faith. Knowledge is a value of its own, and he thought that we should all have more knowledge of other faith traditions, as he had.

II

Religion and Politics in Quebec

Trudeau and the Privatization of Religion: The Quebec Context

David Seljak

In his homily at the funeral mass on October 3, 2000, Father Jean-Guy Dubuc unwittingly drew a line between Pierre Elliott Trudeau the public figure, and the hidden Pierre Elliott Trudeau, the man of faith.

> We know all about Pierre Trudeau's political and public life – now is not the time to go over that – but that will always remain just one facet of his life. The more visible facet of his life.

> But he would go pray with the Benedictine monks near his home on lunch hour; a faithful believer, he would go to his parish church on Sundays. During evening private conversations, he would speak of the Bible; the role of the Church and the transmitting of values he wished to discuss not for a mere intellectual gain, which he certainly could have.[1]

Canadians who knew only the public figure – the politician, author, and intellectual – would have had a difficult time imagining Trudeau as a devoutly religious man. In fact, Trudeau's public record might indicate that he was even hostile to religion. He is, after all, the prime minister who oversaw both the final disestablishment of Christianity in Canada and the creation of a secular Canadian state. As a young intellectual in the 1950s, he opposed the privilege and power of the Roman Catholic Church in Quebec, which had close ties to the conservative Duplessis government. In the 1960s, as a federal cabinet minister, he liberalized the laws on homosexual sex, taking the state out of the bedrooms of Canada, which really meant dismantling the state's role in enforcing Christian sexual morality. He again rolled back the political influence of Christian morality when he reformed the divorce and abortion laws. And when Trudeau championed the 1982 Charter of Rights and Freedoms, he enabled critics to challenge in the courts the continued presence of Christianity in Canadian public schools and other institutions. So Canadians could be excused for imagining that Trudeau was a good son of the Enlightenment, a Canadian Voltaire, so to speak. And they could be excused for being surprised by Father Dubuc's homily. How could someone who had done so much to secularize Canadian society have been so personally religious?

The confusion over Trudeau's own religious identity is rooted in confusion over the nature of the secularization of Canadian society and, more globally, the process of secularization in modernizing societies. Sociologists themselves have done much to promote this confusion. In the 1960s and '70s, they developed a theory of secularization that has since become part of the popular imagination. They taught that as societies became modern, democratic, and rational, religious mentalities declined, the public power of religious communities waned, and religion became an entirely private affair. These three dimensions of secularization were interconnected. As people became more rational and egalitarian, they demanded that reason (science, democracy, and industrialism) replace custom and tradition (religion, monarchy, and feudalism) as the basis of social organization. The power of the churches, identified with tradition and irrational social forms such as the aristocracy, had to be restrained. Consequently, whatever religion was left over in this process became a private affair. Like sex and politics, it was rude to introduce religion into polite dinner party conversation, never mind into parliamentary and public debates. The secularization process, sociologists assumed – and almost everyone believed – was integrated, irreversible, inevitable, and universal. All modern societies would become secular – or so the theory went.

Given that the intellectual establishment had adopted traditional secularization theory as an article of faith in Western democracies after World War II, it is no wonder that Trudeau's critics and supporters alike assumed that he must have been a secular thinker. Trudeau added to the mystique in the early 1960s by advocating the politics of functionalism, an egalitarian strategy that saw reason as the only basis for a prosperous, pluralistic, and democratic society.[2] He wrote explicitly about the need for the privatization of religion and its exclusion from public policy debates, especially those surrounding social issues such as divorce, abortion, and education, but also those concerning questions of economics. Religion, he argued, had to be an entirely private affair, relegated to the sphere of personal choice, individual beliefs and practices, mystical experiences and interiority, family traditions, and voluntary associations. While important public institutions, the churches had to be excluded from political society. In short, Trudeau adopted a theory of secularization in which society is divided into public and private spheres, and religion, like ethnicity, had to be relegated to the private realm. He did not suggest that individuals stop believing – no more than he thought they should give up their ethnic identity. However, as other contributions to this volume demonstrate, he did champion a more rational, individualistic, and "this-worldly" Christianity.

To distinguish the man of faith, the hidden Trudeau, from the public man, we need first to explore the model of secularization that sociologists of religion have completely debunked despite its continued power in the popular imagination. This is an important first step, I want to suggest, because Trudeau's own conception of modern society rested partially on this flawed model. As José Casanova has argued, the traditional theory of secularization always functioned less as a *description* and more as a liberal *prescription* for a modern, democratic society.[3] According to this prescription, public life would become secular, while private life would become the sphere in which individuals could choose freely whether or not to pursue a spiritual life. Trudeau took that prescription to heart and made it the pillar of both his political thinking and his spirituality. Trudeau's deep spiritual conviction that religion had to be a private affair was a product of the struggle over the political modernization of Quebec in the 1950s and early 1960s. This conviction remained foundational to his political and spiritual life throughout his political career. In contrast, the Catholic Church in Quebec evolved quite differently, rejecting both the public Catholicism that justified its privileged status as a "semi-established" church *and* the privatization of religion. In order to help understand Trudeau's approach to religion, I will describe briefly the road he did not take, the path adopted by other Quebec Catholics, including the bishops.

Secularization Theory and the Privatization of Religion

According to the dominant theories worked out in the 1960s, secularization involved three dimensions: the decline of religious mentalities; differentiation or the division of labour; and the privatization of religion.[4]

i) *The decline of religious mentalities*

As people become more rational and scientific, they challenge traditional religious beliefs. For example, they look to evolutionary biology rather than the book of Genesis to account for the origins of the human species. In the face of illness and death, modern people demand medicine not miracles.

ii) *Differentiation or the division of labour*

As societies become larger and more sophisticated, actors in each sphere of activity claim the right to operate free of interference from others, especially religious authorities. In fact, what is popularly called the separation of church and state is better understood as a process by which religion gradually ceases to influence other spheres of society; it also includes the separation of church from institutions in education, health care, social services, the arts, and economic development. These institutions become autonomous and actors in them claim the right to operate according to the demands, values, and assumptions of their own sphere. For example, business people believe that the economy should operate according to market laws (maximum return on investment) rather than religious prescriptions (such as keeping the Lord's Day, which would disallow Sunday shopping and factory work).

iii) *The privatization of religion*

If these institutions are to act autonomously and if society is to be defined by liberty, equality, and reason, religion must retreat from public life. Inasmuch as religious belief and practice did not decline in secular societies, they would have to be relegated to the private sphere of personal choice, individual spirituality, family values, and the ethnic community.[5] Religion would have no public role.

Today, sociologists of religion have refuted the classical theory of secularization. Religion has persisted in the lives of individuals even though it has become less connected to traditional institutions such as the church parish.[6] Furthermore, religious communities refuse to go politely off into what Jacques Grand'Maison has called the "no man's land" of the private realm. Christian churches, as well as other religious communities, enter into public debates on a host of ethical issues ranging from same-sex marriage to economic justice. In fact, only the process of differentiation has been proven, and even that only in the case of the West. In these countries, even religious people have worked toward the separation of church and state (church and the economy, etc.) and the privatization of religion. This is precisely what happened in Quebec, as Jean-Philippe Warren and E.-Martin Meunier show in their essay "*Sortir de la grande noirceur*" ("Leaving the Great Darkness"). In order to promote Christian values, including freedom of conscience, effectiveness in relieving the suffering of the poor, justice, and spiritual maturity, practising Roman Catholics supported much of the transfer of power from the Church to the state during the Quiet Revolution.[7]

Trudeau, Quebec, and the Privatization of Religion

Trudeau promoted secularization primarily in terms of this process of differentiation and its corollary, the privatization of religion. Personally religious, he did not promote the decline of religious mentalities. His passion for separating religion and politics grew out of his experience of the close collaboration of the Quebec state and the Roman Catholic Church in the Duplessis era, sometimes called *la grande noirceur*. Unlike other modern societies, Quebec had, until the 1960s, left a considerable degree of control over the areas of education, health care, and social services in the hands of the churches. For French Canadians these institutions were controlled by the Roman Catholic Church, while a separate set of institutions served English Canadians in Quebec. Moreover, there were Roman Catholic labour unions, workers' groups, credit unions, newspapers, student organizations, farmers' cooperatives, life insurance companies, and nationalist organizations. An army of over 45,000 priests, nuns, and brothers administered these institutions. All of these were supported by the Duplessis government, which defined Quebec as a Catholic province.

Trudeau protested against this arrangement as a type of "feudalism," as if the province of Quebec in the 1950s were some kind of "folkloric" community and not yet an urbanized and industrialized society.[8] Only the relegation of religion to the private sphere, he argued, would allow these institutions the autonomy they needed to be effective, democratic, and just. For instance, in his chapter "Quebec at the Time of the Strike," in *The Asbestos Strike* (1954), Trudeau calls for this differentiation in arenas of politics, economics, education, and culture. French Canadians in all of these areas had to be allowed to operate without interference by the clerical authority. The first step was the rejection of the *clérico-nationalisme* that promoted fatalism, defeatism, social irresponsibility, political immorality, psychological immaturity, as well as an otherworldly and unrealistic attitude to problem-solving. Trudeau argued that Catholic interference in the economy resulted in irrational and ineffective campaigns to address the injustice of the economic inferiority of the French Canadians. He called for the secularization of the trade unions and the cooperative movement because both were restrained by the unrealistic corporatist ideology of the Church and were influenced by a reactionary, anti-modern clergy. Trudeau felt that, once unmoored from the Church, French Canadians could direct unions and promote cooperative initiatives that actually improved their socio-economic status.[9]

For Trudeau, the scourge of religion in politics was tied to the evil of nationalism. In his 1958 essay in the *Canadian Journal of Economics and Political Science* entitled "Some Obstacles to Democracy in Quebec," he lists both religion and nationalism as the primary obstacles (along with English Canadian chauvinism and hypocrisy, he added). Like religion, ethnic identity had its place – that is, in the private sphere. In his widely read *Cité libre* article of 1962, "*La nouvelle trahison des clercs*," Trudeau argued that the nation could be the carrier of a cultural heritage, common traditions, a communitarian conscience, historical continuity, and morality – all of which contribute (at the present stage of human evolution) to the development of the personality. However, like religious values, these belong properly to the private rather than public sphere. He wrote:

> They are more private than public, more introverted than extroverted, more instinctive and savage than intelligent and civilized, more narcissist and emotional than generous and reasoned. They are part of a transitory stage in human history and if evolution takes its natural course, they will disappear.[10]

Public politics, for Trudeau, should be "functional" – in other words, rational, universally accessible, and progressive. Because of their irrational and particularistic nature, religious and ethnic values have no place in public policy.[11] Following this rationalist, liberal theory, Trudeau argued that as society became more and more modern, that is, rational, these particular values were destined for the dust heap of history after they were supplanted by universal values. As a matter of principle, politics and even political morality had to become a thoroughly secular project. Trudeau embraced this model. Indeed, what we now call "identity politics" was anathema to him. The following chart shows Trudeau's prescription for a liberal democratic society that comes out of his rejection of *duplessisme*. It follows perfectly the liberal prescription for the structure of democratic societies[12] – if we understand the term *liberal* in a more general way, applying to all liberal democracies.

Public	Private
Political and Economic Society	The "Personal," Family, Community, Church
Reason	Religion (magic, superstition)
Pluralistic Federalism: citizenship in a multicultural state	Nationalism: ethnic identity rooted in a particular nation
Universal Values: "Functionalism," utilitarianism	Particular Values: ethical, religious, ethnic, aesthetical
Rooted in the Intellect ("modern")	Governed by Emotions ("primitive")
Interested in Scientific Facts	Restricted to Values
Represents Progress: characterized by pluralism, diversity, openness	Represents Backwardness: characterized by unity, sameness, xenophobia

For Trudeau, the public realm – the realm of the state and the market (the twin engines of modernization) – had to be dominated by a universally accessible reason; the putative universality of reason guaranteed that society would be pluralistic and hence democratic. Politically, individuals were conceived of as rational citizens in a culturally neutral state, unfettered, in his "functionalist" model, by religious or ethnic values that clouded the thinking of so many people. Only such a rational society could guarantee that its citizens were moving forward in the great march of civilization.

The enemy in this conception is not religion or ethnic identity per se – only *public* religion and *politicized* ethnic identity: that is to say, nationalism. Kept in their place, though, religion and ethnicity might even be sources of positive values and ideas. For Christians and others who enter the political arena, religion and ethnicity are best left where they belonged – at home.

Anyone familiar with contemporary writing on the public versus the private spheres in modern societies cannot help but be struck by how very close Trudeau's conception was to the classical liberal formulation of the individual and the state. Not all liberals agree on the nature of these divisions. For classical or small "l" liberals and their contemporary followers (some of whom we incorrectly call "neo-conservatives"), only the state apparatus itself and political society belong in the public sphere. In classical liberal theory, the market belongs in the private sphere, hence the term "private property," and the state has no more business sticking its nose in the boardrooms of the nations than it has in the bedrooms. Trudeau, much more a follower of John Maynard Keynes than neo-liberals such as F.A. von Hayek and Milton Friedman, believed that the market was a public institution and hence should be regulated for the common good. His National Energy Program is a prime example of this belief. While there are disagreements among liberals about the exact division and placement of institutions, there is a consensus about the necessity for the creation of a private sphere of personal liberty, a space free of government interference.[13] Conversely, government had to remain free from the interference of religious and ethnic communities. Even believing Christians had to act in public life "as if" God did not exist. In parallel fashion, ethnic groups would have to operate in these public spheres "as if" their cultural values were not universally valid. Trudeau was committed to creating a political framework in which they would be forced to set aside religious and ethnic prejudices and convictions. For Trudeau, this framework was a secular, multicultural Canada.

This model helps us to understand how Trudeau, personally a deeply religious man, could work so hard for the secularization of Canadian society, at least if we understand by that term this process of differentiation and the privatization of religion and *not* the decline of religious mentalities. He could, and did, remain loyal to his Roman Catholicism and French Canadian heritage, but only in his private life. Politically, he rendered both harmless – at least at the level of the state and its awesome power of coercion and organization. The Roman Catholic Church became one social institution among many, just as the French Canadians became one ethnic community among a multitude.

Trudeau and Quebec Catholicism after 1960

Trudeau's battle against French Canadian *clérico-nationalisme* in 1950s' Quebec was the crucible in which his political philosophy was forged. It made him deeply suspicious of both public religion and political nationalism for the rest of his life. For this reason, he did not understand the evolution of a new modern public Catholicism in Canada and Quebec that was not a throwback to the privileged position of the Church under Duplessis. He missed, almost entirely, what I have called the Quebec Church's own "Quiet Revolution."[14]

In 1983, for example, when he was prime minister, Trudeau reacted angrily to the Canadian Catholic bishops' pastoral letter "Ethical Reflections on the Economic Crisis." Responding to the 1982 recession and its sudden jump in unemployment, the social affairs committee of the Canadian Conference of Catholic Bishops criticized the government for pursuing an economic policy that put the interests of shareholders over those of workers.[15] Trudeau dismissed the report and said that the bishops should stick to religion, their sphere of expertise. They were not economists. Their arguments were not rational. The Quebec Catholic bishops defended the letter and especially the right of bishops to participate in the public sphere.[16] They replied that religious leaders had the right to put forward an *ethical* reflection on public policy and that social ethics had been part of the Catholic tradition for close to a century. They argued that, as Christians, they were called to defend the dignity of the human person and if economic institutions and practices violated that dignity they had the right and responsibility to make their voices heard.

The Catholic Church in Quebec refused to adapt entirely to the liberal model embraced by Trudeau. The Quebec Church hierarchy came to renounce both the semi-established position of the Church prescribed by Duplessis' conservatism and the relegation of all religion to the "private life" of individuals demanded by Trudeau's liberalism. A cursory reading of the pastoral letters of the Quebec bishops in the *La justice sociale comme bonne nouvelle: messages sociaux, économiques et politiques des évêques du Québec, 1972–1983*[17] demonstrates that the bishops refused to limit their teaching to private matters of personal morality, piety, and spirituality. They addressed the rights of immigrants and refugees, the priority of the needs of labour over the demands of capital, unemployment, poverty, women's rights, religious liberty, regional economic disparity, and the ecological crisis. The bishops publicly criticized both the Quebec government and society when they neglected the poorest members of society.

The social teaching of the Quebec Catholic bishops is an example of what José Casanova calls a *modern* public religion. Casanova points to the way in which American Roman Catholic bishops talk about the economy and nuclear war as an example of a modern public religion. He contrasts this to the way the same bishops teach on sexuality and abortion. On those questions, they adopt the authoritarian and clerical model of the past.[18] The social teaching of the Quebec bishops – in contrast to some of their teachings on sexuality and women's ordination[19] – demonstrates to what degree they have rejected the liberal model of privatization as well as a regression to pre-modern forms or a rejection of modern values of pluralism and democracy. Religious leaders in such groups do not dictate to believers; they try to persuade through argumentation. They do not ask for special power for the Church but respect the autonomy of the state and political society. They do not violate the values of pluralism and liberty but instead protect those very values by participating as responsible citizens in public debates. Indeed, modern public religions protect the very integrity of a democratic civil society, the undifferentiated sphere of public activity that belongs to neither the state nor the market.[20]

Trudeau could not understand or accept the new Catholicism in Quebec. His experience of the public Catholicism of the Duplessis era and opposition to the *clérico-nationalisme* that kept French Canadians from becoming full participants in modern society convinced him that religion had to be privatized. Only a secular political society, he believed, could enable Canadians to participate as equals in democratic decision-making. Not all Quebec Catholics agreed with him. While these Catholics also rejected the old Quebec and the old Catholicism, they argued that both ethnic and religious values still had something to say to a state and society that were not yet fully rational or just. Consequently, they believed, a modern public Catholicism could make a contribution to Canadian public life.

Politics and Religion in Quebec: Theological Issues and the Generation Factor

Solange Lefebvre

I intend to provide the theological context in which the Catholic Christian faith of Pierre Trudeau evolved. Of course, the cultural, human, and Christian dynamic of Trudeau's faith development can be understood through his Jesuit training and the influences of Catholic intellectuals and religious communities, as our collective reflection explains these dimensions very well. I, on the other hand, have tried to situate Trudeau's faith development in relation to the Second Vatican Council and Quebec Catholicism. The last part will touch briefly on how Pierre Trudeau fits the pattern of his generation, as this is important for understanding the part that Quebec's socio-religious evolution played in shaping his faith.

Trudeau and the Second Vatican Council

In discussing Quebec Catholicism, it is always useful to remember that it was both an impediment to, and a catalyst for, change. From the nineteenth century onwards, through the conservatism of its ruling elite, the Church served to resist change while, at the same time, through its progressive forces, it was able to act as a catalyst for change. Mr. Trudeau illustrated this dynamic aspect of Quebec Catholicism. Around the time of World War II, various currents of Catholic Christian thought, among other factors, began leading up to the monumental transformations of the 1960s. This phenomenon was even more striking in Quebec than elsewhere in Canada, given Quebec's religious homogeneity. One of these deep new currents was the critique that came from *Cité libre* during the fifties. *Cité libre* was challenging a specific type of Catholicism – one that was clerical, defensive, and Jansenist – without rejecting Christianity or Catholicism per se. Pierre Trudeau, like several critical personalities of his time, had no difficulty making that distinction, as illustrated in this excerpt from his famous paper around the time of the asbestos strike. Differentiating between "our" social doctrine of the Church and the doctrine as taught by the popes, Trudeau notes that "the social doctrine of the Church, which in other countries opened wide the doors for democratization of peoples, emancipation of workers and social progress, was invoked in French Canada to support authoritarianism [and nationalism]."[1]

Having enjoyed a liberal education and the opportunity to travel all over the world, Trudeau was aware of the international context. He had socialized with Christian elites, particularly in France where a burgeoning of Catholic intellectual life had influenced his path (the Le Saulchoir Dominican school, Jacques Maritain, etc.). Through these theologians, he and others found a new way of being Christian in the secular world. To situate Pierre Trudeau with respect to the Second Vatican Council, it is important to remember that these theologians, with other European colleagues, had a great influence on the Council.

It is important to stress, from the outset, the pluralism existing within Catholicism, both before and after the Council. The teachings of Vatican II, extraordinarily rich and complex in content, were received in many and diverse ways. It is, moreover, a known fact that the Council documents present more than one perspective on several issues. Even today, this gives rise to bitter controversy, if not outright clashes, between sometimes contradictory theological interpretations. Several aspects of Christian life are involved: from liturgy to vocation, from the Church's relation to other religions to the question of Church and society, to name but a few. It is impossible, therefore, to summarize either the Council or how it was received, and especially impossible to situate Pierre Trudeau with regard to all of these aspects.

I will review here some of the Council's ideas that are likely to shed light on the faith and spiritual life of Pierre Trudeau, public figure and Catholic layman. They are, first, the Church's recognition of the legitimate autonomy of earthly affairs and, second, the specific nature of the temporal order and the discreet nature of the mission of lay people or non-clerics.[2]

The "Relative" Autonomy of Earthly Affairs

The presentations at this gathering demonstrate how the politician was able to keep a certain distance from the positions of the Catholic Church in the public arena, even while taking them into account. This distance is not unrelated to the new relationship between temporal and spiritual matters that had been developing over a number of decades and found new forms of expression at the Second Vatican Council. A new relationship between the Church and the world: this was one of the new directions officially set by the Council and the theme of one of its most famous documents, *The Pastoral Constitution on the Church in the Modern World*, more commonly referred to as *Gaudium et Spes* ("Joy and Hope"). The Council had been prepared for this fundamental discussion not only by theologians anxious to reflect on the relationship between the temporal and the spiritual and on the meaning of history, but also by lay people concerned with the big secular questions, especially in the vast Catholic Action movement (Thils, Maritain, Mounier, etc.). Furthermore, new cultural and socio-political ways of thinking had been developing as technical, cultural, and economic transformation accelerated in the West after the Second World War.

The age-old history of the relationship between the "heavenly city" and the "earthly city" had been a complex and turbulent one, involving rivalry and suspicion, intense debates on faith and reason, and constant battles for supremacy. Now, Catholicism was setting forth, in a conciliar document, the idea of the "rightful autonomy of earthly affairs" (GS 36): that is to say, the recognition that the world and the things of the world have their own particular nature, in accordance with God's will. This concept of autonomy comes closest to the concepts of secularization and secularism, without these actually appearing in the conciliar documents. By "rightful autonomy," the Council wishes to say that this particular nature is also assumed to be dependent on the Creator God and to have, of moral necessity, a reference point in the Creator. For example, the methodological approach particular to science and technology is legitimate and cannot conflict with faith if it is exact and moral.

The Council marks the end of the Church's systematic rejection of secularization, by the decisive orientation it gives to the relationship between the Church and the world. It also does this in the *Declaration on Religious Liberty* (*Dignitatis Humanae*). This declaration involves a revised stand in three major areas: the Church no longer defines its relationship to the state according to a logic of power, it abandons its counter-revolutionary positions by confirming the rights of the human person, and it gives up the Christianity project. Henceforth, state and religion co-exist in an autonomous fashion. As for secularism, it represents a method of deliberately eliminating any reference to religion, and Christianity cannot help but be opposed to this, even if only in the name of religious freedom.

The final aspect of this transformation of the relationship between Catholicism and the world is the theme of dialogue, so important that, at the height of the Council, Paul VI – a great admirer of Maritain – made it the theme of the encyclical *Ecclesiam Suam* (6 August 1964). Through the concept of dialogue, the Council acknowledges the end of assimilative Christianity and views the world as a "dialogue partner" (nos. 80-81). More precisely, Catholicism "lives in the world" and aims to "reach," "purify," "ennoble," "animate," and "sanctify" the culture in its positive elements: "test everything; hold fast to what is good" (Thess. 5:21). This is not, however, about a "separation," but about a "distinction." While declaring it is different, on the basis of its conformity to Christ and the Gospel, Christianity "unites" itself with the world, in the hope of evangelizing it.

Thus, the relationship evolves into one founded on dialogue, even if it is not egalitarian dialogue. The Council defines the parameters: moral soundness and the will of the Creator God. As a result, Catholicism continues to be characterized by various debates over the nature of this morality and this will of God, which it seeks to proclaim in the modern world. The particular case of the Catholic Church in Quebec illustrates this very well.

How the Second Vatican Council Was Received in Quebec

In Quebec, where the vast majority of the population was Catholic and where little importance had been given to developments among the Catholic laity, these changes had an enormous impact. The new teachings, established by the Council and approved by two successive popes, were welcomed with open arms by the predominantly Roman Catholic society. Within Quebec, strong and influential Catholic Action movements had developed through the initiative of progressive Catholic personalities such as Pierre Trudeau, Gérard Pelletier, and others. The new, less authoritarian view of the relationship between Catholicism and the world, and the recognition of the relative autonomy of the world, were greeted with relief. Many Catholics, however, were disillusioned by the publication of Paul VI's encyclical *Humanae Vitae*, which upheld the ban on contraception and reiterated the Church's negative position on abortion, pre-marital sex, divorce, and so forth. It was the appearance of this encyclical that crystallized discontent towards the Vatican. Not only the "dialogue partner" of *Gaudium et Spes* (i.e. the non-Catholic world), but also Catholics themselves did not view "dialogue" the way the Holy See in Rome did, especially regarding matters of sexual morality. These tensions persist to this day, as we can see by the controversies examined in this book – the decriminalization of abortion and homosexuality. The latter, though well after Trudeau's time, calls to mind those debates where he showed himself at once a Catholic and a politician.

A Discreet Christian Faith: The Lay Person as "Leaven in the Dough"

A final theological question deserves to be raised, this time in connection with Pierre Trudeau's discreet faith. Very much a lay person, he considered himself competent in temporal matters and left public discourse on religion and faith to clerics, religious, and others deemed competent therein. According to the Council, the most fundamental mission of lay persons is "to be present to the world" from within, to be "leaven in the dough." Specifically, they are called to "seek the Kingdom of God," "engage in temporal affairs," and "direct them according to God's will" (*Lumen Gentium* 31). These three elements together condition the secular life of the Christian. The search for the kingdom places the secularized world in an essential relationship with eschatology, without which it degenerates into secularism. The temporal domain concerns the milieu of social, family, and professional life. It specifically concerns lay people. Finally, directing temporal affairs "according to God's will" situates human activity within the framework of living the Gospel and following a theological ethic. The first and third aspects of this three-part secular vocation are the responsibility of all the baptized. Although ordained ministers may participate in the secular life of the Church, "by reason of their particular vocation, they are principally...ordained to the sacred ministry."

Trudeau also grew up in a Catholicism that, at least since the Second World War, had promoted a spirituality of discreet Christianity within secular life. For Catholics, for example, the lay apostolate consisted mainly of working *in the world and as from within* for the sanctification of the world, like a leaven (*in saeculo et ex saeculo*). The metaphor of the leaven shows that theological discourse on living the secular life developed in accordance with a theology of discretion, of Christians immersing themselves in a secular world that was more or less hostile to direct evangelization and at odds with Western Christian traditions. Consequently, what became valued was silent testimony, relevant social and political action that avoided proselytizing, the Christian again being seen as "leaven in the dough."

At the same time, this discreet Christianity and valuing of the world and worldly affairs may have contributed in other respects to the decline of religious practice, the dwindling of Christian communities gathered around worship, and a weakened catechesis. In a certain sense, one may thereby have promoted a Christianity that espouses the forms of a privatized modern spirituality. Moreover, it is in response to this discretion and this silence that, ever since the late 1970s, the very faith-affirming images of the public convert, the public figure as a person of faith, and the media-covered pilgrimage have been emerging – within older Christian traditions as well as in charismatic churches.

The Generation Factor

For several years, I have been carrying out various kinds of research on intergenerational questions, transmission, and youth. One particular action-based research study, led by a team from the faculty of theology, brought up the importance of the generation factor in Quebec society.[3] Not only did this qualitative research, which analyzed almost 300 interviews, divide the population into age groups, it also showed that questions concerning one's "generation slot" and relations between the generations (for example, passing on religious tradition, forming new ties) were of great importance to the interviewees. Factors relating to generation proved to be very important, not so much in connection with the life cycle, but rather in the sociological sense: that is, as marking one's experience and historical memory.

The fact of belonging to a generation whose youth was lived during a specific era affected that generation's way of looking at life, the world, and religion, as well as its deepest values. There was a clear dividing line between two main groups: those born before 1940 and those born after (the post-war generation). Another distinction appeared between those born before the end of the 1950s and those born after that. Those born before 1940, like Pierre Trudeau, grew up and lived their youth during a period when Christianity was strong, in an environment where the traditional values of stability and continuity dominated. As mature adults, they were able to integrate modern values with these traditional values.

People born after 1940 belong to the first wave of baby-boomers. Their youth was particularly affected by the great cultural and socio-religious upheavals that took place during the 1950s and 1960s.[4] However, these people remember the period that preceded the great changes and this sometimes creates inner tensions and ambivalence in them, as the transition was so rapid. Individuals born after the end of the 1950s can recall only the cultural revolution of the 1960s with its numerous reforms. It is the generation of the children of the baby-boomers – born during the 1960s and 1970s – that has religious institutions concerned today, in Quebec as well as elsewhere in the Western world, for they appear to be more individualistic with respect to religion, and less involved in faith communities. Consequently, we speak of the "deinstitutionalization" of religion.[5] Only time will tell whether this is a deep trend that is going to persist.

In Quebec, as in most Western countries, the cultural revolution began after the Second World War, on the heels of a baby boom and a new prosperity. Quebec is known for the magnitude of its baby boom and for the speed with which its institutions and values became secularized. In this sense, the so-called Quiet Revolution was a rather violent one! This explains why the notion of "catching up to modernity," which has an almost mythical aura to it in Quebec, flourished there: it showed that modern Quebec had emerged with remarkable rapidity from a Christianity that had been almost entirely closed in on itself. Nevertheless, while daily life and social values in Quebec had been strongly marked by religion, areas such as industry and science had already been undergoing major changes for several decades.[6]

Despite the socio-historical divisions between the generations I have just described, it is important to note that several common dimensions run through to and affect the generations of today. For example, political and religious institutions have, to a certain extent, lost the confidence of all the generations, and individual values seem to be winning out over public values. With respect to social and sexual behaviour, greater freedom is continually sought, with an emphasis on individual rights and the pursuit of personal happiness.

Pierre Trudeau belonged to the generation that was strongly influenced by Christian Catholicism and he remained loyal to a path of deep Catholic spirituality. Like several others of his generation, he succeeded in reconciling many traditional dimensions with very modern elements, by applying an intelligent Catholicism.

As we reflect on the spiritual life of Pierre Trudeau, we also discover the social, cultural, and religious context in which he was raised. He was an authentic lay Catholic who was deeply engaged in temporal affairs; his faith most certainly imbued his remarkable political career with strength, penetrating intelligence, and virtue. Behind the moving stories and anecdotes told by some of his friends and colleagues – with respect to the special attention he gave others, for example – there is no doubt that we can glimpse some of the great hallmarks of the Christian faith. Certainly, these include recognizing the world as having its own particular nature and living a discreet faith. As well, there is the power of this Christian message reflected upon during an entire lifetime: the symmetry between love of God and love of neighbour, the transcendence of the human person created in the image of God.

Trudeau, the great traveller and insatiable explorer of new paths, evoked another aspect of the Council as he participated in an era where opportunities for mobility soared: the acknowledgment that, in the other great spiritual and religious traditions, a truth, a grace – in fact, God's very self – is at work, and the recognition of authentic collaboration between Christians and non-Christians in bringing to fruitful completion their common tasks. This ability to mobilize around humanizing challenges, without attention to cultural or religious differences, is one of the great benefits of the legitimate distinction between state and religion.

Let the Jesuits and the Dominicans Quarrel: A French-Canadian Debate of the Fifties

Jean-Philippe Warren

Maurice Duplessis once declared that it was very easy to rule the province of Quebec: one had just to let the Jesuits and the Dominicans quarrel. Although this image reduces a very broad and passionate debate to a pithy struggle between two religious orders, it may serve as a starting point to better understand the intellectual revolution that took place in Quebec during the 1950s.

In only a decade the province of Quebec witnessed a dramatic change, rapidly evolving from the so-called *grande noirceur* towards a more progressive society. But since industrialization and urbanization were lengthy phenomena in Quebec, because they had provoked tremendous demographic, social, and economic changes many decades before the beginning of the Quiet Revolution, the very name and definition of the *grande noirceur* needs to be explained. How can Quebec be conceived as backward when massive economic and social transformations affecting the North American continent were also affecting the province? How can the 1950s be called a period of strong conservatism when those years actually correspond to an era of unprecedented prosperity for French Canadians?

The mainstream sociologists and historians' answer came as no surprise: "because of the Church," they claimed. The problem was not that Quebec's structures continued to be those of a traditional society in the middle of a modern continent. The problem was that Quebec's collective consciousness was still that of a traditional society, despite the industrialization and urbanization of the province. French Canadians had failed to acknowledge the obvious reality of their own transformation. The old order had taken on an air of unreality. This unreality was to be known under the idea of "cultural lag," a concept borrowed from the Chicago school of sociology, where Marcel Rioux, Hubert Guindon, and Jean-Charles Falardeau had studied. The social structures, transformed mainly by foreign influences, had moved forward while the French Canadian cultural frame of mind still lagged behind.

The fault, historians and sociologists alleged, fell primarily on the shoulders of the Roman Catholic Church. Similarly, the political power of the *Union Nationale* party and of its leader, Maurice Duplessis, was another favourite target of those critics who in the 1950s were trying to redefine the terms of life in Quebec. This political party was also blamed for the prevalent conservatism of the collective consciousness. Nonetheless, it had only "put into practice the conservative doctrines which had existed in Quebec for many years."[1] Duplessis had relied heavily on the numerous priests who controlled the population to impose an outdated political agenda. The Church was the controlling power in the 1950s and it had used its power to bring about the election of politicians who would not oppose its backward policies and outdated values.

According to Maurice Tremblay, for instance, "The Church had adopted a fiercely defensive attitude towards the influences of Protestantism and French modernism, and had thereby succeeded in keeping French-Canadian culture wholly Catholic." Unfortunately, argued Tremblay, "this victory was largely won at the price of a narrow and sterile dogmatism, and an authoritarianism fixed in a conservative mold." French Canada constituted a good example "of that narrow and unproductive ultramontanism which the Church has used as its chief weapon in its general policy of conservatism, and in the defence of French-Canadian Christianity."[2]

This historical framework has been widely used to describe the 1950s until recently. In my opinion, this black-and-white portrait gives a very simplistic interpretation of Quebec's history. Not because the Catholic Church did not possess the influence it was believed to have; indeed, it is difficult to argue it was anything less than the main institution of French Canada. The Roman Catholic Church controlled many aspects of human life that have now been turned over to the state. It had its hands in labour unions, schools, publishing houses, newspapers, social clubs, agricultural circles, hospitals, charitable organizations, and, last but not least, the parish. I am not trying to convince you that the

Church's impact on French Canadian history was unanimously positive. Quite obviously it was not.

My thesis is that the Quiet Revolution cannot be understood without taking into account the struggle occurring within the Church itself. The 1960s saw the victory of one religious faction over another, and not the victory of atheist and agnostic forces over the Catholic Church.

Some commentators will say that the result was the secularization of Quebec and the demise of the Church as the main French-Canadian institution. I agree completely. And this explains why it has taken so long for historians and sociologists to acknowledge the major role played by the Roman Catholic Church in this process of secularization. They have failed to see that the Quiet Revolution, to use an expression popularized by Marcel Gauchet in *The Disenchantment of the World*, corresponds to a religious end of religion.

To make matters clear, I will draw on a typology that had a very direct and personal truth for people growing up in the 1940s and 1950s. In his book *Le poids de Dieu*, Gilles Marcotte recalls how, when he was younger, the Catholic students divided themselves in two groups: those in favour of a more conservative ideology rooted in nationalism and authority, and those in favour of a more progressive ideology rooted in universalism and freedom. The first group I will call "traditionalist"; the latter group I will call "Personalist."[3]

The traditionalists were attached to the ideology established at the First Vatican Council. It was based on the assumption that authority prevents chaos, and that the best social order is authoritarian. In Quebec this religious stream of thought was taken up by the nationalist circles, so that the fight against the modern individualistic ideology was recycled into a fight against the Protestant and Anglo-Saxon influences.

Trudeau belonged to this traditionalist doctrine through his father, a lifelong Conservative and a close friend of Camillien Houde, and through his education. At the age of twelve he entered Collège Jean-de-Brébeuf, a Jesuit institution for elite French-Canadian boys. Although the overall pedagogical approach was centred on a conservative nationalist ideology and a careful Cartesian logic based on Thomism, Trudeau met professors there who were to have the greatest intellectual and spiritual influences in his student years.

Father Rodolphe Dubé, better known under his pen name, François Hertel, was the author of the revealingly titled book *Pour un ordre personnaliste*. He was one of those who acquainted Trudeau with philosophical and artistic subjects, which had been banished from the classic colleges' curriculum. He opened Trudeau's eyes to a world that was kept hidden from students because it was considered to be decadent or hostile to religion by other staff members of the Collège. As for Father Jean Bernier, another of Trudeau's professors, he recalled introducing "Plato as a model of intellectual courage." Plato, he said, "caused the Greeks to pass from a mythical to a rational mode of knowledge."[4]

One should always remember that this passage from myth to rationality did not occur overnight, and François Hertel's ideology at the time was more ingrained in traditionalism than he was willing to acknowledge in the 1960s. When Trudeau stated that he had "always detested" nationalism, and when François Hertel argued that his teaching aimed at proving the superiority of tolerance, they were telling only half of the truth. In *Le Beau risque*, a novel published in 1939 (in which many readers have recognized Trudeau as the main character), Hertel wrote the story of Pierre, a boy from Outremont who was a student in a classic college and indulged in an idle and "provocative for provocation's sake" adolescence. The young Pierre broke with his family background when he realized that the French-Canadian nation was in danger and needed to defend itself against foreign influences, such as the American Jewish culture. In this novel, Hertel imagined what he thought should be his student's future and intellectual career. For Pierre Elliott Trudeau he dreamt of a life of struggles to protect the besieged French-Canadian nation. Was not Father Rodolphe Dubé's pen name taken from one of Dollard des Ormeaux's companions? François Hertel died defending the French colony from the attacks of so-called savage Indian tribes. For Father Bernier, only the enemy had changed.

In 1937, Pierre Elliott Trudeau joined a secret society, the *Loges des Frères Chasseurs*. The activities of the society are not well known.[5] Suffice to say that it organized riots in Montreal to denounce the control that the English community was exercising over the city and the province. The ideas of the members of the small movement were simple. First, they wanted French Canada to prove its true Christianity by establishing an integral Christian social order. Second, they asked for the conversion of every soul to the spirit of the new era. Third and lastly, they pledged to work for an independent Quebec.

As we all know, Trudeau supported Jean Drapeau in 1942 when he campaigned against the conscription of French-Canadian youth and their enrollment in an army fighting a so-called imperialist war. For Trudeau, there seemed to be no real difference between Nazi Germany under the Führer, fascist Italy under the Duce, and Canada under Mackenzie King. In an enthusiastic speech, he declared the Liberal foreign policy "sickeningly dishonest." "The people [of Quebec]," he said, "are being asked to commit suicide."[6]

Within ten years, Trudeau changed his mind completely and performed a perfect reversal from almost everything his professors at Brébeuf had taught him. In particular, he came to challenge their moral philosophy and their political agenda. In brief, he strongly contested the authoritative morality, the corporatist doctrine, and the nationalist stance of the French-Canadian traditionalist elites. This he did, not only through his travels and studies at Harvard and the London School of Economics, but also through his readings of the preeminent members of the Personalist movement – a revolutionary Catholic political stream of thought led by Emmanuel Mounier, among others. Indeed, when he decided to join the Liberal Party in 1965 and had to summarize his political philosophy, he declared that he had always preached a "Personalist conception of society."[7]

This Personalist philosophy was not intrinsically Catholic, but in the particular historical context of Quebec its teaching was inevitably mediated through a Catholic culture. Its paradoxical result was to give Catholics weapons to fight the Church in the name of the true Christian tradition. It gave believers the right to question the Church on its own ground. The Personalist philosophy, to use an expression coined by Guy Cormier, was a kind of "anticlericalism from the inside." This *glasnost* and *perestroïka* provoked results very similar to those experienced in Russia in the 1980s.

In the 1930s and 1940s, the traditionalists perceived the economic and social crisis as a crisis of civilization. They lived under the impression that the prevalent chaos stemmed from a collapse of order. For example, the freedom indulged by rich capitalists, the liberty they had to set the wages and organize the economy as they saw fit, caused the worst consequences. The social ties were broken, traditional solidarity was replaced by a competition of all against all, the respect of rights and duties was reduced to a respect of cost-efficiency, and the equilibrium between the rich and the poor was crushed by capitalist appetites for ever bigger profits. In the opinion of traditionalists, this freedom was no freedom at all. It led to a new kind of enslavement, the worker bending under the iron law of demand and supply. In this system, the labourer was defined as nothing more than a simple commodity. Assimilated to butter or shoes, he could be sold for a price on the market.

This supposedly false notion of freedom had to be replaced by one that would not contradict the necessary respect for authority. As paradoxical as it may seem today, traditionalists believed that people had to obey to be free. Without authority men and women would not find freedom, only chaos. They would not be promoted to be masters of their lives; they would be diminished under a tyranny of chaotic desires and aspirations. Hence, what was needed was a promotion of authority, whether this authority be of the parents, the breadwinners, the proprietors, the priests, or, ultimately, God. "All authority other than God's own," argued one of the most preeminent French-Canadian philosophers of the 1930s, "comes from divine authority.... The idea of authority born of the free will of man, and constituted according to human calculations alone, has thrown into the world a social conception which is only a cause of trouble and a source of instability."[8]

Because of this conception of authority, the traditionalists were opposed to liberalism, whether political, social, or economic. Politically, they did not entirely trust Parliament and representative democracy since they did not recognize that people themselves are sovereign. Socially, they generally perceived change to the social order as a threat to the ancient harmonious and peaceful way of life. Economically, they favoured a strong and authoritative regime, leaning toward Italian fascism or Spanish corporatism and using Franco and Salazar as models. Corporatism became at the end of the 1930s the panacea to French Canada's problems. Not only did corporatism impose order on chaos, but it also realized a sort of independence within the Canadian frame. Corporatism promised to reproduce a traditional society that was not opposed to progress and modernization, and it also pledged to build a symbolic wall around French Canada that would isolate it from the rest of North America.

The Personalists broke ranks with the traditionalists on the notion of a new definition of authority and freedom. In the 1950s, the Personalists' goals remained the same as before; they wished, as Trudeau once wrote in *Cité libre*, "to testify to the Christian and French Fact in North America." Nevertheless, the question was no longer to impose official Christian structures to a pagan people. The challenge was to transform passive French-Canadian Christians into real, dynamic, open-minded, virtuous, and heroic Christians. Rules, regulations, and restrictions produced "external Christians": superficial, normalized, lip-servicing, bourgeois Christians. Personalists argued that a true Christianity was a Christianity of the heart and not a Christianity of sermons and morals. To keep the Christian faith alive, the traditionalists had covered it under a glass bell. But this, the Personalists declared, was the best way to kill it. For them, faith blooms in open air, nourishing itself from various sources, even the most surprising ones.

If the person was first, this meant that the group was second. That led the famous French-Canadian philosopher Charles de Koninck of Laval University to write a book bearing the revealing title *Personalism Against the Common Good*. For him there was no doubt that Personalism was a tool in the hands of those who wanted the destruction of the old traditional order. At worst they were anarchists; at best they were fools.

One of the intellectuals most profoundly shocked by the Personalist philosophy was Lionel Groulx. For Groulx the individual was only an atom of the larger organism. Each person was first and foremost a member of the race. Each person was moulded in a specific culture and one's very thoughts were rooted in the national soil. There was no escaping it: either you were for the nation, and thus accepted its commands and rules, or you were against it and were either a traitor or a degenerate and uprooted human being. This traditionalist nationalism explains the violent xenophobia of the time, which fills the pages of such publications as *L'Action nationale*, *L'Ordre nouveau* and *L'Action catholique*. It also explains how this nationalism could dissolve the individuals into a special destiny – the preservation of Quebec's French and Catholic society. French Canada had a mission: maintaining "the luminous heart of religion and of thought" in a materialistic and pagan North America.

With this context we can better understand the campaigns in favour of democracy in the 1950s. Furthermore, we can better understand Trudeau's comment that French Canadians did not want democracy for themselves, and that English Canadians never wanted democracy for French Canadians. Indeed, English Canadians were the first to benefit from this authoritarian climate. Until 1960, for example, the Montreal *Gazette* was a strong supporter of Duplessis. Each editorial was an opportunity to congratulate the premier on his sound political agenda and his great handling of the social crisis. *The Gazette* applauded, for example, when the *Union Nationale* Party sent in the mounted police to beat up the workers during the Asbestos Strike.

The Personalists believed the French-Canadian people had to be educated in democracy. This is why, in 1956, Trudeau became the vice-president and later, briefly, the president of *Le Rassemblement*, an organization aimed at furthering the cause of democracy in Quebec. In *Cité libre*, Trudeau wrote that "Democracy first! should be the rallying cry of all reforming forces in the province." Many Catholic intellectuals agreed. Within the priesthood, Father Dion, Father Lévesque, Father Poulin, and Father O'Neil were busy trying to convince their countrymen of the importance of developing a true democratic spirit, convinced that faith would suffer otherwise.

Democracy was the first step in the establishment of a Personalist society. But two other steps had to be taken before such a society would materialize. On the one hand, the policies of a real social democracy had to be put forth. On the other hand, the idea of federalism had to be rediscovered as a way of fostering tolerance in a world of growing diversity.

Social democracy was the Personalist answer to the corporatist cry of the 1930s and 1940s. The traditionalists had believed that the struggle between work and capital would be solved by the implementation of a corporatist regime. In Canada, the implementation of such a regime seemed a distant dream. In European and South American countries, its successful implementation seemed a materialized nightmare. Refusing to build a society based on an abstract conception of the group (the race, the social class, the state, the nation, etc.), the Personalists were advocating a social democracy in which each person would be served according to his or her needs and his or her rights.

In the aftermath of the Second World War, in Quebec as in France, a left-wing Catholicism was winning its battle against a conservative Catholicism. French-Canadian Personalists went so far as to collaborate with communist militants and Trudeau himself declared that the province had to be ready for socialism. Those declarations were, however, uncommon. Mainstream Personalism stayed within the borders of Christian democracy.

At a provincial level the Church controlled the social institutions; therefore the only state willing to move toward the establishment of social democracy in the 1950s was the federal one. It is thus not surprising to see that many Personalists invested in the federal governmental apparatus and became – as Pierre Elliott Trudeau did briefly within the Privy Council Office – high-ranking civil servants working to put in place social programs and policies to remedy such problems as unemployment, illness, bad housing, and retirement. A decade later, when the provincial government finally put forth its own programs and policies, Personalists who had attended schools of social, political, and economic sciences were anxious to exercise their technocratic skills and quickly invaded the Quebec bureaucratic elite as well.

A great number of those who participated in the Personalist philosophy were trained in Canadian Catholic youth movements. *Cité libre*, for example, was founded as the unofficial voice of the *Jeunesse Étudiante Catholique*, of which Gérard Pelletier had been president for many years. These Catholic youth movements were organized according to a federalist structure, a translation of a new and modernized concept of the subsidiary notion of the state. In the Church doctrine, a subsidiary state had to respect the natural divisions of roles and functions in a given society. It did not try to replace the family or the parish by a governmental apparatus if the family and the parish could fulfill society's needs by themselves.

The federalist state was no different from the subsidiary state except for its distrust of traditional society's inefficient organization. The Personalists were convinced of the need to rationalize society and make every social sphere functional. In their minds, the federal system corresponded to a decentralized state, capable of adapting itself to each person, while at the same time corresponding to a functional bureaucracy capable of administering the economy with a minimum of injustice.

In the aftermath of the Second World War, the Personalists discovered Keynesian economic organization. The Keynesian theory not only confirmed their views about social democracy but also strengthened their belief in the need of an efficient federalism. It showed that the autonomous policy pursued by the provincial state was no longer suitable in an industrialized society. When Maurice Duplessis declared that "the legislature of Quebec" was "a fortress" that had to be "defended without failing," the Personalists could oppose him on the grounds of a new definition of the economic and political organization of a modern state.

Politically, the provincial government was no longer the seat of French Canada. It was only a level of administration, centred on the needs and aspirations of each person, whatever the person's religion or language. Economically, the provincial government was no longer the locus of decisions. In a Keynesian economy, power lays in the hands of the central government.

For all the reasons mentioned above, Personalism fostered a revolutionary movement that had a tremendous impact on French-Canadian society. In fact, Personalism abolished French Canada all together. From then on, only a political community could define a society. Citizenship was no longer intertwined with language or religion. The purpose of the state was no longer the preservation of the race, but the flowering of each person thanks to the implementation of various social policies, including a Charter of Rights and Freedoms revealingly called in French the *Charte des droits de la personne.*

By privatizing religion and dissociating the Catholic Church and the state, the Personalists believed they would help establish a real Christian social order and build a French-Canadian society that would not be only externally and ritually Catholic. The result, however, was an almost total secularization of Quebec in the span of a few years. The state replaced the

Church as the supplier of social services. And the religious faith was henceforth confined to the private sphere of life.

Instead of Christianizing Quebec, Personalism stripped French Canadian Catholics of an important institutional support. The less the Church became important, the less faith played a central role in French-Canadian lives. Thus, because of their religious beliefs, the Personalists built a modern society that ultimately marginalized and dissolved their religious beliefs. They succeeded in their attempt to enlarge freedom and implement a social democracy, but this came at a price – the loss of the underlying principles for which those reforms had taken place.

Pierre Elliott Trudeau and the *JÉC*

Marc Nadeau

In 2002, thousands of young people converged on the city of
Toronto for one of the great moments of contemporary Catholic Action:
World Youth Day. Today it may seem that the place of Catholic Action in
the lives of young people – and even in the lives of adults to a certain
extent – is rather limited, at least compared to what it was in the past.
While the two movements – World Youth Days and Catholic Action (of
which the *JÉC* was part) – are indeed different in nature and scope, one
could claim that they are similar in terms of their ability to mobilize.

There was a time when Catholic Action movements were at the
forefront of social and intellectual life for Quebec youth. During the early
decades of the twentieth century, from 1935 to the mid-1960s, young
Catholics in Quebec heard and followed the beat of a stirring and rallying
movement. It was called *la Jeunesse Étudiante Catholique* (Young Catholic
Students) or simply the *JÉC*.

In the summer of 2002, I had the pleasure of doing research in the
archives of the *JÉC* paper. This was enjoyable work in more ways than
one. I discovered several pieces by Gérard Pelletier, who was one of the
masterminds of this Quebec movement. It also afforded me the opportunity to consult eloquent writings by Pierre Juneau and Roméo Leblanc,
from which I shall quote later.

Before I take a closer look at the movement's monthly newsletter, it
is important to say a few words about the movement.

The *JÉC* is one of the numerous Catholic Action movements born
throughout the world, starting in the 1920s. In 1922, Pope Pius XI
published the encyclical *Urbi Arcano*, in which he proposed that the gap

between the Church and the masses should be closed. It was after the publication of this encyclical that organizations like the *JÉC*, the *JOC* (*Jeunesse Ouvrière Catholique*), and the *JAC* (*Jeunesse Agricole Catholique*) were established. The *JÉC* appeared in Quebec in 1935.

JÉC members were suspicious of the Jesuits, who had begun another Catholic Action movement called "*l'Association catholique de la jeunesse canadienne-française*," a rival movement that was elitist, nationalist, and conservative. The *Jécistes*, for their part, were supported by the Dominican Fathers, the Oblate Fathers, and the Fathers of the Holy Cross.[1] As we are reminded by André Bélanger, "the *JOC* and *JÉC* movements were introduced into Quebec at a decisive moment in its history: the economic crisis gave rise, in almost all Western societies, to a moment of fundamental reconsideration."[2]

It was natural to the *JÉC* to use the Church as its cornerstone. In their biography of Pierre Trudeau, Stephen Clarkson and Christina McCall describe how members were recruited by teaching nuns and priests who had observed their intelligence and devotion.[3] Furthermore, the *JÉC* refused to be involved in any political activity and thus rejected any association with the prevailing nationalism. The organization's work, however, "stopped short of the social realm to which its members would later be so committed. In this respect, they remained quite separate from real life."[4] In other words – and this is quite natural – the *Jeunesse Étudiante Catholique* limited their action to the sphere of the student world. Their incursions into the social arena were in fact quite timid.[5]

And, in contrast to other Catholic Action movements, which appealed mainly to the moral values of its members, the *JÉC*, for its part, appealed to their knowledge. By way of illustration, the theme of their 1951 annual campaign summarized the essence and philosophy of the movement very well: "The idea of 'possessing the world' through intellect represents an attitude that would have been absolutely foreign to *JÉC* predecessors. It summarizes a humanist vision according to which human beings create their future, on the basis of what they have observed and understood."[6]

The *JÉC*, André Bélanger reminds us, was a movement that encouraged young lay people in Quebec to expand their ideological horizons.[7] But that is not all: "the *JÉC* of the 1940s and 1950s served as an *ideological matrix* for quite a succession of progressive [representatives]."[8] Although Trudeau was never a member of the *JÉC*, it constituted a veritable training ground for the future administration of the government he would lead. It included Gérard Pelletier, as well as Jeanne Benoît, Maurice Sauvé, Charles Lussier, Roméo Leblanc, Pierre Juneau, and, of course, Marc Lalonde. And

Clarkson and McCall remind us that it was Gérard Pelletier who would serve as liaison between Pierre Elliott Trudeau and some former *JÉC* members.[9] It is likewise important to mention in passing that individuals such as Father Yves Congar and Emmanuel Mounier had an influence on the movement.

The *JÉC* was an important and visible locus of socialization for the up-and-coming Quebec elite, and continued to have this role until the mid-1960s. With regard to influence, André Bélanger explained:

In actual practice, they [the members of the *JÉC*] were barred from taking charge of the social destinies of the collectivity. It would require the emergence of the *Cité libre* before any inroads into this forbidden area could be attempted.[10]

As we know, Pierre Elliott Trudeau would be much more involved in this second ideological "vector."

Let us now look at the movement's paper, *JÉC*, which in September 1946 changed its name to *Vie étudiante* ("Student Life") and continued publication until 1964. In its pages, one finds "articles on literature, film and the arts in general."[11] Events of a more social nature are less present – except for a few references to strikes, for example. That being said, "the face of the community does not show through in the pages of [the *JÉC* and] *Vie étudiante*, which is almost entirely devoted to the perfection [or fulfillment] of the person."[12] The emphasis is on individualism, the personal initiative of each individual.

Apart from the future members of Pierre Elliott Trudeau's immediate entourage mentioned earlier, Guy Rocher, Fernand Dumont, two future PQ ministers (Camille Laurin and Pierre de Bellefeuille), and Paul Gérin-Lajoie contributed to the publication. Even Robert Bourassa makes a brief foray into the pages of *Vie étudiante*.

There is only one text by Pierre Elliott Trudeau, which appeared in August of 1944. The topic of his text was the canoe expedition. Here, the future prime minister extols the virtues of this activity for those who practise it.

What are the benefits of this venture for one's character? Allow me to make use of an old distinction and I will tell you that the mind will come away from it not more rational but more reasonable; for during the experience, the mind will have learned how to work in natural conditions of productivity.[13]

Some excerpts from texts written by Pierre Juneau and Roméo LeBlanc help to illustrate the orientation of the *JÉC* paper. Juneau wrote:

77

Prevailing over all these arguments is one fundamental law: the requirements of reality over a "plutardiste" ["someday"] culture. We are working within time, as Richard says, on a project which must endure; already here and now we can put our hard-working hands to the task of building the everlasting City.[14]

We can already sense the desire and the determination to be involved within a greater whole. Following in the same vein, Juneau also defines the principles of reality in the December 1946 issue:

Granted, it is important to know all the moral principles to be upheld, but, precisely in order to better uphold them, it is also important to know the laws that govern the country's concrete situation, from the points of view of economics, industry, agriculture and so forth. Now, this does not fall under the mandate of Catholic Action. However, those who belong to Catholic Action must nevertheless consider one day moving beyond the limits of their current framework so that, with all their Christian energy, they may become committed to the study and resolution of the political problems of the country and the world.[15]

Finally, in 1949 the young Roméo LeBlanc penned a most interesting article entitled "Through the lens of the living":

If today, for example, our initial reaction to a situation like the asbestos strike is not one of sympathy for the strikers, if we have already reached the age where we do things gradually, don't want to upset anything, and want to keep the "established order," then at forty we will probably be among those who view all claims, all unforeseen demands as the bold behaviour of troublemakers, disturbers of the peace, and poor, envious revolutionaries.[16]

Here, too, we sense impatience for involvement, and even the high priority placed on it. In that same text, the future Governor General of Canada wrote:

Concern about the problems of the people is not just the domain of clergy and social science students. It is an attitude of life that must be urgently developed and nourished. Otherwise this concern will be [no more than] a dialectical topic, the paternalistic snobbery of educated people toward the uneducated.[17]

It would be interesting to go back over all the texts written by the future colleagues of Pierre Elliott Trudeau, but time precludes such a perusal. Nevertheless, we can draw two conclusions. First, the inner circle of the future prime minister was influenced by *Jeunesse Étudiante Catholique*. Second, we sense, especially from the comments by Pierre Juneau and Roméo LeBlanc, that the *JÉC* intended to move society forward. This intention would become fully realized in the years that followed. The *JÉC* was a movement of very great importance, not only in the history of Quebec and Canada, but also in the personal journeys of many who would become Pierre Elliott Trudeau's close political companions.

Discussion

B.W. Powe: There were two times in Pierre Trudeau's political life when he broke off with his former friends. The first was in 1963, when he decided to fight really hard the nationalist trend in Quebec and he made Pierre Vadeboncoeur, among others, his enemy. Vadeboncoeur had been his closest friend at Brébeuf in the 1950s. Then he broke with a former friend in the summer of 1965 when he announced that he would run as a candidate for the Liberal party. I think that one reason Pierre Trudeau decided not to be engaged in the NDP anymore was his pragmatic approach to politics. I believe him when he said that it was impossible to fight for changes inside the NDP; it would never be elected and it had no roots in Canada from coast to coast. If reforms had to be made – and according to him urgent reforms were needed – then I would say that the Liberal party would be the best carrier for those reforms. I am not sure that faith played a role at all in this aspect of particular engagement and involvement. I think he looked at politics as a pragmatist and he decided that it was time for something to be done. He was right in that he foresaw that the NDP did not have a chance, at least in the short term, in Canada. Faith really has nothing much to do with that.

David Seljak: Trudeau's circle at *Cité libre* was very disappointed with his decision. What I am going to say is speculation. David Martin, in his book *A General Theory of Secularization*, says that French Catholicism – that is, in France – was global, total, and oriented towards power. Therefore it generated a mirror image in a republican movement that was totalizing, and global, and oriented towards power. I wonder if the authoritarianism of French-Canadian Catholicism is not mirrored in Trudeau's own approach to power. Someone's psychoanalytic speculation suggested that there was a strong authoritarian streak in his family, so I will offer a sociological one as well.

Stephen Clarkson: My question is for Professor Warren. You said that Personalism, in practice, led to its own contradiction or self-destruction. Could you elaborate?

Jean-Philippe Warren: First, I would like to offer a word about what has just been said linking Trudeau's ideology and his involvement as prime minister. I think he would have endorsed Newman when he said: "If I had the choice as a Catholic to say cheers to my own personal conscience and cheers to the Pope, I would, as a Catholic, prefer to say cheers to my own conscience." It is sometimes difficult to draw the line between what is simply a personal choice and what belongs to a Catholic ideology. You can be in favour of freedom, but is freedom really only a Catholic value? I am not sure about that at all.

To answer your question about the contradictions of Personalism, I have absolutely no nostalgia coming back to the 1950s, but I think that this was a choice that led to the Catholic Church's demise – it cannot do without the institution itself. When the person says, "Okay, let's forget to act as a Catholic who advocates our Catholicism, let's just act as a Catholic in the privacy of our hearts," I think that the Catholic Church is making a bet that it will surely lose, as Solange Lefebvre suggested. Catholics need the institution. It is not like any other religion where you can rely only on private beliefs.

Stephen Clarkson: So it is destructive to the Catholic Church but not to Quebec. I thought you were implying that those values disappeared, whereas I would have thought that Personalism was quite successful in its long term goal.

Jean-Philippe Warren: Yes, I am happy that Personalists lost their bet. To answer your question directly, I think that it helped build a modern Quebec, and we have to applaud the reforms that were made in the 1950s, '60s and '70s. But if we look as an observer at what happened to the Catholic Church and its destiny, we have to say that you cannot have a humanist culture without an institution passing on humanist values, the same way you cannot have a Catholic faith without people teaching you about the dogma, the rules, without pressing you to go to church. You will not find on your own, as they believe, a true Catholic faith.

Stephen Clarkson: The gist of this conference is to lift up the hidden Pierre Trudeau, so we are emphasizing his faith and the influence of Catholic thought on him. But we have to remember the background to this conference: that Trudeau was a liberal; he was a great lover of the liberal tradition. We are always talking about a conversation between the two traditions, and that cannot be lost.

Gregory Baum: Personalism was a movement in France; Emmanuel Mounier was involved in it, as was Catholic Action. This was not an effort to dismantle Catholic sacraments or institutions; it was a movement that emphasized that people must make personal choices, and that people are responsible agents in a social sense. It distinguished itself from liberalism and individualism on the one hand, and from Marxist collectivism on the other, in searching for human social understanding. It was for freedom and engagement. I do not think the theory proposed by Max Weber – that once Christianity becomes concerned with this world this leads to secularization – is applicable. Weber argued that this happened to Protestantism, and the Protestant ethic became "this worldly." That is, religious energy was moved into changing things in this world, and Weber thought – without sufficient evidence, I would argue – that this was the cause of secularization. You still have the same theory, and a number of sociologists who support it. Because it made people independent of the institution, religion faded away. I am not convinced by this. I think that if we want to look for reasons why people moved away from religion, we have to look for other causes. At least I want to put a question mark behind the theory that Personalism initiated the decline of the Christian practice.

Solange Lefebvre: I agree that Personalism is not related to this enormous transformation in religious institutions everywhere. We call this individualization. It is not just related to liberalism or to Personalism; it is too complex.

Jean-Philippe Warren: Is it a good thing that these reforms have been made? Absolutely, yes. Were the results exactly the ones that the Personalists in the 1950s expected? Not really. And the Personalists themselves have written books and articles to say that this is not exactly the society they wished for. Are we in a better society now because of Personalism, openness, tolerance, industrialization, and so on? Of course we are. Was it the society they foresaw in the 1950s? Was it the Christian society that they designed intellectually for Quebec? I don't think so.

Gregory Baum: I agree, but I would say that to account for the rapid secularization of Quebec and for the secularization that began in Ireland in 1985, you have to look at the convergence of a number of different factors. This is a complex process; several trends are coming together in a particular way that deserves to be analyzed very carefully.

David Seljak: We see in the United States a broad acceptance of Protestantism, and yet the United States is a very religious society where rates of participation are very high. So the European experience of secularization has not been universal. You have to look at different trends, not simply the Catholic or the Protestant culture. I think because we are talking about religion, this panel is kind of a corrective to other analyses – as is Jean-Philippe's book – that look at those structural trends and emphasize them to the exclusion of religious culture. That is why this panel is focusing on religious culture. The one law or rule David Martin names in his book is that the closer the relationship of church to state before the great jump to modernization, the more secular the society will be afterwards. Furthermore, the lower the participation rate, the lower the attendance rate and the lower the membership rate after that period of modernization. Accordingly, the great secularization in Quebec is often seen as a direct result of that close relationship between the Church and the Duplessis regime in the 1950s. You can see the same thing in France, Italy, and a variety of other countries where you had a very strong Catholic government with close collaboration with the Church prior to rapid modernization occurring.

Jean-Philippe Warren: The question is not to judge the progress that has been made. The problem is to try to understand why in 1960 everybody was Catholic in Quebec, everybody went to church, and by 1966 the drop was already dramatic. Why were priests happy to be priests – or at least that is what they told people around them – and then when the state took over Church-run institutions, such as education and health care, why did they decide to become bureaucrats and marry and have children? What was good about it, and why was it important for them to realize themselves inside the family? The Personalist movement was saying this is what a human being should do: you should not be a priest, to be a priest is bad, you are away from the people, you are an abstract person, you do not realize yourself as a person; you need to love someone, to have children, and so on. So the Personalist ideology had a huge impact, not because it brought phenomena that were not there before – those phenomena *were* there – but because it legitimized a movement towards the modernization of Quebec. The idea of Personalism – that you should not educate your children in the Catholic faith because it would imprison them in the faith, would indoctrinate them in the faith, and would be propaganda, and that you should let your children do what they want to do and they will discover by themselves the Catholic faith at some point, has, in my opinion, not materialized. But are we better today in Quebec than we were before?

III

The Man and His Beliefs

The Man's Formation in Faith

Jacques Monet

Much has already been said about Pierre Elliott Trudeau's formation at Collège Jean-de-Brébeuf and the influence of Emmanuel Mounier's Personalist philosophy on him. Also discussed was the important role played by the *Jeunesse Étudiante Catholique* in the spiritual formation of so many of his French-Canadian friends and associates. I thoroughly agree with all this, of course, and presuppose all of it in my remarks.

I will concentrate on Mr. Trudeau's years at Brébeuf and propose to do a Jesuit reading of his spiritual formation there, concentrating on a few important moments in its development. I say "Jesuit" because apart from the first religious formation he received at home from his practising Catholic parents, especially his devout mother – a formation reinforced by the *Clercs de Saint-Viateur* at the Académie Querbes – it is the time he spent at the Jesuit Collège Jean-de-Brébeuf in Outremont that most marked his religious beliefs. It was there that he would learn how to articulate his faith to himself, that he would adopt the way in which he would reflect on it for the rest of his life, and that he would form habits about how he would witness to it in practice.

* * *

First, a word about Jesuit education.

The Jesuit educational system is based on a set of pedagogical principles worked out in the late 1500s by a group of Jesuit college teachers and theologians in the spirit of the Spiritual Exercises of St. Ignatius Loyola, the founder of the Jesuit order. The aim of the Exercises is, first, to develop in each individual person a close, affectionate – indeed a loving – friendship with the person of Jesus Christ as both the model of human life and the inspiration for one's service to others. Second, it is to integrate into this relationship with Jesus Christ all other relationships and concerns, including the teachings and traditions of the Roman Catholic Church. The system was published in 1599 as the *Ratio atque institutio studiorum Societatis Jesu* (the *Ratio Studiorum* – Plan of Studies – for short). It has remained basically unchanged ever since, and it is still followed in most schools directed by Jesuits. It was updated in 1832, in 1946, and then after the Vatican Council, after which it is often referred to as the "Jesuit Educational Paradigm." In any event it was certainly in full vigour at Brébeuf in the 1930s when Pierre Trudeau was there between the ages of twelve and twenty.

The object of the *Ratio* is the total and harmonious education of the whole person – mind, body, and soul. It is not the acquiring of knowledge, but the fullest development of all of a student's talents: intellectual, physical, and spiritual. That latter "religious" dimension is the main one, meant to permeate the entire system. Ideally the graduate of the system will be motivated

a) to seek and find God in all things, all being good, and to be chosen, or accepted, with a free will as a gift from a loving God;

b) to relate personally to Jesus Christ (God incarnate) as a living human person and then to articulate and defend this faith; and

c) to participate actively in human society for the service of others.[1]

The curriculum prescribed by the *Ratio is* usually graduated over eight years in a typical Jesuit high school and college. It includes courses in the classics, the arts, languages, and humanities; these are preferred to mathematics and sciences because they are seen as the best instrument to promote intellectual and moral growth. The courses in philosophy and "natural theology" are meant to develop spiritual insight. All courses are supplemented by many extracurricular activities: debates, elocution contests, study groups – especially by academies or clubs for small-group discussion about art, books, cinema, journals, music, painting, political and public affairs, theatre, and "missions." All of this is designed to help the mind enter into other cultures by understanding the genius of a language; to train it to reflect autonomously, and thus be better able to give leadership in service; and finally to enable it to reason through every question, and so appropriate the answer into a lifelong conviction. All this is "food for the mind."

The *Ratio* also includes a well-developed program of sports and physical activity. The purpose, in addition to strengthening the body, is to help learn the acceptance of success and failure, to become aware of the need to cooperate with others and to use one's best qualities for the advantage of the whole. Every Jesuit school thus typically has a full program of competitive sports and games as well as gymnastics, dramatic pageants, and plays. Most, especially in North America, also incorporate all or several of baseball, basketball, boxing, fencing, football, judo, karate, lacrosse, running, skiing, swimming, tennis, or yoga.

Those familiar with Mr. Trudeau's biography will recall how he became an admired skier and tennis player at Brébeuf, after being the captain of the junior hockey team. In his *Les Années d'impatience,* Gérard Pelletier relates how, on his first meeting with Trudeau (a chance encounter on Montreal's Cherrier Street in the early summer of 1941), he found Trudeau bursting with intelligence and muscle, "un athlète de première force."[2]

Finally, and principally, the *Ratio* insists that the curriculum nourish the soul. It incorporates into the schedule a daily low mass, as well as high mass and benediction on Sundays and feast days; daily morning and evening prayers; such regular devotions as the rosary, the way of the cross, and the nine first Fridays; weekly confession; and several preached three-day retreats and at least one eight-day retreat in the senior years. Each student is to have an assigned spiritual guide (if he has not already spontaneously chosen one) with whom he meets at least once a month for spiritual conversation. There are also planned spiritual academies for group discussion on the New Testament, on religious books or Church documents (such as Pius XI's *Quadragesimo anno* on social justice, which came out in 1931), on dogmatic or moral questions, and for debating cases of conscience, in which participants propose solutions to ethical dilemmas. Thus virtue gives its quality to knowledge. Thus the individual student is formed in attitudes and a set of values that strengthen active religious practice, ideally for life.

Such was the worldwide Jesuit educational system.

Now, Brébeuf and the young Pierre Trudeau. The *Ratio Studiorum* was in place at the college, which had just opened in 1928 for the boarders of the much older Collège Sainte-Marie (founded in 1848). There, the Jesuit system was also coloured by much of the intellectual atmosphere of Montreal in the 1930s. The overall *nationaliste* climate, tinged with anti-Semitism and corporatism, then prevalent in the other colleges in the province of Quebec, may have been more intense at Brébeuf because of the very close association of the French-Canadian Jesuits with Henri Bourassa, two of whose sons had just joined the order in 1931, as well as with the editors of *L'Action nationale,* which began publication in 1933. *Nationalisme* was also nurtured by the debates and historical pageants organized at the college in 1934 to celebrate the 400th anniversary of Jacques Cartier's "discovery" of Canada and, in 1937, to mark the centenary of the *Patriotes.* On the other hand, it may also have been tempered by Jesuit international involvement (such as the Jesuits' French-Canadian mission to China, which began in the 1920s), as well as by visits to the college of prominent French, Spanish, and Latin American Jesuit professors and writers – all objects of much exchange in the student academies.

The presence of a number of francophone students and teachers, usually fluently bilingual, from outside Quebec (the French-Canadian Jesuits had exchanges with their colleges in Sudbury, Saint-Boniface, and Edmonton) was another balance to the narrower Québécois *nationalisme.* One such individual was Jean-Baptiste Boulanger, who particularly impressed the young Pierre Trudeau. He recounts in his *Memoirs:*

> At the age of ten, he had written a biography of Napoleon that had earned him a medal from the Académie française. A native of Edmonton, he was fluent in three languages: French, English, and Ukrainian. We decided together to read over one summer the great works of political writing – Aristotle, Plato, Rousseau's *Social Contract,* Montesquieu, and others – and to exchange letters giving each other our impressions and our comments on each of the works we read. Boulanger knew more than me in this field, and that was why I hung around him.[3]

Another Quebec outsider was a young Jesuit scholastic who taught Pierre Trudeau *belles-lettres.* Robert Bernier, twenty-five years old when he came to Brébeuf from Saint-Boniface in 1935, was a Franco-Manitoban who, Trudeau said, "had a great influence on me."[4] In class, but especially in the academies, Bernier helped Trudeau in his reflections on the works of Locke and Tocqueville (which he had read earlier), and introduced him to Lord Acton, a Catholic liberal historian for whom "the Church was dearer to him than life."[5]

The point, I think, is that despite the *nationaliste* climate at Brébeuf, there was a current of what has come to be recognized as *"la gauche chrétienne."* This had a profound influence on Pierre Trudeau's spirituality.

This liberal current was certainly carried in the teaching and influence of Bernier who was at the college for the last four years of Pierre Trudeau's time there. Mostly, however, it was transmitted to him in the enthusiasm of another young Jesuit scholastic, Rodolphe Dubé, who was full-time at Brébeuf from 1931 to 1934, and returned part-time periodically between 1935 and 1939 as prefect of some of the academies and as *animateur* of a number of student clubs. It is Dubé who introduced Pierre Trudeau to the French spiritual writer Emmanuel Mounier and to his philosophy of Personalism.

Because there are so many references to Personalism in so much of what has been said and written about Mr. Trudeau, allow me to insert here a brief summary of Mounier's ideas by his biographer Donald Wolf. It may help to understand better what will follow.

Mounier's Personalism was based on belief in the person as a spiritual being, maintaining his existence by adhering to a hierarchy of values freely adopted and assimilated. The person lives by his own responsible activity and interior development, unifies all his activity in freedom, and by creative acts develops his individuality and vocation. The person freely involves himself in the world while maintaining a spiritual detachment from, and transcendence over, the material aspects of civilization. Personalism means "engagement in action" in contemporary civilization.

In October 1932 he founded the journal *Esprit*, in which he applied his philosophy of Personalism to the contemporary social, political, and cultural problems of the France of his day.

In Mounier's thought, a Personalist political order would be based upon a pluralistic society. The resulting democracy would be limited by the spiritual person and the rights of the natural societies that compose the nation.[6]

Rodolphe Dubé was twenty-six when he came to join the staff at Brébeuf, and during his years there, under the pen name François Hertel, he published a book of poetry (1934), a volume of essays (1936), and a novel on life at the college, *Le Beau Risque* (1939); he also worked on preparing what became a 300-page book of reflections: *Pour un ordre personnaliste,* published in 1942. The character of the protagonist in the novel, and the fine descriptions of his maturing in self-discipline, progressive initiation into prayer, and growth in the responsible use of freedom, are obviously modelled on Pierre Trudeau. In any event, Hertel's presentation of the great classical authors of world literature, his flair for the dramatic, and his sense of fun all proved very attractive to the young Pierre.

Hertel took Pierre and half a dozen of his friends under his wing. There followed academies for discussions on Alexandre Dumas, Dostoyevski, and Léon Bloy; essay topics on Sophocles as the greatest dramatist of all time *and* a winner in the Olympic games; long hikes in the woods on Mount Royal or through the architecture of Old Montreal; fierce games of hockey (the challenge was to not utter a single swear word throughout the game); directions on how to meditate the Gospels, on how to organize one's thoughts to avoid distractions, on how to talk with God. It is Hertel who suggested that Pierre keep a spiritual diary to record his successes and failures in meeting the challenges he set for himself. It is he who dared Trudeau to develop both his willpower by mental self-discipline and physical exertion, as well as a spiritual motivation in his determination to excel. "To an extraordinary extent," Mr. Trudeau later wrote in his *Memoirs*, "Hertel was our guide."[7]

This was certainly true for the introduction of Personalism. Hertel brought to the academies and to class the few articles in *L'Action nationale* that André Laurendeau, recently returned from France, was devoting to Mounier's thought, as well as copies of the new periodical *Esprit*. He also stimulated discussions on the writings of Jacques Maritain, who in 1933 began teaching at the Pontifical Institute of Medieval Studies at the University of Toronto and was thereafter a frequent visitor to the Université de Montréal. He recommended *Pour un humanisme intégral* and helped students analyze it after its publication in 1936, underscoring how Maritain related history, culture, art, and poetry to theology and religious experience.

* * *

After graduating from Brébeuf in 1940, Pierre Trudeau continued his reading and, dare I say, his prayer. Later, in 1945 at Harvard, he completed the search he had begun with François Hertel. "My adherence to Personalism," he wrote in his *Memoirs*,

> was not the result of a sudden flash of insight. Quite the contrary it was the outcome of a long reflection. [It was a philosophy] that reconciles the individual and society. The person is an individual enriched with a social conscience, integrated into the life of the communities around him and the economic context of his time.... It was thus that the fundamental notion of justice came to stand alongside that of freedom in my political thought.[8]

During Trudeau's stay in Paris a year later, the spirituality of Personalism became a firm conviction. He met Emmanuel Mounier briefly and by coincidence, but he talked often with Mounier's close colleague Henri Marrou, the well-known historian of the early church, and much more frequently with François Hertel, who was staying in Paris. (Hertel would leave the Jesuits in 1947 and Canada in 1949.[9]) Through Marrou and Hertel, he was also in touch with such liberal theologians as Marie-Dominique Chenu, Yves Congar, Jean Danielou, and Henri de Lubac. He would be part of the moment that would bring Congar to write years later: "Anyone who did not live through the years 1946–1947 in the history of French Catholicism has missed one of the finest moments in the life of the Church."[10]

Hertel brought Trudeau and Gérard Pelletier together again, the latter being in Paris working for the *jéciste* "Fonds mondial de secours aux étudiants." A dedicated worker for the *Jeunesse Étudiante Catholique,* and a sincerely committed churchgoer, Pelletier could see the crying need for change and reform in Quebec. He was very discouraged, however, by the Church's entrenched conservatism and apparent refusal of new ideas. The tempting answer seemed to be Marxism, but he could not embrace it. "*Ma préoccupation dominante était religieuse,*" he later wrote.[11] Pelletier and Trudeau discussed this in at least four or five long conversations. He had barely heard of *Esprit,* and even less of Personalism. Trudeau showed him there was a Catholic way to reform; he had thought it through and believed it could be found in *la gauche chrétienne* [the Christian Left], in Personalism, in *Esprit,* and in the writings of Mounier and Maritain.

The following year at the London School of Economics, reading Acton once more and introduced to Newman for the first time, Trudeau again reflected on *la gauche chrétienne,* on his conversations with Pelletier, on the spread of communism and its challenge to his Catholic faith. At Harvard he had chosen as a doctoral thesis topic "The interplay between two doctrines, Marxism and Christianity." He would never even begin that dissertation, but now his Personalist conviction had hardened. Again, quoting from his *Memoirs:*

My reflections as a student undertaken at Harvard, Paris and London reached their conclusion at LSE. When I left this institution, my fundamental choices had been made. I was to acquire more knowledge and to encounter countless options throughout my life. But my basic philosophy was established from that time on, and it was on those premises that I based all my future decisions.[12]

In *Cité libre*, founded in 1950, he applied to the Quebec context the full strength of his Personalist conviction. This was done with the *jéciste* Gérard Pelletier and the help and direct support of their friends from Paris: Henri Marrou, by now a regular visitor to the Université de Montréal; Paul Vigneau, who had also worked with Mounier in founding *Esprit* and often travelled to Montreal at the turn of the 1950s; and Albert Béguin, Mounier's successor as editor of *Esprit*, also in Montreal often during those years.

All this – Brébeuf, Harvard, Paris, the LSE, beginning *Cité libre* – was early in Mr. Trudeau's life. In 1950, he was just beginning his thirties.

* * *

Life went on, with the outward signs – discreet but real – of Mr. Trudeau's strong faith apparent to whoever would see them: the spiritual group discussions he held regularly for years with Dominicans in Ottawa and in Montreal; the exchanges over the writings of Chenu, Congar, de Lubac, Pierre Teilhard, Edward Schillebeeckx; reliving the heady days of post-liberation Paris; appropriating the teachings of Vatican II; the spiritual retreats at Saint Benoît-du-Lac; and meditation at the Benedictine priory on Pine Avenue in Montreal. All this was evidence, to my mind, of a man firmly rooted in a close friendship with Jesus Christ; a man spiritually dedicated to seeing God in all things; a man ever searching out how to integrate all of his intellectual, physical, and spiritual experiences into one whole for the service of others.

This was towards the end of Mr. Trudeau's journey. But the search remained very close to the lessons learned in the beginning at Collège Jean-de-Brébeuf.

The Unending Spiritual Search

Ron Graham

Generally I find that, apropos of the theme of the conference, there has been both more than meets the eye in the subject matter and in some cases less than meets the eye. Let me talk about the first: that which is more than meets the eye. What we have heard, of course, is the importance of the subject of religious spirituality. I think we can draw from that that virtually every public figure deserves a conference like this about this very important sphere of their life. It is particularly important in terms of Pierre Trudeau because he was an intellectual, because he did think long and hard about these issues, and because he was by every definition a man of faith. It is clear, from what we have heard, that this faith, these beliefs, this intelligence did not necessarily relate to any of his policies as a leader of the government. There was a very clear difference between his beliefs and some of his government's programs, which mostly emerged from his firm belief in democratic pluralism. It was not his role, as a believer in one tradition, to impose those beliefs on anyone else in this society, because we are a multi-religious, multicultural, multi-ethnic society. As Allan MacEachen says in Part V, he was clearly operating in a political context, and he was respectful of that context. There were things that he could do and things that he could not do.

I do not think we can point to any part of his career and say, "He did this particular action because he was a Roman Catholic." More to the point, his Roman Catholicism is relevant and pertinent because it serves as a framework for his thinking about all the issues that came across his desk, as Tom Axworthy explains [see Part V]. It was an intellectual construct, his individual personality, his total spirituality that was operating through his faith. As Michael Higgins pointed out, it came clearly through the many strands operating in Quebec: the Jesuits on his way of thinking, the Dominicans on his philosophy, the Benedictines and their contemplative mode, and Personalism in terms of social action. One larger framework was not mentioned; it is a dicey area, and I do not think any self-respecting academic would go there without great trepidation. I only venture there to offer an idea, more than to state anything as fact. This is the idea that there is a Catholic ideology, a Catholic ethic at work: a bigger framework in which he was navigating.

We know, of course, through Max Weber, the concept of a Protestant ethic in capitalism – that there are ways of thinking inside Protestantism that are applied to economics and social thinking. It is less clear, at least in my reading, that this idea of an ethic has been applied as clearly to Catholicism. Obviously, there is a good reason for this absence, because Catholicism is such a complex and international force. Even within Canada it is clear that an English-Canadian Catholic ethic is probably different from a French-Canadian one. Even within French Canada, the ethics of Jeanne Sauvé or Gérard Pelletier are vastly different from those of Pierre Trudeau or Marc Lalonde. They are not total and they are not universally the same, but nevertheless there is something there that I think touches on the theme of this conference. I put it out to the academics that a Catholic liberal is not the same as a Protestant liberal nor, I would suggest, is a Catholic atheist the same as a Protestant atheist. Yet, they meet at some level, as Mr. MacEachen says; there is a place at table where his traditions coming out of Cape Breton meet those traditions of Jean Marchand coming out of Quebec City. That is the type of area that I want to talk about for a minute. To do so I want to step back into an even bigger picture, to put Pierre Trudeau in that context.

Trudeau was very familiar with the work of Louis Hartz, the political philosopher at Harvard who taught him, and also Ken McCrae, a Carleton University professor whom Pierre helped on one of his key essays on the founding of new societies. Both Hartz and McCrae postulate that fragments of old cultures and old societies come into the new world and become new cultures in that new place. When they talk about French Canada, they describe it as a fragment of seventeenth-century feudal France. It moved here at a time of the great Counter-Reformation. It managed to miss both Voltaire and the French Revolution, and it entrenched itself throughout the nineteenth century on both the survival of French Canada and on the power of the Church. It was a very ultramontane Church, more so by that point than the Church in France and most of the world. McCrae and Hartz list some obvious, almost cliché-ridden, definitions of the characteristics of this fragment: strong central authority, order versus liberty, obedience versus conscience, the collective against the individual, ideals versus reality, mercantile or interventionist, and planning versus free enterprise.

I still would argue, and I am willing to stand corrected, that this Church attitude was still predominant in Quebec when Pierre Trudeau was growing up in the 1920s and 1930s. Despite the small liberal schools within Catholicism, despite modernization, despite new communications, it was still there, because the Church still controlled so many of the social institutions and wielded so much power. The Church had allied with nationalism; authority, community, idealism were the personifications of the Church at that time. What is extraordinary in the history of Quebec is that religion, even when it died, transformed that ethos into Quebec nationalism, as Pierre Trudeau himself wrote about. You can make a jump directly from Maurice Duplessis to René Lévesque or even Pierre Vallières, and you can see the transmission of these broad Catholic values where the authority figure is dead. What was left is the brotherhood of mankind. You can see this not only in Quebec but in Catholic societies around the world. You move very quickly from feudalism to communism, for example, without ever stopping at liberalism in between, because the intellectual framework in which they are operating has certain similar values in terms of authority, collectivity, and so on.

When Pierre Trudeau was growing up in this environment in the 1930s and 1940s, that is what he was hearing and that is what he was getting, particularly at Brébeuf. You remember the famous line of the Jesuits, "Give me a boy before the age of ten and I will have the man for life." Well, there is something to think about in that, because my argument would be that so much of what is said about Pierre Trudeau in this book were constructs that happened from 1945 on, after he was already in his twenties. These he superimposed on this base. I know that base was mitigated by all kinds of personal factors in Pierre Trudeau's life: for example, the influence of Franco-Manitoban Father Bernier, who taught Trudeau to read Locke and Montesquieu and Lord Acton is an important fact. The worldliness of Pierre's father is another factor. The Scottish mother and a bicultural and bilingual household is also obviously a factor, even though she was a very devout Roman Catholic. Perhaps most astonishingly, as Stephen Clarkson said, were Pierre's deep psychological reactions to the death of his father.

I am not totally comfortable with psychological projections, but in this case I talked to Trudeau about the impact of his father's death on his own ideology. He recognized the personal importance of this event, but also its impact on his concepts of authority. At a very tender age, just at the age where he was about to come into some sort of manhood and probably rebel against a very oppressive and authoritarian father, his father died. The rebellion that he could already feel welling up within himself was directed, first of all, towards God – he was very angry with God for killing his father. Second, when he got over that, he harboured discomfort at all authority. Whether it was throwing snowballs at a statue of Lenin in Moscow, or running off in the middle of conferences when everyone was expecting him to speak, he just hated the idea of authority imposing something upon him. This would flare up in a very adolescent way, as Trudeau himself recognized. That was obviously an important part of the psychological makeup that mitigated against his Catholic upbringing.

Nevertheless, it was a Catholic upbringing of that period, of that era, of that place. His liberalism, whether it is Personalism or whether it is an anglo-liberalism that came through his readings at Harvard and at the London School of Economics, I would suggest, was an intellectual construct on top of this base. He believed in liberalism but he forced it intellectually onto the base with which he had grown up, and it came late in his life. Most of his writings in *Federalism and the French Canadians*, for example, are based on readings from that post-1940s period, and most are readings in the English language. Nevertheless, so much of the turmoil of that intellectual debate was based on this idea of authority – that was the issue that really drove him in those days. Where should authority be? Why should I obey it? How much should there be? He was wrestling with liberalism on top of the great Catholic issue of authority and the role of the individual therein.

Let us jump ahead to 1970. He is there as prime minister, and very clearly settling into that cabinet in the mythical image of French power. There was not just Trudeau, but so many very powerful French Canadian cabinet ministers and advisers in his office. So what is French power all about? It is clearly not just about language or even language rights and, I would suggest, not even just about seats from Quebec. Nor is it really about the agenda of that particular cabinet. I would suggest that French power, because of the concentration of power in the hands of so many francophone Quebeckers who had come out of this tradition, was a different way of doing business and looking at society than had gone on before under Lester Pearson. It was more or less interventionist, *dirigiste,* as it was expressed in Quebec at that time. It was concerned with big ideas and big principles and big concepts and ideals. As John Godfrey says, it was based on the very Jesuit idea of *voir, juger, agir* (see, judge, act). I have spent most of my time writing about Pierre Trudeau, trying to overcome the three big myths about him: that he was an autocrat, a centralizer, and an interventionist. All three have been exaggerated. He believed in participation and consensus, as opposed to being an autocrat. He believed in federalism and decentralized the federal state more than any other prime minister, and in that regard was not a centralist. I think he was reluctant about a lot of the interventionist measures that his government took. He was, in his writings and to an extent instinctually, very much a free enterpriser because that was part of individual liberty.

Why, then, was he seen as a dictator? One reason might have been because it suited the opposition and the press at that time. The opposition in particular, and the nationalists in Quebec, wanted to see him as a centralizer. Conservatives wanted to see him as an interventionist, and people who had lost leadership inside the party wanted to see him as an autocrat. So his opponents propagated this idea of him, and the press picked it up. The second reason was that Trudeau did believe that the state had to act: *agir* was the purpose of the game. To act, it had the right to govern, and because he was at the centre of his theatre of government, he therefore defended the centre. Had he been a provincial politician, we would have a different image of him. The downside of the right to govern, as I saw it, was that he seemed to me to be comfortable with dictatorships of the left and right: Cuba, China, or Burma, for example. I remember an extraordinary moment, having lunch with Trudeau one day. He had just come back from Burma, and he said that the junta had found out that he was in town and they invited him to have dinner. It was shortly after the Tiananmen Square massacre, and they were telling him that the Chinese had picked up from them, the Burmese, how to handle their dissidents. Pierre for a moment found this an amusing story in which to be caught. I thought that this was a very unusual take on it and we talked about it. Even though it was not democratic, it came out of this belief that the state had a right to govern and that order was important in society, as well as liberty.

The third reason he was viewed as a dictator, I would argue, is that he made liberalism into absolutism. I remember the time of the Charlottetown Accord, where Chrétien was trying to find a way to negotiate a compromise and Trudeau was so heavily against the idea of a distinct society that Chrétien in private called Trudeau a fanatic on this issue. The War Measures Act was clearly, as Trudeau argued in defence of his actions at the time, a defence of order in a democratic regime against terrorism. The absolute in that case was not individual liberty or civil rights, but the ability of the democratic state to survive in the face of terrorists. Also very interesting was his idea of the general will, seen throughout the text of the Charter of Rights: the will of Canadians, the Canadian community. The will was not in Quebec, nor in the provinces, nor in the interest groups: but there was a general will of Canadians. That was part of his argument behind the Charter. It was a collective of Canada, a community of Canada.

The fourth reason he was seen as a dictator was, of course, his personality. He could not resist a challenge. He was extremely competitive. He enjoyed the Socratic dialogue, and he took no prisoners when he was engaged in it. He was best in crisis: he was cool; he was reflective; and he could be incredibly intimidating to his cabinet ministers, to his office staff, and to anybody else who got in his way. He could be cold, he could be cruel, he could be self-centred, and he could be mean. In that sense, I would argue, he was a very Catholic intellectual.

Would I say more or less? I think we can exaggerate, and are perhaps in danger of exaggerating, Pierre as a spiritual or a religious person. His spirituality was one aspect of a multifaceted personality and a multifaceted character. It may be an important part, but it was not necessarily the most important part of his personality. You could have a conference on nature and Pierre Trudeau, or an equally interesting one on art and Pierre Trudeau and talk about his deep love of poetry, painting, dance, and music. You could talk about the martial arts and the discipline he brought to that. You could talk about sex and Pierre Trudeau.

Mostly, I think, we project these things onto him because anybody coming into contact with him, and even through seeing him on television, recognized very early on that this was what the Chinese called a Superior Man. He was very Chinese in that sense; it was a Confucius thing. I remember talking to him about how the harmony of society was part of the harmony of the universe, and how politics was an ethical issue and required a sense of duty. He also picked that up from Montesquieu: knowledge, discipline, travel, the makings of a superior citizen, Superior Man. That is a given to anybody who knew him.

A couple of other things were equally clear. Certainly, he was not mystical. I do not think he had any time for the type of New Age ideas that were floating around, or even the mystical traditions in a lot of the old religions. He was not, as has been made clear, a member of the JÉC. He never wanted to be a priest, as far as I know, unlike a lot of his contemporaries. He never wrote about religion and theology. He never studied under Father Georges-Henri Lévesque at Laval, like Marchand did. Furthermore, he was not a seeker. Early on, a very close friend of his said, "Oh, ask him about his travels, his travels were a pilgrimage.

When he was in the Middle East and going towards the east he studied Zoroastrianism and got involved in all kinds of esoteric teachings." So I asked Trudeau about it, and he denied every word of it. His travels were sociological – that was his word. He wanted to see how societies worked, he wanted to learn about different cultures, he wanted to see the world. It was not a pilgrimage in the sense of a man seeking something. In fact, as far as I can understand, he already got what he was looking for and got it early. He had a faith based on reason: St. Augustine, Pascal, Thomas Aquinas. He had nothing new or original to say about that, so he did not write about it.

Finally, by his own admission, he was an extremely humble man. On a deep level, he never claimed to be wise, or to have the answer to anything, particularly on spiritual issues. Yet we projected that onto him: the "three wise men" who go to Ottawa; Richard Gwyn's famous title *The Northern Magus*; that he was a magician, that he was a shaman, that he was a sage. His enemies even thought he was Satan – you remember the thing about his licence plate being 666. I asked him about that, too, and he had never heard of it before; he said that was what the insurance people had sent him. More than anything, we were projecting this onto him because of his superiority, and we projected that because we are spiritual searchers ourselves. We thought even better of him, knowing that it was learned and not natural to him. He had learned those skills; he had developed his mind, his body, and his superiority; and that was more intimidating and more impressive still.

I think we project the idea of him being a "wise man" or wise onto his silence. Being with Pierre Trudeau was often to be with silence. I remember one lunch, sitting with him, and wondering how long we could go without either of us saying a word before he would speak. We went through an entire bowl of soup, two of us in a restaurant, waiting for the other person to say something, and he seemed totally unfazed. I realized we were going to go through the entire lunch without him saying a word. Finally, I gave up and spoke. There was very little small talk in him; it was a huge emotional reticence. He confessed to me once that he saw his inability to express his emotions to outsiders and even to loved ones as a weakness, and not a strength. There was the legendary privacy we have been hearing about in the sense of a discreet faith. There were also huge defensive barriers he had put up, by his own admission, at the time of his father's death, when he was a puny, vulnerable, beat-up little kid. He learned these powers and these defence mechanisms so the world would no longer be able to hurt him. He recognized that this also was a weakness and not a strength in himself.

Then it was his old age when his mind began to go. I remember the lunch when he said, "I fear going gaga." That fear of going "gaga," of getting up and saying something that might peter out into nothing, or losing his train of thought in the middle of it, kept him silent near the end. That is the power of what the Jungians called the Withholding Parent. I know the phenomenon because my own father was a withholding parent, the same type, the same generation, about the same age as Pierre Trudeau. It was a generational thing as well as a cultural thing, where you did not project out, you did not say what you were feeling; you kept it to yourself. In that keeping to yourself, people projected their own insecurities onto you and that gave you power. "Does he like me? Am I boring him? Am I smart enough to be sitting at this table with him? Am I amusing enough? Am I good enough? Am I disciplined enough? Can I compete?" These were pressures that almost everyone, including his wife, as she wrote in her memoirs, talked about. In that emptiness, in that silence, in that withholding that he was a victim of by his own admission, we project wisdom: this all-knowing seer, this judgmental father, this piercing intellect who is going to be able to see into our souls and judge us, this omnipotent human being who also happens to be either prime minister or former prime minister. Certainly I felt like that. The lunches with him were like being at a table with the gods: the conversation was so excellent, the thought so precise, the level so interesting, the twists so unexpected. And yet I felt unworthy to be there because the carrying of the conversation was on my shoulders.

I learned a trick early on with Trudeau, while we were doing the television *Memoirs*. The first session was done over the course of a week, rotating one day in English with me and one day in French with a journalist from Quebec. We would ask the same questions, on the whole. I discovered very early in the process that if I asked the soft question, "I am genuinely interested in finding out what you were thinking at this period in time," I would get a wonderfully deep, thoughtful, honest answer. The French journalist was more confrontational and wanted to challenge him about this, that, and the other thing, and you would get wonderful television but it was all smoke and no substance. When I learned that, I realized that he would tell me anything – this legendary privacy was not really there if you just asked the question in a way that made him believe that you sincerely wanted an answer and were not just looking for a fight. When I asked questions that way they revealed an extremely tender, polite, vulnerable, decent, kind, patient gentleman. I knew the other side of him. I had seen the other side in the political realm, but I never saw that once in all the time I was with him. It was clear that the only conditions of our being there were that they would be off the record in his lifetime, but after that he recognized that he belonged to history. He was not sure how history would judge him, and he did not care particularly, but he recognized that he belonged to history – he just did not want to be bothered during the rest of his life. That was the condition of these questions over a dozen years.

Finally, we get to the moment, a terrible lunch, three days after Michel's funeral. I had helped him write the condolence notes that he sent out to people who had sent him letters. The letters were overwhelming, numbering about two hundred. I tried to express to him that these letters were a sign of love to him, that it was a way for Canadians to say "we loved you" or "we appreciated you" and "while you are still alive we are going to use this tragic occasion to say this to you." He understood and accepted that, and was grateful. We went into an Italian restaurant, and the waiters and everybody who went our way were tiptoeing around the subject: "Do I dare interfere? Did he tire of the subject? Does he want to talk about it?" The waiters embraced him as he came in and did not say anything. We sat down and shortly afterwards I said, "How are the boys doing?" He said, "They are doing better than I am," and then he started to talk about what he was going through. He was going through a crisis of faith. He could not find the reason why God had killed Michel. Why had God taken Michel and left him an old man on earth? What was the reason for that? And worse, "Am I responsible for Michel's death because I encouraged him to be fearless?" He was tormented and he was at a crossroads. His faith, which he had built on reason, had been demolished. I do not know what his confessor or his spiritual directors were telling him at that time, but I could not tell him, "This is a test of God to try your faith," because it was nonsense in his grieving to say that. All we talked about was the idea that every spiritual path, no matter what it is, is at the core to get beyond your ego. You have to penetrate the shells and the barriers. You have to learn how to cry. You have to learn how to love. You have to learn how to become dependent on other people. You have to surrender these barriers and the self you have built up over decades of living. Reason will never get you the answer; you have to go through this dark night of your soul to find out what is making you what you are.

I do not know how it ended. I do not know if he ever regained his faith. I do not know if he ever found his balance. I do not know if he found wisdom near the end. I suspect, based on the person I saw during that lunch, that he did not.

In the Bible they talk about the three great temptations of Christ in the desert. Metaphorically or mythically these personified different things: stone was wealth, the kingdoms of the earth were secular power, and "Are you the son of God? Throw yourself off!" was spiritual pride. It was my conclusion, at the end of Pierre Trudeau's life, that he was a superior human being: a great searcher, a powerful man. He had survived the first temptation, and when they offered him temporal power in the kingdoms of the earth that is where he went. I also believe that he was an old soul and that we will be seeing him again.

His spiritual search is not over.

Faith in Conversation

Nancy Southam

A year ago I completed a master of divinity degree at Weston Jesuit School of Theology in Cambridge, Massachusetts. I could probably also add that I won the award for taking the longest to finish the said degree. In the last five years of Pierre's life, he and I were neighbours in Montreal. I would come home from studying and we would get together for lunch or dinner or a walk. He was fascinated by what I was studying and with what the most recent Jesuit theologians were saying. I cannot imagine that he really loved it every time we talked about theology, but the poor guy got it for five years from me. A lot of the conversations were private, but I will very briefly share with you a couple of ideas that we talked about.

Certainly we talked a lot about the Bible: the various interpretations, the various translations, the different audiences for whom the suspected writer was writing. I had a problem with what I call Paul's "Mail" in the New Testament – Paul's Letters. I would occasionally rant and rave about my opinion on Paul and this became an in-joke with Pierre. I would get going on something, and he knew I was probably wrong. He would say, "So, are the Jesuits still trying to convert you?" I should explain that I am Anglican, and that I am quite happy in my faith.

Another area that we discussed was moral theology. I ended up developing an interest in the virtue of mercy, and subsequently wrote my thesis on that subject. I knew nothing about moral theology, let alone Catholic moral theology. It was not just about good and bad behaviour; it became goodness and rightness, and there was a distinction between right behaviour and good behaviour. I think he was very interested in the virtue of mercy because I do not think it had really been explained to him at Brébeuf. There was a new interpretation that was developed by one of my teachers at Weston, in which he defined mercy as "the willingness of someone to enter into the chaos of another in order to ease their pain." So we discussed that often.

The study of theology got very frustrating because it is trying to describe or define something that is essentially ineffable, indescribable: God. You can have all this theory and interpretation but, at the end of the day, it does depend upon your faith, what you believe. I do not think you know what your faith is, how wide or deep or unshakeable it is, until something tricky happens to you. Of course, in Pierre's case it was that awful mid-November morning in 1998 when the two RCMP officers came to his front door to tell him about his son Michel's tragic accident. I remember much about that time. The night before the memorial service I went over to see Pierre. I did not say much, but I just sat with him while they planned the service. One of the boys asked Pierre if he would read something at the service: Paul's famous bit on the resurrection, 1 Corinthians 15, which is often used in funerals. He said to me, "They have asked me to read this; what do you think?" I did not think the question was about whether or not it was the right reading. I thought the question was more like, "Do you think that I can handle this?" I remember looking at him, and I said, "I do not think you can get through this." Here was a very strong but broken-hearted, shocked, wounded father who had obviously had a brilliant career making speeches in front of a lot of people. But this was the one time that he had to speak and I did not think he could do it. He wanted my advice and I gave it to him. Of course it was wrong. At the memorial service the next day, he got up from the pew and he walked up to the pulpit. Stooped over, he started off in a low sort of quiet voice. As he was reading the words, it was absolutely clear to me that he believed every word of what Paul wrote on the resurrection.

That is one personal example of Pierre's faith. In the couple of years between Michel's death and Pierre's death, we spent a lot of time on the Book of Job. It is a very complicated book, but one way that I tried to help Pierre with the loss and the grief he was suffering was by pointing out that Job had had great patience. I really think that Job is a model of the faithful human being; he rants and raves at God but he never gives up his faith. Over the course of many conversations, I discussed with Pierre how there is a way of seeing God as the only character in the book that allows Job to grieve. While his so-called friends rambled on about divine retribution, God was the only character that was silent; not absent, but silent as a presence.

I gave him articles that I had to read in my studies; I decided one day to give him a book by Roger Haight that I had been taught but that I found wholly complicated and did not understand. I gave Pierre the book, assuming that he would not understand it. Not only did he get through it once, he read it twice before giving me an analysis of the entire book. Pierre understood it all completely.

We read poetry after that.

IV

Trudeau, Politics, and Faith

Faith and Politics

Rt. Hon. John N. Turner

Pierre was a committed Christian, a convinced Catholic, although he did not wear it on his sleeve. He had an ecumenical view of the Christian faith, fully supported Christian unity, and was multicultural in his view of the country. He felt that politics had to reach out to the wider good, the common good.

We spent very friendly times together. I knew Pierre well before we entered Canadian politics together, and he was always a practising Catholic. One Christmas Eve, he phoned me and asked, "John, are you going to midnight mass tonight?" I said, "Geills and I are going to be there." He said, "Where are you going to go?" I said, "To Our Lady of Mount Carmel." "Margaret does not want to go to church in French tonight," he replied. "She would like to come with you, if you will take us to your church." I said, "Show up at 11:30 and you will be with us at midnight mass." So I called Father O'Rourke, who was the parish priest and said, "Don't let this disturb you but I am going to give you a little advanced warning of this. The prime minister of Canada and Mrs. Trudeau are going to be at our church tonight." He said, "Jeeessssus!" I said, "You don't have to change your sermon. Whatever you were going to say, say it. Just leave the usual row I have in the fourth or fifth row for the four of us, recognize his presence and Mrs. Trudeau's presence, leave room for a couple of Mounties at the back of the church and everything will be just as if he weren't there." Anyway, it went marvellously. It was a great midnight mass and of course the next morning Justin was born, on Christmas Day 1971.

When Pierre won the leadership of the party in 1968, running against great stalwarts like Allan MacEachen and myself, he became prime minister and asked me to succeed him as minister of justice. That ministry involved the issues of abortion and homosexuality. Of course, I was a practising Roman Catholic – as was Pierre – so I had to face these issues in terms of personal conscience as well. I am going to take you through a brief history of both issues.

* * *

The amendment on abortion meant that abortion would no longer be a crime where "the life or health of the mother was in danger." The effect of this amendment was to establish a statutory defence to the procuring of a miscarriage *if* three conditions were met. First, the operative procedure was carried out by a qualified medical practitioner, that is, a doctor. Second, the operative procedure was performed in a hospital accredited by the Canadian Council on Hospital Accreditation or in a hospital in a province approved by the provincial minister of health. Third, a therapeutic abortion committee appointed by the management of an accredited or approved hospital consisting of not less than three qualified medical practitioners certified in writing that in its opinion the continuance of the pregnancy would be likely to endanger the life or health of the mother. That was a pretty organized procedure, but it was not a reform as trumpeted by Pierre Trudeau. Quite frankly, when I looked into it, it merely codified into statutory form what the courts in all the English-speaking countries had been deciding for more than half a century. I received a written opinion from the federal department of justice that confirmed that in Canada, the United Kingdom, the United States, and Australia, for over fifty years the courts had never allowed a prosecution against a doctor or a mother where her health or life would have been in danger because of carrying the child. I then sought three outside legal opinions to the same effect, and I chose three prominent Catholic lawyers whom I knew very well. First, John O'Brien of the O'Brien-Holme-Nolan firm in Montreal, who, while I was president of the Junior Bar in Montreal, happened to be the president of the Bar Association de la Province de Québec. I also got an opinion from Jack Weir of the firm Weir & Foulds in Toronto, who later became president of the Quebec Bar Association. The third opinion was from my hometown of Vancouver: C. Francis Murphy of the great firm Farris, Vaughn, Wills & Murphy. After their own independent research, all three firms duplicated the opinion that I had received earlier from the department of justice. The amendment of abortion was not a change in the law; it was just rendering statutory what the courts had been deciding for fifty years.

I then met with the executive of the Canadian Conference of Catholic Bishops (CCCB) for discussions at Cercle Universitaire on Laurier Avenue in Ottawa. The CCCB chairman at that time was Alex Carter, the bishop of North Bay and the brother of Toronto Archbishop Emmett Carter. I showed him all the opinions, and for twenty minutes these were circulated. The conclusions were very succinctly drawn, and Alex Carter said to me, "Gentlemen, I think John has convinced us. Let's have a drink." Thankfully, I was not representing the Presbyterian Church. The Catholic Church never again intervened on that issue.

During the early 1980s I was out of government, having resigned in 1975, and was practising law in Toronto. Archbishop of Toronto (later cardinal) Emmett Carter,[1] my tennis partner in those days, asked me to have lunch with him. He said, "I have been told by my counsel that this Charter that Trudeau is proposing could jeopardize the abortion issue." I said, "Well, I have not really looked into that, your Eminence, but why don't you go talk to Trudeau?" So he went up to see Pierre in Ottawa with his legal opinion. The next day he came back and told me that he felt he was unsuccessful with Trudeau, and he left it at that. Of course the Charter was passed, and fifteen years later the Supreme Court of Canada used it to strike down the abortion legislation that I had been responsible for on Trudeau's behalf. This legislation itself had been the Church's last and best defence on the abortion issue, and the Charter had thrown that into jeopardy.

* * *

I inherited another piece of criminal law from Pierre – that homosexuality was no longer to be a crime if it was a private act between two consenting adults. It is worth quoting some of the House of Commons debates to illustrate the arguments that I made at the time. On April 17, 1969, I explained:

> Mr. John Turner (Ottawa-Carleton): In private. In other words, when acts are committed in private between two consenting adults, these acts, however indecent or repugnant or immoral, should remain a matter for their own private consciences and not a matter bringing into play the Criminal Code of Canada. The conduct contemplated in this clause, homosexual acts between consenting adults in private, is repugnant to most of us. It is repugnant to the great majority of people of Canada. I resent

very much the argument of some members of the opposition that this legalizes homosexuality.

Mr. Marcel Lambert (Edmonton West): Of course it does.

Mr. Turner: It surely does nothing of the kind. The clause does not endorse such acts. It does not promote such acts. It does not advocate such acts. It does not popularize such acts. It does not even legalize this kind of conduct.

Mr. Lambert: It legalizes it. Of course it does.

Mr. Robert Stanfield: Would the minister permit a question for sake of elucidation? I understood him to say the attitude of the government was to leave these acts entirely within the realm of private judgment. If this is so, how can such conduct possibly be illegal?

Mr. Turner: With the greatest respect, I think that is a bit of sophistry. The Leader of the Opposition (Mr. Stanfield) was not present throughout the debate yesterday, although I presume he read *Hansard*. The argument put forward by some members of the Opposition was that the effect of this clause was to legalize or condone a standard of conduct which to most of us is physically and morally repugnant. It does nothing of the kind. It merely lifts the stigma of the criminal law from a certain type of conduct which we consider to be private conduct which ought not to be within the purview of the criminal law. That is the purpose of the clause.

It is our view that it is not the purpose of the criminal law to probe into the private lives of individuals where the public order is not involved. Here I come to another argument, and in this I believe a good many members of the House will support me. A penal law is not a good law unless it is an enforceable law. A law which is not enforceable is not a good law. And it is our judgment that a law against the kind of conduct contemplated in clause 7, acts between consenting adults in private, is unenforceable, indeed that attempting to police this type of conduct by probing into the private lives of people would bring the whole system of law into contempt and disrepute and thereby contribute to making the law less credible. I believe that public order would be better served by the amendment to the code which we propose.

May I thank you for your indulgence, Mr. Speaker. I appreciate that hon. members opposite have suggested in rather strong terms that law and morality ought, where possible, to be synonymous, public law and strictly private morality. However, I cannot accept that. I suppose that in a perfect society where one would have unanimous opinion as to what is morality and what are standards of good behaviour[,] this might be so. But the problem of trying to render synonymous law and morality is then we come down to the question[s]:

Whose morality?

Whose standards of behaviour?

...Who is to attribute blame?

Who is to say what is moral and what is immoral?

Who is to decide when moral responsibility exists in terms of freedom of will, and when it has to be diluted in human terms because of environmental or physical causes?

We believe that morality is a matter for private conscience. Criminal law should reflect the public order only. Despite the fact that most of us in our personal convictions have a complete repugnance to the conduct from which we are lifting the taint of criminal law, this does not to my mind interfere with the validity of the principles that we are trying to submit to the House.[2]

In other words, Trudeau's legislation, which I inherited, did not legalize homosexuality or render it into a separate marital estate. That needs to be perfectly clear in judging Trudeau's faith – on both of these issues. On the abortion issue he did not change anything. On homosexuality he did not recognize the act; he just took the criminal code away from private conduct. On May 12, 1969, I said in the House of Commons:

I want to repeat what I said on second reading: all that is immoral has not been and is not now criminal. I agree with and support the view that in the field of sexual behaviour the basic function of the criminal law is to preserve public order and decency. It is to protect the citizen from what is offensive and injurious and to provide sufficient safeguards against the exploitation and corruption of others, particularly those who are especially vulnerable because they are young, weak in body or mind, inexperienced[,] or in a state of special physical, official or economic dependence. Where potential violence, corruption, public order or the total integrity of society are involved, or where the general consensus of what is right and wrong is involved, then there is a connection between law and morals. In those certain areas of private behaviour which are more properly left to the conscience, which are in private and do not involve public order or the corruption of others, particularly the young, we are of the view that this is no place for the criminal law.[3]

Homosexuality never became an issue with the Catholic Church. The Canadian Conference of Catholic Bishops never raised it as they did the abortion issue. At that time, abortion was the far more difficult situation; the Church did not raise homosexuality because the bill did nothing to enhance the legal status of the homosexual unit. By contrast, it provoked far more attention in the House of Commons than did the abortion debate. The third reading got pretty rough. Mr. Diefenbaker made one of the roughest speeches that I have ever heard in the House on that issue. He was looking at me and said, "I have known that man since he entered the House. Why is he carrying this issue? I know why he is carrying it; he has got a dagger in his back and on the hand of that dagger is the hand of the prime minister." I thought the best remark of the debate was Réal Caouette's contribution: "Being homosexual is now okay, as long as it is in private between consenting Liberals."

To summarize, Pierre Elliott Trudeau believed that law and morality were separate issues; I am telling you that in neither the abortion issue nor the homosexuality issue, which he introduced and which I successfully piloted through the House of Commons, were those issues at stake. There was nothing new in the abortion situation, and there was nothing that raised homosexuality to a separate legal status. Law, he and I believed, should deal with public order, whereas morality was a matter of private persuasion. He encapsulated it in words that the country never forgot: "The state has no place in the bedrooms of the nation." Throughout all of this time, and until the day he died, his private faith in Christ remained firm and intact.

Slow to Leave the Bedrooms of the Nation: Trudeau and the Modernizing of Canadian Law, 1967–1969

Andrew Thompson

In December 1967, then Minister of Justice Pierre Elliott Trudeau uttered what would later become one of the most memorable phrases of modern Canadian politics: "The state has no place in the bedrooms of the nation."[1] At the time, he was in the process of proposing sweeping reforms to the Criminal Code of Canada. His goal was to modernize Canada's criminal laws, some of which were more than a century old. Specifically, he wanted to reduce the state's role in regulating moral behaviour. Ultimately, he desired a criminal code that differentiated between "sin and crime."[2] Still, Trudeau proceeded with caution with his reforms. Above all, he was as much a pragmatic politician as he was a philosophic thinker. Perhaps better than any of his predecessors as minister of justice, he understood that separating moral and religious values from the law was easier said than done, even in an increasingly secular and pluralistic society. In doing so, he showed that the law and morality are clumsy yet inseparable partners; the former is inevitably connected in some way to the latter. Moreover, he showed that reform can, in some cases, be just as polarizing and as exclusionary as maintaining the status quo.

The reforms that Trudeau sought were ambitious, controversial, and above all overdue. Among many amendments, he sought to legalize therapeutic abortions and the dissemination of family-planning materials. He also advocated decriminalizing homosexual acts between consenting adults. And, in a separate piece of legislation, Bill C-187, he proposed reforms to the divorce law that included a number of new grounds for divorce, the most contentious of which was the open-ended concept of "marriage breakdown."[3] Many Canadians welcomed with great enthusiasm the prospect of removing the state from the private affairs of individuals. Not surprisingly, in taking on the challenge of overhauling the criminal code, Trudeau quickly came to embody this excitement.[4] Here was a politician who was prepared to redefine the relationship between the individual and the state, to make Canada's laws reflective of the times, to secularize them, to reshape them according to contemporary needs, not a Victorian past. Although Parliament only passed Bill C-187 before breaking for Christmas in 1967, Trudeau's assault on the criminal code continued as prime minister. Inspired by his vision of a "Just Society,"[5] he and his minister of justice, John Turner, tackled these issues once again in May of 1969 with a second omnibus bill, C-150. Just as before, the aim was to bring Canada's laws in tune with the needs of a modern nation.

Trudeau's reforms were more than an exercise in updating antiquated laws. For him, they were about a balance of needs. His principal aim was to forge a society that encouraged individual self-fulfillment. Yet he also recognized that the purpose of the law was not to undermine any shared religious and philosophical values of Canadian society. While the reforms reflected Trudeau's commitment to the protection of civil liberties against undue encroachments from those in authority, they endorsed neither unbridled individualism nor moral relativism. Included in the legislation were what he believed to be reasonable limits upon individual behaviour. He understood that good governance required that the moral norms of society not be discarded in the process of removing the impediments that interfered with individual rights and freedoms. Canada in the late 1960s was becoming more and more diverse, and with this phenomenon came changes in the attitudes of the nation about the purpose of the law. Trudeau knew – indeed, he believed – that traditional Judeo-Christian values no longer offered sufficient justification for state involvement in the private lives of Canadians.

Of course, these were not easy reforms to make; that many of the issues remain contentious three-and-a-half decades later is evidence of this. At the centre of these changes were divisive moral and religious debates that affected large segments of the population on both sides of the issues. Given the controversies, Trudeau faced the difficult challenge of drafting laws that were reflective of the realities of Canadian society, but that did not necessarily sanction a particular behaviour still considered in many circles to be taboo. Defining this equilibrium was not easy, particularly as heated emotions and charged rhetoric were commonplace. Those who opposed the changes either exhorted the potential moral and ethical dangers of liberalizing the law or chastized the government for not liberalizing it enough.

Not unexpectedly, Trudeau proceeded with care. His reforms came at a time when there was little consensus of opinion concerning the point at which the individual's rights gave way to the larger needs of society. His wariness was evident in the final version of the amendments, as neither the divorce reforms nor C-150 were bold overhauls of the criminal code, but rather minor adjustments that codified existing practices. And they were a product of compromise: imperfect and sometimes vague, yet reflective of a middle position between competing extremes. Nevertheless, their acceptance was at least a step in the direction of Trudeau's vision of a liberal democracy that protected individual rights and respected the plurality of the nation.

Alas, his victory was short-lived. Although not the only controversial component of the reforms, the changes to Canada's abortion law were particularly problematic, as the state's involvement – or lack of involvement, depending upon to whom one spoke – in the procedure ignited divisions within the country. Moreover, it soon became apparent that the changes, despite being politically expedient, were inadequate. They were ambiguous, open to both broad and narrow interpretations, and inequitable in their application. In essence, the new law did not translate well into practice. Consequently, over the next two decades, Canadians on both sides of the issue responded by challenging the constitutionality of the laws in the nation's courts. And in 1988, almost two decades after the 1969 reforms, the Supreme Court of Canada struck down the law, ruling that the restrictions placed upon women seeking an abortion violated their rights under the Charter of Rights and Freedoms. Thus, what had begun in the late 1960s as a series of calls to relieve the state of the task of regulating moral behaviour quickly turned into long and cumbersome disputes over the validity of the laws themselves. In the process, Canadians were asked to decide whether the state still had a legitimate – if perhaps diminished – place in the nation's bedrooms.

* * *

Almost immediately after the laws were liberalized, Trudeau (as well as Turner) began to face tremendous criticism from many within the Catholic Church – and certain Protestant denominations as well – for his apparent disregard for the teachings of his faith. But Trudeau's commitment to individual liberty and limitations on state authority can be traced back to his days at Collège Jean-de-Brébeuf and at Harvard. In their biography of Trudeau, Christina McCall and Stephen Clarkson credit these institutions for having fostered within Trudeau a love of intellectual rigour based upon reason and logic. These schools exposed him to such seventeenth- and eighteenth-century liberal political theorists as Montesquieu and de Tocqueville, whose ideas about checks and balances upon state authority resonated deeply within him. Moreover, they introduced him to the contemporary ideas of Carl Friedrich and Charles McIlwain concerning the importance of individual rights as the cornerstone of any democratic system.[6] It was during these formative years that he developed his reliance upon rationalism rather than emotional conviction as the basis for understanding the world, eventually leading him to adopt his now famous motto "reason before passion."

While Trudeau's schooling satisfied his intellectualism, the ideas that he was attracted to were often at odds with his Catholicism. Although he was raised to be a devout Catholic, he was also suspicious of the "political superstition and social conservatism" of the Catholic Church during the Duplessis era, when it had aligned itself with the government in order to maintain its influence within Quebec society.[7] McCall and Clarkson suggest that Trudeau was able to reconcile his feelings and distance himself from the actions of the Church while still remaining true to its teachings by turning to Personalism, a sect of Catholicism that began in France in the 1930s as a reaction to the rise of fascism and communism. Led by Catholic intellectuals such as Jacques Maritain, the appeal of Personalism was that it reduced the importance of the Church hierarchy by stressing the development of the individual in matters of both faith and active participation in society.[8] Personalism not only spoke to Trudeau's sense of anti-clericalism and individualism, but more importantly enabled him "to maintain both the certainties of his faith and the obsession with personal freedom that had taken hold of his imagination."[9]

The combined effect of Trudeau's love for intellectual rigour and his attraction to Personalism was evident throughout much of his political thought during the 1960s, as he advocated a system of rule of law in which the state did not interfere with the individual's ability to pursue personal growth and fulfillment. He advocated a society in which the laws allowed individuals to decide moral issues on the basis of their consciences. In 1965, when discussing the purpose of the constitution, he wrote:

> the state must take great care not to infringe on the conscience of the individual. I believe that, in the last analysis, a human being in the privacy of his own mind has the exclusive authority to choose his own scale of values and to decide which forces will take precedence over others. A good constitution is one that does not prejudge any of these questions, but leaves citizens free to orient their human destinies as they see fit.[10]

Ultimately, he envisioned an expanded bill of rights embedded within the constitution that would hold government powers in check by obliging those in office to "guarantee the fundamental freedoms of the citizen from interference, whether federal or provincial."[11]

Thus it is not surprising that in 1967 and again in 1969, Trudeau attempted to relieve the state of the burden of policing what were effectively moral offences, not criminal ones. For him, the government neither had, nor should it ever have had, the jurisdiction to regulate such behaviours. Of course, putting ideas into practice is rarely, if ever, a fluid process. Despite being an idealist as a thinker and as a philosopher, Trudeau's sense of pragmatism as a legislator often tempered his actions when it came to altering the criminal code. He understood the religious implications of what he was proposing. Moreover, as a practising Catholic, he was well aware of the Church's reservations about his efforts to grant greater individual liberties to Canadians; and particularly those liberties that were perceived as having the potential to harm the moral fabric of the nation.

* * *

Beginning in the late 1960s, the Canadian Catholic Conference (CCC), the national organization for the Catholic bishops of Canada, now known as the Canadian Conference of Catholic Bishops, presented a number of submissions to the federal government outlining the Church's positions on contraception, divorce, and abortion, all of which were in the context of the Second Vatican Council.[12] Its stance was generally a balanced one. It recognized the need for laws that reflected the views and ambitions of a pluralistic Canada, not simply those of the Church. Still, it warned that circumspection was in order. Like Trudeau, the CCC also struggled with the question of how society's laws might strive for the "proper balance between personal and social needs."[13] It began by suggesting that while the Christian legislator had a duty to govern temporal affairs according to his or her conscience, any decisions should be informed by the Church's teachings. In deciding whether a moral offence should also be considered criminal, the CCC set out four criteria that politicians might use as guides for their decisions. First, the act in question "notably injures the common good." Second, any law pertaining to the act in question had to be enforceable. Third, the law had to be equal in its application to all Canadians, meaning that one segment of the population would not be unduly targeted. And fourth, the most important requirement, the law "should not give rise to evils greater than those it was designed to suppress."[14]

On the issue of legalizing contraceptives, the CCC conceded that reform was necessary. Although the Church did not endorse the dissemination of birth-control materials, the current law found in section 150 of the criminal code failed to meet the conditions outlined in criteria two and four. In the CCC's view, the law prohibiting the spread of family-planning information was unenforceable, and great harm could come from any attempts to police what was to all intents and purposes a relatively minor offence. It was particularly concerned that the state not be in a position whereby it would have the authority to use family-planning education as a condition upon which married couples might be eligible for welfare assistance. Any measure of this nature, it argued, would pave the way for possible encroachments against the family that could potentially "result in unnecessary moral damage and social discord."[15]

On the issue of divorce the CCC took a harder line. Not surprisingly, its position was that marriages were indissoluble. Although couples could legally obtain a divorce if one or both of the partners had committed adultery, in the eyes of the Church only the passing of one of the partners could break the bonds of holy matrimony, and only in what were considered to be "grave situations" did it permit a separation between husband and wife.[16] In its briefing to parliamentarians, the CCC stated, "We cannot over-emphasize that an indiscriminate broadening of the grounds for divorce is not the solution to the problem of unhappy marriages."[17] In its view, the laws also needed to protect the family, not simply weaken it. Any opening up of the criteria for divorce had to be accompanied by positive measures designed to ensure that a couple had the necessary assistance to salvage their troubled marriage. Even so, the CCC did not dismiss outright the government's initiative to insert the concept of "marriage breakdown" into the legislation. It believed that the proposed reform allowed for the introduction of counselling and reconciliation services, as well as marital-education programs for those about to be wed. Nevertheless, the CCC was hesitant to endorse the proposed changes, believing that the new law did not do enough to protect the well-being of any children caught in the middle of a divorce. Moreover, it was suspicious of the courts' new abilities to use broad and open-ended criteria for deciding cases. Instead, it argued that each case should be decided based on its own merits. Otherwise, if certain safeguards to protect the family were not included, then liberalizing the law could result in "problems more serious than those it seeks to control."[18]

Trudeau was conscious of these fears, even though arguments rooted in the rights of the individual – not moral or religious criteria – were the basis for his government's positions. On the issue of contraceptives, the government made it clear that legalizing distribution did not mean that it now had an obligation to provide funding for such activities.[19] With Bill C-187, Trudeau wanted to relieve the state of the task of dictating the terms through which marriages could be broken. He told Parliament that the primary purpose of the legislation was to make husbands and wives equal before the law. Thus, he refused to define the concept of "marriage breakdown," choosing instead to allow the courts to determine its meaning based upon "evidence or proof of the existence of specified matrimonial situations."[20] He also made it very clear that, like the Catholic Church, he too did not want his legislation to undermine the family as an institution. Although he was expanding the criteria for divorce, he assured Parliament that in the event of marital breakdown it was still the state's responsibility to "surround the family with maximum protection" by requiring the courts to attempt to reconcile the two parties.[21]

Similar tact was evident in the government's position towards homosexual acts between consenting adults in 1969. The government was quick to point out that although such activities no longer constituted an indictable offence, Parliament was in no way approving of such behaviour. In his defence of the omnibus bill, Turner explained, "These amendments remove certain sexual conduct between consenting adults in private from the purview of criminal law. There is one point which I cannot emphasize too strongly in this regard. It is that Parliament would not, in enacting these amendments, be condoning this type of conduct."[22] In his memoirs, Trudeau later explained that this discretion was necessary. Although he believed that the state could not justify such an intervention into the private lives of Canadians, he "also had to make it understood that in decriminalizing a given action, the law was in no way challenging the moral beliefs of any given religion."[23]

* * *

Nowhere was the tension arising from this delicate balancing act more pronounced than with the proposed changes to the criminal code relating to abortion. Prior to 1969, Canadian law on abortion dated back to 1892, and was explicit in its condemnation of the practice of inducing a miscarriage: all abortions were illegal, no matter the circumstance. The maximum sentence for any individual found guilty of performing the operation was life imprisonment. Trudeau's changes simply allowed for very controlled exceptions to this position. Section 251 (originally section 237) stipulated that abortions would be legal only if the pregnancy threatened the "life or health" of the woman. In order to avoid criminal sanction, two major criteria had to be met. First, the operation had to be performed at a hospital that was either accredited to do so by the Canadian Council on Hospital Accreditation or given approval by the appropriate provincial minister of health. Second, the procedure had to have the written approval of the hospital's Therapeutic Abortion Committee (TAC), which consisted of at least three medical practitioners, none of whom could be the doctor performing the operation.[24]

On this issue the Canadian Catholic Conference's (CCC) position was firmly entrenched. In its view, life began at conception, was sacred, and was inviolable. It deemed that the state had a duty to see that the fetus was protected at all costs, even in cases in which the mother's health or life was deemed to be in danger. To do otherwise would be to "sacrifice a greater value for a lesser one."[25] More specifically, the CCC insisted that the proposed changes to the law were too broad, and that if allowed to pass would eventually lead to "official recognition of 'abortion on demand.'"[26] It suggested that if the government was to liberalize the law it must also provide positive reforms aimed at reducing the social and economic barriers that might tempt a woman to seek an abortion in the first place. Thus, it advocated a social safety net that allowed for greater welfare assistance to unwed mothers, better access to daycare centres, more support for adoption services, and increased research aimed at aiding those individuals and families who were coping with mental illness and physical handicaps.

Despite the views of the Catholic Church, the government stood its ground on the need for reform. In the House of Commons, Turner deflected numerous calls from the opposition for the inclusion of a series of additional criteria aimed at watering down the proposed new law. These included prohibiting women under the age of twenty-one from procuring an abortion, restricting hospitals with less than four hundred beds from performing abortions, and making it mandatory for hospitals' therapeutic abortion committees to include a psychiatrist and even a member of the clergy.[27] To this last condition, Turner responded, "the decision to be made by the committee is a medical decision. That does not stop a woman from seeking spiritual help." Implying an absence of spiritual integrity to the government's rationale, Progressive Conservative MP Walter Dinsdale countered, "This is straight humanism."[28]

Although the government downplayed religious and moral arguments against moving forward with the legislation, it was quick to point out that, as with the other amendments in the omnibus bill, it was not sanctioning the procedure, and that it was sympathetic to the fears expressed by opponents of the reforms. Indeed, Trudeau's private convictions were not that different from the position laid out by the Catholic Church. In her memoirs, *Beyond Reason*, Margaret Trudeau revealed that her husband was staunchly opposed to abortion.[29] But Trudeau also believed that private convictions should not be the basis for governance in the public realm. Despite his personal views, he recognized that the old abortion laws were out of touch with the realities of Canadian society.

Still, given the controversial nature of the changes, it is not surprising that his government was sensitive to the charge that it was taking Canada down the path towards abortion on demand. In a rather defensive move, Turner told Parliament that the proposed reforms neither "authorize[d] the taking of fetal life" nor "promoted abortion," but instead "simply remove[d] certain categories of abortion from the present place they have on the list of indictable offences."[30] In essence, the government argued that the law was a compromise: abortion was to remain the only medical procedure found within the criminal code, yet the changes recognized that there were times when an abortion needed to be performed in order to protect the life and health of the woman.

Predictably, few on either side of the debate were satisfied with the government's middle ground. Ed Broadbent of the New Democratic Party was particularly critical of Trudeau for not going far enough with the changes to the criminal code. Even though all of the political parties had supported the reforms, Broadbent attacked the government for what he believed were responses that did little to challenge the status quo in any meaningful way. His main charge was that Trudeau lacked a liberal vision of Canada. In a 1970 pamphlet entitled "The Liberal Rip-off: Trudeauism vs. the Politics of Equality," Broadbent referred to the prime minister as a "swinging Mackenzie King who wanted a with-it generation to accept a conservative program with a clear conscience." He then described Trudeau as a "Liberal for our season," who was content to play it safe and not take any political risks. "Like all political conservatives," he continued, Trudeau "sees governing as the art of keeping the ship afloat, not as a skill in getting to a pre-selected port."[31]

Of course, these attacks downplayed the pressures facing Trudeau's administration and the difficulties involved in drafting new human rights norms. However, there was something to be said for his argument that the reforms in the omnibus bill were not as bold as they might have first appeared. At the very least, the fine balances that Trudeau had sought between protecting the freedoms of the individual while maintaining the needs of society were imperfect and ambiguous, particularly on the issue of abortion. Soon after it was passed, the limitations within the law became apparent once it was put into practice.

In the early 1970s, the government began to look at how well the law was operating. Its intent had been to protect both the rights of the fetus and the well-being of the woman. In May 1971, the department of national health and welfare conducted a review of Canada's abortion law, and found that because the legislation did not specifically require hospitals to establish TACs, only 120 of the 453 accredited hospitals, and only 23 approved hospitals had done so.[32] Because the law did not compel mandatory participation, not all Canadians had access to the service. In part, this was a consequence of the stipulation that at least four physicians had to be involved in the decision. In practice, this meant that few hospitals outside of the large metropolitan centres had the necessary personnel to establish a TAC in the first place.

There were other controversies as well. Beginning in 1973, the abortion debate reached a whole new level of intensity as the United States Supreme Court ruled in *Roe v. Wade* that the constitutional right to privacy found in the 14th amendment meant that the decision to terminate a pregnancy belonged to the woman and her doctor, provided it occurred within the first trimester.[33] In the companion case of *Doe v. Bolton*, the same court ruled that Georgia's law requiring approval from a TAC of an accredited or approved hospital was unconstitutional.[34]

In Canada, the law was put on trial as well, this time by Dr. Henry Morgentaler, a physician from Montreal and the president of the Humanist Association of Canada. Morgentaler was arrested on August 15, 1973, after Montreal police raided his clinic. A day later he was arraigned on six charges of violating section 251 of the criminal code, including performing an abortion on a distraught woman from Sierra Leone who feared that carrying the pregnancy to term would bring her tremendous hardship. This was not the first time that Morgentaler had run into trouble with the law for performing abortions; he had been arrested in 1970, but the charges were dropped after the Quebec Court of Queen's Bench ruled that police had used illegal methods of seizing evidence. The 1973 case was particularly important, however, because it challenged the constitutionality of Trudeau's reforms to the criminal code. As in the United States, the trial centred on the woman's control over her body and tackled the issue of whether a woman's health included her emotional and mental state, not simply her physical well-being. Unfettered by his newly acquired notoriety and unafraid of the spotlight (on Mother's Day 1973, CTV had aired a tape of him performing an abortion for its television crews), Morgentaler was unrepentant. Thriving off of the intensity of civil disobedience,[35] and willing to be a martyr for his belief that a woman had the right to control her own body, he remained undeterred by the prospect of imprisonment.

During the trial, his lawyers stressed the inequities of the law, arguing among other things that section 251 inadvertently made it more difficult for women to procure an abortion because it violated a woman's right to privacy and not all women had the same access to abortion services. They argued that section 251 was therefore inoperative according to sub-sections 1(a) and 1(b) of the 1960 Bill of Rights, which guaranteed "life, liberty, [and] security of the person" (arguing that while privacy was not mentioned explicitly it was implied in this sub-section), and "the right of the individual to equality before the law," respectively.[36] Moreover, they contended that Morgentaler's actions were legal under the common-law defence of necessity and section 45 of the criminal code, suggesting that a competent physician could perform an abortion in emergency situations if there was no other reasonable alternative available. The jury agreed, acquitting him on November 13, 1973.

The government of Quebec, however, was not in favour of the decision. It appealed to the Quebec Court of Appeal on the grounds that section 45 could not be used as a defence against section 251, since Parliament had already outlined the conditions in which therapeutic abortions were legal. Subsequently, the jury had been misdirected by being allowed to use it. This time, the Court of Appeal sided with the government. The justices were unanimous in their ruling that the original trial judge, Justice Huggessen, had erred in permitting the necessity defence to stand because Dr. Morgentaler had neither proven that there had been a "real and urgent medical need," nor had he "made any effort, as was his duty, to find out why this woman couldn't comply with the law."[37] In a highly controversial move, it overturned the acquittal and convicted Morgentaler.[38] His lawyers appealed to the Supreme Court. In the meantime, Huggessen suspended his sentencing, waiting for the outcome of the appeal; however, the Supreme Court ruled that Morgentaler was to appear before the judge for sentencing since he was no longer an innocent man. On July 25, 1974, Morgentaler was sentenced to eighteen months in prison. To make matters worse for him, on March 26, 1975, the Supreme Court confirmed the Quebec Court of Appeal's ruling in a 6 to 3 decision. Meanwhile, a series of new trials was initiated against him for similar charges. Interestingly, in all of these cases he was again acquitted by the juries.

Despite the favourable ruling for the government, the Morgentaler trials revealed significant flaws in Canada's abortion laws, flaws that the Trudeau government felt at least compelled to acknowledge if not act upon.[39] It did two things. On July 3, 1975, Minister of Justice Otto Lang proposed new legislation that would prohibit a jury acquittal from being reversed, and on September 29, 1975, Trudeau appointed Robin F. Badgley to chair a commission to discover whether the law was operating equitably across the country. The second action was more controversial than the first.

To no one's surprise, the Badgley Commission found that there were indeed tremendous discrepancies in the application of the law. One of the principal problems was that, when drafting the law, the federal government had decided not to define the term "health," preferring instead to allow the TACs to base their decisions on the medical evidence before them. While this decision made sense on a theoretical level, the lack of direction led to a wide variation of interpretations between TACs. Some took guidance from the World Health Organization, which defined health in broad terms as "a state of complete physical, mental and social well-being and not merely the absence of disease or infirmity." Others considered mental health only if there was evidence of "psychiatric disorders associated with physical conditions, psychoses, or long-term neuroses."[40] As a result, the ambiguities in the law and the variances in opinion between medical practitioners meant that a woman's chances of successfully seeking an abortion were largely dependent upon the makeup of the hospital's committee. The situation was an ironic twist of fate for the pragmatic Trudeau. In the process of securing individuals against the arbitrary use of authority, he had effectively enacted a law that not only accommodated arbitrariness, but encouraged it.

There were other problems with the law. Expensive costs for the procedure that provincial health care plans did not cover meant that middle- and upper-middle-class women had greater access than did lower-class women. Moreover, guidelines for establishing TACs differed between the provinces, and given the controversy surrounding the issue, few hospitals – either religious or secular – wanted to be associated with the procedure. Consequently, only a small percentage of hospitals had gone to the trouble of setting up a committee, and most of these were in the major urban centres.

There were delays as well. With the bureaucratic procedures outlined in the law, coupled with the limited resources facing most hospitals, the commission determined that the average period of time between a woman's first consultation with her physician and the procedure was about eight weeks.[41] As the operation became more dangerous with every passing week, many women sought to avoid the TAC altogether by having the operation performed in the United States.

Finally, the inequities were compounded by the newly elected Parti Québécois government's 1976 decision not to prosecute any qualified doctor in the province who performed an abortion in a private clinic.[42] The reasons were that Quebec's public hospitals could not meet the demand for abortions, there was no evidence that private clinics were more dangerous than hospitals, and after Dr. Henry Morgentaler's third jury acquittal in 1976, the chances of convicting a doctor in Quebec seemed unlikely, if not impossible.[43]

In light of its findings, the commission's conclusion was somewhat unexpected. Like the Supreme Court of Canada, it too found that the problem was not with the law but with "the Canadian people, their health institution and the medical profession, who are responsible for this situation."[44] In essence, it blamed poor socio-economic conditions and regional disparities for any inequalities. By so doing, it let the federal government off the hook; it did not ask Parliament to revisit the 1969 changes to the criminal code.

In part because of the controversial recommendations of the commission, the issue did not go away for Trudeau. Throughout the rest of the 1970s, he was hounded about the government's policy, both inside and outside the House of Commons. By the end of the decade, the controversy was clearly weighing on him. In June 1978, Conservative MP Jake Epp asked him whether, in light of it being the United Nations' year of the child, he would consider reviewing Canada's abortion laws "so that children will be given the greatest gift of all, namely, the gift of life." Trudeau responded flippantly. "Mr. Speaker, it is not for the government to give the gift of life to children: that is done by God and by the parents."[45] He deflected further criticism by suggesting that fault for the rise in the number of abortions lay not with the federal government for drafting poor laws, but with the provinces for not doing enough to enforce them.

His cavalier attitude aside, Trudeau's distaste for reopening the debate surrounding Canada's abortion laws was understandable. Virtually since it came into force, the law had caused headaches for his government. In his attempt to find middle ground in 1969, he had paid a price for opening up this proverbial Pandora's box. Despite the criticism, it was still safer politically to let the status quo stand.

The irony of the controversy surrounding the abortion laws, however, was that it was Pierre Elliott Trudeau who was responsible for the striking down of section 251 of the criminal code, albeit indirectly. The true watershed moment was not 1969 but 1982, when the Canadian Charter of Rights and Freedoms was entrenched in the newly repatriated constitution. During the negotiations leading up to the Charter, Campaign Life, a pro-life organization formed in 1978, contended that sections 7 and 15 (which covered the security of the individual and equality before the law respectively) would pave the way for abortion on demand unless they were amended to include the explicit legal rights of the fetus. Trudeau disagreed – or at least he did so publicly – maintaining that the Charter would not be the instrument used to settle the debate between pro-life and pro-choice camps. In fact, he was able to convince Emmett Cardinal Carter of this in the spring of 1981. In April of that year, the *Globe and Mail* reported that Cardinal Carter had publicly dissociated himself from Campaign Life after receiving assurances during a private meeting with Trudeau and again in a letter from the department of justice that the Charter would not override the current provisions found within the criminal code. Later, in an article that appeared in the *Catholic Register*, Cardinal Carter wrote, "While I am not satisfied with the protection accorded to the unborn, I do not consider the proposed charter as worsening the position."[46]

Not everyone was convinced that Trudeau's assessment of the impact that the new charter would have on the judiciary in Canada was sound. In the autumn of 1981, he was forced to defend his government's position before Parliament. On November 27, 1981, he told the House of Commons:

the Charter does not say whether abortions will be easier or more difficult to practice in the future. The charter is absolutely neutral on this matter, and according to the interpretation of senior officials and agents of the Department of Justice and according to the minister himself, under the constitution the

House retains the right to amend the Criminal Code, which is the statute affecting the issue of abortion.[47]

Consequently, he opted not to amend the proposed constitution, despite the calls to close any potential "loopholes" within sections 7 and 15.

Not surprisingly, little time passed before the courts were forced to rule on section 7's potential impact on Canada's abortion law. In the Saskatchewan Court of the Queen's Bench in 1983, lawyer Joe Borowski took the attorney general of Canada and the federal minister of finance to court on the grounds that section 251 of the criminal code was unconstitutional because the term "everyone" found in section 7 included the fetus.[48] He also avowed that the law violated sections 12, 14, and 15 of the Charter, suggesting that abortions were "cruel and unusual punishment," that fetuses were denied a fair hearing from the TAC, and that they were denied equality before the law.[49] Acting on behalf of all taxpayers, he then suggested that, because all abortions were subsequently illegal, the transfer of money from the federal government to the provinces for TACs was also illegal.

Borowski's logic was less than compelling. The Honourable Justice Matheson dismissed these arguments on various grounds, suggesting that he was advocating "indefensible legal conclusions."[50] The case was not insignificant, however. In the process of making his decision, Matheson reaffirmed earlier court decisions that the law did not recognize fetuses as legal persons, meaning section 7 of Charter would not decide the abortion debate in favour of the rights of the unborn. But the matter was not closed. Borowski was granted leave to appeal to the Supreme Court of Canada.[51]

Those, like Borowski, who had predicted that the new constitution would eventually lead to the removal of abortion from the criminal code soon found that their fears were well founded. In the late 1980s, Dr. Morgentaler again appeared before the Supreme Court of Canada, this time because he and two other doctors had been arrested on charges of conspiracy to procure miscarriages by setting up a private clinic in Toronto. As before, Morgentaler had been acquitted by a jury.[52] Once again, the government challenged the decision in the higher courts. The Supreme Court was now asked to consider seven questions pertaining to the constitutionality of section 251, the most important of which dealt with potential violations of the Charter. On January 28, the Supreme Court ruled 5 to 2 that Canada's abortion law was unconstitutional because it violated "principles of fundamental justice" and "the security of the person" found in section 7 of the Charter. In her judgment, which was the strongest in its wording, Madam Justice Bertha Wilson wrote that "Section 251 is more deeply flawed than just subjecting women to considerable emotional stress and unnecessary physical risk. It asserts that the woman's capacity to reproduce is to be subject, not to her own control, but to that of the state. This is direct interference with the woman's physical 'person.'"[53] It was a powerful ruling. Abortions were no longer criminal offences and hospital TACs no longer had any legal authority to decide whether or not a woman qualified for an abortion. Proponents of a woman's right to choose were elated, opponents enraged. Many in the latter category questioned the legitimacy of judicial activism in Canada in the Charter era.

Nevertheless, the ruling was not a complete endorsement of abortions on demand. The Supreme Court acknowledged that Parliament still had an interest in protecting the unborn. However, it failed to offer any substantial guidance that might assist Parliament in coming up with new laws that were in keeping with the Charter.

After the decision, the Mulroney government drafted new legislation to replace section 251 of the criminal code. Bill C-43: An Act Respecting Abortion eliminated the requirement that a woman first obtain written approval from a TAC. Furthermore, the proposed new law minimized any ambiguity surrounding the term "health" by stipulating in very clear terms that its definition encompassed physical, mental, and psychological health.[54] But this is where the clarity ended. Abortion was still considered to be a medical act performed for health reasons, and the Supreme Court had recognized that society has a vested interest in protecting the fetus. Because the majority in the Supreme Court had submitted three separate rulings, however, the government lacked any meaningful direction on how to proceed. Understandably, it was reluctant to dictate the terms by which a woman could seek an abortion for fear that the courts would once again strike it down as being unconstitutional. Furthermore, Bill C-43 did not recognize any rights for the fetus, again out of fear of another constitutional challenge making its way through the courts.[55]

In the end, the government's efforts were moot. Bill C-43 was defeated in the Senate by a tied vote of 43 to 43. Afterwards, the Mulroney government divorced itself from the issue. No government has touched it since.

* * *

The battles at the Supreme Court aside, the reforms to the divorce laws in 1967 and the omnibus bill of 1969 did not represent sweeping changes to Canada's criminal code. Nor did they necessarily "give rise to greater evils." They were negotiated amendments that tried to accommodate widely divergent views. If, by the passage of these laws, Trudeau was responsible for opening the door towards a "decline" in Canadian's moral conduct, it was only because in opting for a middle position he left the nation with ambiguous and open-ended laws that were susceptible to broad interpretations.

The reforms that he sought were not bold. They were a compromise founded on his understanding of Canada as a pluralistic, modern society. They embodied his struggle to balance his desire to protect individual rights while still honouring the traditional values of the nation. And they revealed a side of Trudeau that was cautious and pragmatic, yet unwilling to let his private Catholicism dominate his public actions. Besides, Canadians themselves were not in agreement over how much the state should intervene in the practice of a particular behaviour, whether divorce, birth control, homosexuality, or abortion. The changes to the criminal code were small steps towards modernizing Canada's laws, steps that were palatable with those Canadians in the middle of the political spectrum. While the state may not have had any place in the bedrooms of the nation, it was slow to leave them completely.

Trudeau and the Bedrooms of the Nation: The Canadian Bishops' Involvement

Bernard Daly

The sociologist in me hesitates somewhat in the face of all this for reasons that I will come to later. My main reservation is that this topic is reductionist, partly because Trudeau and his government colleagues were reductionist in how they dealt with the legislative changes in compartmentalizing and separating issues. Clearly, the laws in question touched more of the Canadian household than just the bedroom. It must also be pointed out that Trudeau was not solely and personally responsible for changing these laws; others have said this and I will not stress it.

I emphasized this point in an article published by the *Catholic Register* on November 20, 2000, just after Trudeau's death. I was commenting on remarks in some church circles, which continue to be uttered, that Trudeau opened the floodgates on abortion. Trudeau cannot be fairly singled out this way. His government and cabinet colleagues (some of whom have contributed to this collection), as well as Catholic parliamentarians not in government at the time, all had a voice in the process. So did every Catholic doctor and lawyer in the country. Members of the bar association and medical association had led the push for the legislative changes before the matters came to Parliament.

Here I will review how the Canadian bishops were involved in this process. I think it is important that some points be clarified, and I will conclude with some hypotheses or questions for discussion or for further research.

Early in 1966, as others have said, Parliament began to discuss amending article 150 of the criminal code, which made it a crime to distribute or sell contraceptives.[1] This was for the House of Commons' Standing Committee on Health and Welfare that held hearings and invited the bishops to present their views; they did so in September 1966. The statement said in general that if article 150 was repealed by Parliament in view of the common good, there should be legal safeguards against irresponsible sales and advertising, there should be no government-backed birth-control programs, and contraceptives should not be forced on the poor as a condition for financial help.

Before the government presented any legislation on that matter, the question of divorce reform came up, this time studied by a joint Senate-Commons committee. On April 6, 1967, the bishops presented their brief to that committee, which in midsummer brought in a report that included a draft Divorce (Extension of Grounds) Act. After that, a joint church committee reviewed the 1600 pages of testimony that had been given to the committee. The inter-church group summarized its analysis in a statement to the minister of justice about the proposals for reform of the divorce laws; members of that group met with Trudeau on November 8, 1967. They noted that divorce and reform of divorce of laws often had been presented as subjects that deeply divided Canadians. Catholics were opposed to divorce, other Christians accepted it, it was argued, and so there was no commonality. However, the analysis of what these Canadians had actually said in their testimonies showed there was broad agreement on the need for legislative reforms that would provide more adequate social means to deal with marital troubles. It was agreed that the civil law on divorce should be reformed. It involved, the church people felt, as others argued, serious questions of collusion and so on. However, Canadians also shared the view that lifelong marriage was the ideal and that there should be adequate preparation for it with public support. The brief added that even the best marriage sometimes needs counselling services, which should have public funding. Reconciliation efforts are often affected and should be part of any legal proceedings dealing with faltering or broken marriages. The brief ended with this affirmation: "It is the duty of the state to strengthen marriage and family life. It should be the declared intention of the federal government as an example and incentive to those at other levels of responsibility to apply itself earnestly to progressive, positive updating of all laws and social programs affecting marriage and the family."

There was never any indication that the department of justice or any level of the government of Canada took these Christian joint-church proposals seriously. The 1967 divorce debate showed that most MPs and senators, Catholics included, saw no need for the state to establish a comprehensive social framework to support marriage and family life as jointly advocated by Canadian church bodies, including the Bishops' Conference. Even as Trudeau was hearing such views about divorce law, the Commons Health and Welfare Committee took up the matter of abortion. Asked in 1967 for a brief on abortion law, the bishops set up a drafting committee of bishops, theologians, social scientists, lawyers, and married couples. The final meeting of the drafting committee was set for December 20, 1967, to appear before the committee on January 23, 1968. On December 19, 1967, the Health and Welfare Committee unexpectedly published an interim report. So, at the meeting the following day the bishops' committee tried to integrate something from the interim report into their brief. On December 21, the government published the omnibus bill of amendments to the criminal code, including a section on abortion. So much for what the bishops thought. Instead of giving their views to legislators preparing the bill, the bishops now turned their minds to giving all Catholics some pastoral direction on the draft bill already published. They nevertheless agreed to meet the standing committee on March 5, 1968; their pastoral was published on February 7, 1968.

This brings me to some questions arising from Mr. Turner's remarks. I agree in general with his summary of what the law at the time aimed to do, and I agree with what Andrew Thompson said. About his private meeting with the executive members of the conference headed by Bishop Alexander Carter, however, Mr. Turner said, "The Catholic Church never intervened on that issue again," meaning (I presume) abortion. I find that truly astonishing because, after their first brief, the bishops published at least twenty other briefs on the question of abortion as well as various press releases and telex messages, until Parliament in January 1991 "gave up the ghost" and left Canada with no law of any kind on abortion.[2] Mary Jo Leddy, theologian and writer, looking back on those years, has noted:

> the bishops have articulated the rights of the unborn as an issue of justice for the most vulnerable in our society – those literally without a voice. They have affirmed that these rights are integral to a vision of a good and just society…. In effect, the bishops have presented a profoundly countercultural position that contains an inherent critique of capitalism and consumerism. This biblically founded vision has been integrally linked to economic and social changes that would commit all of us to sharing the cost and responsibility for raising children in this society.[3]

To return to the discussion of Trudeau in particular, I was pleased that Nancy Southam disclosed as much as she did. Trudeau wanted to be private about his religious life, but for people to protect the privacy after his death is to risk having him misunderstood or misrepresented. The man deserves full disclosure now. Where, for example, did he stand on the question of the social place of traditional Catholic values? The bishops and the clergy in Quebec, including leading Jesuits, were trying to fashion an urban Catholicism to replace a fading rural Catholic culture at the time Trudeau was attending Brébeuf College. Some Quebec laity, seeking more autonomy, looked to intellectuals in France for new ideas. "Thanks to two French thinkers, Jacques Maritain and Emmanuel Mounier," Trudeau explained in his *Memoirs*, "I never came to believe in the doctrine of absolute liberalism."[4] But there remains much ambiguity in this statement. After all, Maritain and Mounier did not agree on how Catholic values should be expressed in temporal society. For example, in May 1953, the Quebec bishops wrote about Mounier and his publication *Esprit*: "an unwholesome breath of freedom seems to be stirring in some groups. According to them, people must be freed from Church domination. A campaign in favour of the review *Esprit* has begun. This is pure Protestantism under a new form."[5]

To fully explore Trudeau's convictions about lay freedom from Church domination, the views of other members of the Canadian government at the time must be examined. For example, Mark MacGuigan (later a cabinet minister) wrote an essay against what he called "episcopal interference with the political prerogatives of the laity" – an explicit commentary concerning relations between politicians and bishops, and (by extension) all Christian pastors.[6] Did other Catholics in government disagree with MacGuigan? What stands did Trudeau take in such debates that reflect his faith and spirituality (presuming that there were such debates)? Indeed, did the government have a sincere interest in learning the bishops' views about laws on conception, divorce, and abortion? Or was the invitation extended to the bishops only as a political tactic on the part of legislators whose minds were already made up, shaped by other influences?

Under the Canadian parliamentary system, much of the information we need to answer these questions is hidden in cabinet and caucus secrecy. How accurately do such minutes convey the values underlying the positions taken? Even what happened on the floor of the House of Commons and Senate – which has always been public record – may have been skewed by the rules binding party members to support government policy.

Furthermore, I think there needs to be more exploration of Trudeau's views on freedom. Was there a contradiction involved here? In *Memoirs* he declared himself to be an interventionist on economic matters. The hand of the state was needed to modify the "hidden hand" of the market for the sake of the weak and underprivileged.[7] However, he apparently stood for untrammelled personal freedom in what he reduced to "bedroom" matters. Did he see common-good interest in economic relations, but only matters of individual good, reduced to freedom, in personal relations?

The bishops took "a seamless garment" approach, stressing that matters such as divorce and abortion touched both the common good and individual rights and responsibilities. Trudeau appears to have "divided the cloth," stressing only individual freedom in laws touching personal matters. "The issue of freedom had obsessed me since high school, in my first year of philosophy," he said in *Memoirs*. "It was my conscience I wanted to obey, taking precedence over even the commandments of the Church or the rules of [Brébeuf College]." He recalled that, later in life, "the fundamental notion of justice came to stand alongside freedom in my political thought."[8] Is there any similar evidence that for him any qualifying value stood alongside freedom in matters of personal behaviour?

Finally, were Trudeau and his Catholic colleagues in Parliament at that time up to date on Vatican II teachings that their bishops proposed in their briefs? Or were they still living in accordance with the mind of the pre-Council church? This is particularly relevant because the bishops presented Vatican II texts with their briefs on the substantive questions, specifically linking them to new Council teaching. Central to this teaching was the Vatican II concept that laity and hierarchy "each in its own way shares in the one priesthood of Christ,"[9] so that "everything said about the People of God is addressed equally to laity, religious and clergy."[10] They therefore discussed the mission of the Church in the modern world, and the role of lay Catholics in that mission; this was new teaching on both points. Never before in the 2000-year history of the Church had a general council studied those two topics. The entire text of Chapter 4 of Part 2 of the Vatican Council's *Pastoral Constitution on the Church in the Modern World* was attached to the bishops' 1966 brief on contraception and their 1967 brief on divorce. The laity, the Council stressed, "are given this special vocation: to make the church present and fruitful in those places and circumstances where it is thought through them that she can be the salt of the earth" – for example, in Parliament.

"Thus, every lay person ... is at once the witness and the living instrument of the Church itself."[11] The text it attached to the briefs said bluntly:

> Let [the laity] be aware of what their faith demands of them in these matters and derive strength from it; let them not hesitate to take the initiative at the opportune moment and put their findings into effect. It is their task to cultivate a properly informed conscience and to impress the divine law on the affairs of the earthly city. For their guidance and spiritual strength let them turn to the clergy; but let them realize that their pastors will not always be so expert as to have a ready answer to every problem (even every grave problem) that arises; this is not the role of the clergy; it is rather up to the laymen to shoulder their responsibilities under the guidance of Christian wisdom and with eager attention to the teaching authority of the church.[12]

The mission of the Church, the Council said, "is not only to bring men the message and grace of Christ but also to permeate and improve the whole range of the temporal."[13]

Therefore, "at the time when new questions are being put and when grave errors aiming at undermining religion, the moral order and human society are rampant, the Council earnestly exhorts the laity to take a more active part, each according to his talents and knowledge and in fidelity to the mind of the Church, in the explanation and defence of Christian principles and in the correct application of them to the problems of our times."[14] The bishops in 1890 or in 1950 might have ordered every pulpit to tell the members of Parliament how to vote. The bishops in 1966 told Catholic MPs that they were the Church in Parliament, and in the temporal arena they had the first responsibility to impress the divine law on the business at hand: namely, in this case, Canadian law on contraception, divorce, and abortion. What did these MPs understand of this post–Vatican II perspective, however, and how should the Church be present in Parliament?

The Bedrooms of the Nation: A Commentary

Hon. Otto Lang

The broad thrust of the title of this conference and the notion of Pierre Trudeau's spirituality attracted me a good deal. I had more reservations about the specific subject.

What I saw as one of the most emphatic characteristics in Pierre Trudeau was an unbelievable respect for the dignity of the individual; he showed it in many ways. I call it the evidence of his spirituality because, while it may be possible for humanists to reach a conclusion of respect for individual dignity, I have always found it very hard to see how that can be true without some significant remnant of self-centredness in the scope with which they approach these issues. I therefore believe in the logic of the respect for the dignity of the individual reflecting a continuum from God to the soul to the individual. I am also satisfied that Trudeau was extremely comfortable with that basis and background for his respect for individual dignity, which he saw as something rich in the person and also as very fundamental for democracy. Why else would you respect the vote and each vote in a similar and basic way?

I saw this evidence of his respect for the individual dignity in his way of speaking to people. When addressing an individual, he always spoke to them directly. He was never thinking about another problem or to whom he would speak next. This was a bit of the magic about him and his relationship with people.

I saw it also in the cabinet room very early on. At the University of Saskatchewan, I had been used to the university council where, when someone said something that was verging on the stupid, the general approach was to move right on with the discussion, ignoring it completely. That was the polite way of handling that comment; the discussion went on. I was just newly in the cabinet room in Ottawa when a comment in a serious debate could have matched this description. True to form, the next minister immediately began to speak as though that remark had not happened. But Pierre put up his hand and said, "Just a moment. I do not think we understood what was just said." And I thought, my God, he is going to unveil the remark in all its blessed stupidity. But instead he probed until he found the gem that was really the intention of the person who had made the comment. That was the credit he gave to the intention and dignity of the person who made the remark. I developed my own "one-liner" for general purposes from that: "the stupider the thing you think you've heard, the more likely it is you've misunderstood."

In his politeness over the years in the cabinet room he showed his belief in that dignity of the person. My greatest problem with him – I don't know whether my colleagues here would see it the same way – was his patience. This is not the way people generally think of him. When he was speaking to the press, for example, he did not necessarily see journalists as being well intentioned in their comments and remarks, so he gave as good as he was getting. But he was patient, and he would hear people out.

I saw his respect for individual dignity in a most telling way one day as we left a huge meeting on Western development in Saskatoon. We were leaving with the usual crowd of RCMP around us; it was, after all, in the West and in some of his more difficult days. Suddenly Pierre Trudeau spotted a little old Aboriginal woman, and he just stepped through the group of RCMP (to their dismay) and spoke to her. He said a few words to her in Cree. Whether he did it so that he could have that communion with a person in that way I do not know, but he was paying all of his attention to her and in that moment tears came streaming down her face.

That is part of what I see as the basic spirituality of Pierre Trudeau: individual dignity in the context of pluralism. The other fundamental matter I want to talk about is the issue of morality versus the law. What I saw in Trudeau was a tremendous practical approach to issues, a practical reasoning through to right approaches. Law and morality may coincide, and perhaps should not contradict, but each has its own sphere of operation. When looking at issues that the law may or may not deal with, one of the things you have to bear in mind is the inefficiency of the law, the cost of the process, the randomness of the ability for it to be applied, the fallibility of the judges or those who are working to enforce the law. In all these cases you see morality has a superior place. It is not dependent on randomness; it exists wherever the individual acting in conscience exists. It is not subject to fallible judges and is therefore efficient and cost-free. Where the law is attempting to enforce morality, in situations where some people are unwilling or opposed, it is like a dam holding back water under pressure, and the danger is always present that the water will break through.

In terms of whether an issue should be dealt with by moral teaching or the law, I have a feeling that Pierre Trudeau had a smile somewhere in his mind as he thought of the proper obligation of the bishops and the clergy to preach, and teach, and persuade – even more so when there is no law that tries to enforce itself upon the conduct involved. Is that not the better way to go? We need the law, of course, in areas where we are protecting individuals and property, and protecting order against disorder. But we should be very careful about where we employ the law. Abortion was, of course, a delicate issue; under the circumstances, I think, more so than for changes in the law regarding homosexuality, because many people can rightly see the need for the protection of a being in those circumstances. Should or could the law therefore intervene?

There is this other thing about the law: the randomness of effectiveness and enforcement poses a problem. I have to confess that, in that cabinet room as we debated these changes (many of which had been debated before I got there and had moved along some distance), I had serious reservations and issues to debate in my own conscience. I do not quite agree with John Turner's view that the law was not being changed because it was enunciating what had in fact resulted from the courts. By putting the doctor committee in place, as an authorization and a clearance, it probably made it easier for abortions to occur. I had that dilemma with the law. But it was a fact that we were in a situation where jury after jury, let alone judge after judge, would find a way to acquit persons who on the basis of the facts appeared to have been guilty of the offence that existed in law. Therefore, when one of them finally did convict, this caused another problem because of that randomness. I think, to a large extent, this moved Pierre Trudeau. But above all, the fundamental thing to bear in mind was his tremendous respect for individual dignity, which I see as the sign of his spirituality.

Discussion

Gregory Baum: I listened very carefully to remarks about how Catholics, wrestling with contemporary issues, develop and arrive at new positions. I am conscious of the evolution of Catholic social teaching and Catholic ethical teaching. I belong to this old generation that still remembers when Catholic teaching did not recognize religious liberty. In the nineteenth century, Catholics looked upon the modern state as problematic. Popular sovereignty and the separation of church and state were rejected, and therefore human rights were rejected. There was an evolution, and theologians, politicians, and Catholics in many countries wrote about this. Some of them criticized the Catholic Church, and eventually at the Second Vatican Council the Catholic Church endorsed the human rights tradition on theological grounds. Today, I am very grateful to Pope John Paul II, who has become a champion of human rights in all parts of the world.

So I think that Catholic teaching changes as Catholics wrestle with contemporary issues. I would argue that the Catholic position on women and sexuality is being wrestled with at this time. Many Catholics are not in agreement with the official teaching on women, and many Catholics do not agree with some of the traditional sexual teaching. So it is very interesting to listen to what happens in Parliament, and to what happens when Catholics get together to wrestle with how to respond to concrete issues that happen in their society. I think this development will continue to go on.

David Seljak: Stephen Clarkson offered a kind of psychological analysis of Trudeau's authoritarian streak. I offered a sociological one. While we are on the topic, we might talk about the spirituality of the War Measures Act, an act in which I do not think we really saw respect for the dignity of the human person. I would contrast Trudeau's own position with that of Claude Ryan, who spoke out against the War

Measures Act very courageously, saw it as a violation of civil liberties, and wrote about this in *Le Devoir* and Catholic journals such as *Maintenant*. For Ryan this was a terrible violation of respect for the human individual. I think that we have to remember that there are at least two sides to someone as complex as Pierre Trudeau.

Otto Lang: Let me tell you, first of all, that I am not sure I ever saw a cabinet decision as easily unanimous as the one we took with regards to the War Measures Act. If I put it into the context of September 11 happening in Canada, with a slightly additional context, our problem at that time in Canada was that the desire to protect human liberty and freedom had led the previous government to remove a lot of the effective intelligence activity that police services had performed to ensure that they were aware of particular groups and sects. This represented the "common sense" infiltration of groups to be sure you knew when difficult activities were about to happen. We did not have very much good information about the FLQ cells in the province of Quebec at that time, how many more times they might strike, and what would happen. And we had a Quebec government that was not handling the situation very well. It really was this uncertainty – and I take the New York scene and put that into a Canadian context – where we did not know how many groups of terrorists there were. We suspected there might be a certain number of others ready to strike, but we did not have information about it. What would we do? At that point, we decided that a slight withholding of civil liberties would be appropriate. We would have liked to have had another act in the books, because the War Measures Act was like having to use the atomic bomb in order to fire a rifle in the selected area. That is perhaps putting a low value on the arrest of suspected people whom we did not know but were worried about. There was clearly a critical need to move, and in that context I think it made good sense. Certainly we saw it that way in the cabinet at the time.

David Seljak: To compare the October Crisis to September 11 seems to stretch things rather to a point. I just can't see the parallel.

The second point is that, as I recall, when the cabinet papers were released in 2000, Quebec newspapers reported that the RCMP deemed the threat to be not as great as Trudeau thought. They suggested that Trudeau's original list of detainees was much longer and larger than the police authorities thought it should be and so it was cut considerably. What I am focusing on is that, even in the cabinet, as I understand it based on the newspaper evidence, Trudeau's response when it came to the question of Quebec nationalism was a very firm authoritarian response that he did not show in other contexts. I think that this is something that is a throwback to his religious upbringing, and something that comes from a chaotic family situation. But I don't want to do too much of a psychoanalytic exercise here.

Otto Lang: And particularly you shouldn't, because it was a cabinet decision and it wasn't by any means Trudeau's decision alone. As I said, it was not as though it was a difficult decision; it was easy because of the evidence we had and did not have. I think it is a lot like the situation in New York. You could say that in the World Trade Center attacks, a lot of people were killed, whereas here we only had two kidnapped of whom one was subsequently killed. But we did not know what capability there was for the FLQ seizing more people and, as I said, there was instability in the Quebec government scene as well, which preyed upon us a good bit. I did say at the time that the real worry was not another politician, but if they had kidnapped Maurice Richard we would have been in serious trouble!

Tom Axworthy: On the point of the War Measures Act and comparisons with September 11, we should never forget that prior to October 1970 there had been a long pattern of violence in Quebec. It was not simply the political kidnapping and murder that October, but before that there was a long history of armed robberies, armouries had been broken into, mailboxes had blown up, a whole series of crimes had been committed, and the Montreal police went on strike. The cabinet, as it looked at the culmination of that violence in a political kidnapping, would not be looking at an isolated event; they would be looking at a pattern of violence where reasonable people could say, "We are not quite sure what is going on here. There may be something far larger than any of us realize, and therefore we had to make a choice to have order as the precondition of freedom." One could never have freedom in a situation of anarchy, without an agreed-upon framework of law, and it was that framework of law that seemed to be under duress in Quebec. Therefore, I do not think that the decision to invoke the War Measures Act in any way reveals an authoritarian complex. I think it revealed a true appreciation of freedom, which is that you need an agreed-upon framework of law in order for us to make all of our individual choices.

Richard Alway: Certainly, the events of 1970 left a huge mark on the Canadian consciousness, but in the practical order I recall that there were written requests from the premier of Quebec and the mayor of Montreal asking the federal government to take action. And, as Otto Lang says, the only legislative tool that was available was a very blunt instrument. When you use such things in that kind of circumstance, the result is often somewhat more drastic than you really intend. What I would like to do is invite further discussion about the way in which Mr. Trudeau wrestled with the significance he placed on the individual and the dignity of the individual, and the sense he would have had with respect to Church teaching and his responsibility as a committed Christian and practising Catholic. Otto, do you feel that there is at the moment any particular pressure on Catholic legislators in that sense?

Otto Lang: I would say no. I am not sure that it is easy to apply even a statement like that to a given situation. Certainly the laws that are before our legislators in parliaments have more to do with broad economic and social issues within a context that is open and acceptable all around. Individual issues might arise, I suppose, more for a provincial legislator than for a federal one, whereas the law may be said to be neutral from a moral point of view by not making abortion a legal matter. It might be a more complicated issue, with various financing going forward to the systems of abortion, clinics, and the like. In the provincial context, then, this could be a more serious issue that would have raised it for me as a former federal legislator.

Bernard Daly: I think the statement that Richard Alway referred to needs to be compared with what the pope said in his encyclical on life. A section of that encyclical would take precedence over the statement from the one department to the effect that a Catholic legislator has to deal with the practical realities of what kind of law can be passed in a given situation, and this was in effect the position of the Canadian bishops. When he was president of the Canadian Conference of Catholic Bishops, Bishop Lebel spoke out publicly about this because, as many of you know, the bishops were very much under attack by some members of the Church for failing to be aggressive enough about the teaching and law on abortion. There were those who wanted every Catholic member of parliament excommunicated, and so on.

There is a quote from a 1988 statement, one of the ones that John Turner missed, that states,

> The society which accepts abortion as a solution to present problems whether personal or social is also a society which abuses its children, lays waste the environment, risks nuclear war and implements economic policies in which the immediate benefits to some now, will be dearly paid for by many in the future. All of us are attempting to live as if there were no tomorrow. Persons who are still in the process of coming to birth

are a real reminder to us of the fact that for the some the future is just beginning.

Now, the bishops insisted that it was for the legislators to devise the way that Canadian society as a whole, through law, would somehow deal with these issues. But there was never a specific call to criminalize the actions of a woman, for example. The position that I hear in that statement would have to be compared with the pope's own position.

Otto Lang: The encyclical is *Evangelium Vitae*, which came out in 1995. I agree with that, and I think the kind of sense that we have of ecclesiology here is interesting because Bernard has explained that the Catholic bishops in Canada have had – I am not sure that nuanced is the right word – but, a broad position with the many aspects they have tried to teach. As Gregory has said, evolution in the Church can even take place within Parliament, through the speeches and actions of parliamentarians viewed over time. This is all part of the church community moving.

Tom Axworthy: On the connection between Mr. Trudeau's views on freedom and clericalism, and his advocacy of using the state in terms of economic freedom, I think he believed strongly that what was important, as Otto Lang has talked about, is the dignity of the individual. He believed the individual should have the maximum amount of choice, both in terms of morals and ethics, and also in terms of the objective conditions of life. If you believe in having a maximum amount of choice, so that individuals can make their own definition of the good for themselves, then in terms of the law his views on the Church and anti-clericalism, and the amount of freedom and choice that existed under the law in the 1940s and 1950s, he would say that the results were rigged – that there wasn't real freedom of choice because the attachment to pluralism was less than it should be in Quebec.

Therefore, this explains much of his anti-clericalism at that time, because the Church seemed to be allied with authoritarian forces. However, once you achieve freedom of religion and of the press, as enabling conditions for individuals to make choices, then that objective condition has been achieved. Added to this, of course, is the concept of negative liberty. Trudeau was a tremendous believer in T.H. Green and positive liberty, the idea that in order to expand choice it should not only be about morals, but also about having the ability to live a good life. In Trudeau's analysis of the economic system, it was rigged or unfair economically in Quebec in terms of individual choice in the 1940s and 1950s. People did not have maximum choice because poverty kept them in fetters. Therefore, the state may have been a part of the problem in Quebec and had to be removed, and poverty was a problem whereby the state could be an enabler to try to bring more equality. So I do not think there is a contradiction. Trudeau's ultimate goal was to expand the degrees by which individuals could have real choices, and in one case it meant taking the state away and the other meant using it as a mechanism for change. I think he was rather agnostic about the use of the state, except as means to try to expand human freedom: restricting in one case, but allowing it to exercise some measure of regulation on the market on the other.

V

Faith, Politics, and Personal Experience

Reflections on Faith and Politics

Hon. Allan MacEachen

I have never had, in my political life, a discussion bringing together political realities of life in Canada and the spiritual dimension. I intend to begin by looking at the quotation from Pierre Trudeau beginning with "I naturally asked myself questions." It is found in an interview conducted by "Ed" and reprinted in the United Church *Observer* of September 1971. Now, Ed may stand for Editor, but Ed's identity is not disclosed as he conducts this interview. From the flow of the interview, it is a safe bet to conclude that Ed did not know Mr. Trudeau very well; otherwise he might have probed Mr. Trudeau's faith perspective more skillfully. Ed began: "Now I am going to get personal. I have been told you are a devout Catholic. I do not know whether you are a devout Catholic or not." Well, it was not a good start. The word "devout" was not a good choice, certainly not for the cerebral Mr. Trudeau. His response to these questions was predictable; he began a dialectic:

Trudeau: "I honestly do not know what they mean by a devout Catholic."

Ed: "Well you are a believer and you go to church?"

Trudeau: "Yes."

Ed: "Does that make you a devout man?"

All predictable.

Finally, Mr. Trudeau shifted the ground of the interview from devotion to belief and said, "I believe in life after death, I believe in God and I am a Christian." In making this declaration, he drew upon portions of the Apostles' Creed, which begins, "I believe in God, the Father almighty," and concludes with the words, "the resurrection of the body and life everlasting." He said it all; he could not have said more. It was all there: his declaration of faith. It is more than accidental that in defining himself he avoided devotion, which signifies practice, and relied upon the creed, signifying intellectual assent. When I read this interview by Ed, I was amused first at the predictable dialectic and then I was edified by this profound profession of faith that he made so easily.

Mr. Trudeau was highly disciplined in his use of time, words, food, and drink. His discipline stood out; even in his lifetime when people asked me about Mr. Trudeau I emphasized his discipline. Discipline comes from a force within the person; therefore it is not surprising that in Ed's interview he states, "I like to impose constraints on myself." In his self-imposed regime, Mr. Trudeau excelled.

I must declare that despite my conversations with Mr. Trudeau – I sat for years as his deskmate in the House of Commons and sat next to him in the cabinet – and despite all these conversations we had. We never discussed fundamental questions of faith and resurrection and so on.

I do remember on one occasion Mr. Trudeau sat next to me and talked about his visit to the Vatican, where he had an interview with Paul VI – that agonized pope – and he was full of sympathy for him. Trudeau described the pope as "beleaguered." We were aware of each other's faith, after he and others got over the incongruity of a Catholic with a blatantly Scottish name. Everybody thought I was a Presbyterian. The Scottish Catholic escaped the influence of John Knox. It is well known that Mr. Trudeau went to mass, whether travelling in China with Jacques Hébert or visiting Cape Breton with me. Sunday mass was a must for Pierre Trudeau. That Cape Breton event took place at Stella Maris parish church in Bernash, on August 1, 1971, the same year as his interview with the United Church *Observer*. The pastor, Father MacCloud, had been a classmate of mine at St. Francis Xavier University and cooperated fully with the service. Of course, Fr. MacCloud and his family were great Liberals. In my class at St. Francis Xavier there were 48 graduates, 12 of whom became priests; we also produced one United Church minister. I preferred politics to the priesthood, and I must admit that in my long political life, with my association with my constituents, I heard more confessions than the combined efforts of my priestly classmates!

Mr. Trudeau had a lot of events scheduled in Cape Breton, but the church service was not listed on the official program and was not covered by the media. Later on that beautiful August Sunday, Mr. Trudeau opened the Gaelic gathering at St. Anne's, Cape Breton. He was garbed in the Elliott kilt, a gift to him from the Liberal caucus. In packing for the journey, Mr. Trudeau forgot to include his sporran. "What should we do?" he asked. I said, "Go ahead." Well, it was not good advice. His photograph in the kilt without a sporran was widely shown in British newspapers – he got exposure, and it was not only media exposure! Following the event he quietly confided to me that he could now understand why a sporran was necessary in wearing a kilt.

In my era, and in my area, politicians were expected to treat religion with deference and respect. When lapses occurred, my constituents were not amused. One such lapse involved Mr. Trudeau during the 1972 election campaign. In the election of 1968, the "Just Society" was a Liberal campaign slogan. Indeed, citizens of Canada could be forgiven if they concluded that the "Just Society" was just around the corner. I was visiting door-to-door in the fully Presbyterian county of Victoria, in the fully Presbyterian district of Little Narrows, with the thoroughly Presbyterian warden of the county, Mr. Kenneth Matheson. Standards were stern in that area, and we were doing important business. We arrived at this one door, and the lady of the house was obviously ready to leave. She was dressed with her handbag and said she was going to a church meeting. She said, "Sit down." She was ready to delay, and began the conversation herself by saying, "We have always been Liberals in this house. It suits us to be that way. Not that we think we are better than others." I thought that was an unnecessary admission, however, but I continued to listen. She went on, "I am not pleased with your prime minister." Mr. Trudeau had suddenly become *my* prime minister. She then opened her purse and handed me a newspaper clipping, reporting Mr. Trudeau's reply to a heckler in his campaign in southern Ontario. "Mr. Trudeau, what happened to the Just Society?" the heckler asked him. And he replied, "Ask Jesus Christ, he promised it first." When I rose my head on reading that clipping, my prospective supporter said, "Mr. MacEachen, I regard that as blasphemy."

When I became a member of the House of Commons in 1953, Louis Saint-Laurent was prime minister. My recollection is that Mr. Saint-Laurent referred at times to God in his public utterances. Later on, I recall Paul Martin Sr. urging Lester Pearson to mention God in his speeches from time to time. Mr. Pearson was reluctant. Throughout my political career, politicians were disinclined to invoke God and religion in the discharge of their public duties. Faith, belief, religion, was a private matter, and the single regular manifestation of faith in my years in the House of Commons and the Senate was the daily recital of prayers for which we stood at the beginning of the daily session. Monique Bégin recounts that in her eight years in the cabinet she heard a reference to religion only once. That occurred in a report on the census containing data on the religious composition of the Canadian population. I shall quote Monique because she makes an amusing reference to me in her observation. She said, "The minister responsible for the agency Statistics Canada was telling Prime Minister Trudeau that for the first time, citizens who identified themselves as Catholics formed the majority of Canadians. No comment was made, but the face of Allan MacEachen, the deputy prime minister and a staunch Catholic from Nova Scotia, more precisely from Cape Breton, showed what could only be interpreted as pleasure at a long overdue revenge against history." So watch the expression on your face! Although Mr. Trudeau may have been seen as a devout Catholic by Ed, and I as a staunch Catholic by Monique, we were not given to mixing our politics and our religion in the conduct of public office.

We neither hid nor displayed our religion, but we were certainly not Godless. The mixing of politics and religion in the Canadian context is not the thing to do, or has not been the thing to do. For Canadian politicians it was generally an uncomfortable mixture. One time, when Mr. Pearson was the leader of the opposition, I accompanied him to Halifax, where he addressed the Canadian Foreign Policy Association. Frank Doyle, the managing editor of the *Halifax Herald*, assuming that Mr. Pearson went to church regularly, called me and said, "Mr. Pearson is likely going to St. Matthew's church and I would like to cover him and have a photographer there." I conveyed that message to Mr. Pearson and he was not at all pleased. In fact, he was clearly unhappy at the notion that the church or religion should be involved in his political life. He finally consented, however, and lo and behold, the photographer did not show up.

Another example of the sensitivity to the mixing of religion and politics was driven home to me in a particular way as minister of labour in the Pearson cabinet. Saint Benoît-du-Lac, a monastery in the province of Quebec, applied for a grant under the Municipal Winter Works Program. The program was funded by the federal government to help municipalities provide new facilities and jobs for unemployed workers. Such requests from municipalities were approved as routine; in this case, not so. Officials turned down the application despite the vigorous, repeated representations by the abbott made by phone, letter, and visits to Ottawa. So insistent were the representations that I decided to look at the file myself to discern the reluctance. My investigation revealed the following: first, the abbey had acquired the status of municipality under Quebec law, and enjoyed the same privileges as any other municipality. We just could not get over that. A monastery was a municipality, certified to us by the minister of inter-governmental affairs. But what about the monks? We discovered that the monks – or some of them at least – were registered as unemployed in the local manpower office and were assigned to jobs from time to time as tradesmen.

So there it was. I said, "This is unusual but nevertheless, under the law, they qualify; Saint Benoît-du-Lac is a legitimate applicant." I could have made that decision on my own, but I felt so sensitive in reaching this conclusion, fearing a headline in the Montreal *Gazette* reading "Staunch Roman Catholic MacEachen gives a grant to Saint Benoît-du-Lac" that I went to cabinet. Trudeau asked, "Boys, ladies, what do you think?" Well, the case was solid and we approved the grant, but I will never forget the look on Mr. Pearson's face. He regarded my submission as a distasteful intrusion, undoubtedly wishing that he had a minister of labour with better judgment.[1]

Now, what I have described as sensitivity to religion in Canadian politics, Monique Bégin describes as silence. She writes, "In Canadian politics, one great silence is religion. No politician in contemporary Canada would ever speak insistently about religion. All public figures consent to a wise silence." We could all agree with her when she argued, "Bringing religion into the public arena is dangerous and potentially explosive should it result in the favouring of one church as an institution over another." About Mr. Trudeau she wrote, "I do not recall any occasion when Mr. Trudeau in his role as a public figure referred to his faith." Obviously, Monique was not a regular reader of the United Church *Observer*.

The reticence of Canadian politicians to go public on matters of faith and religion is not an obligation imposed by any articulated and commonly accepted doctrine of the separation of church and state in Canada. No such declaration can be found ensuing from the first amendment in the classic judgment by the Supreme Court of the United States, where this separation is carefully articulated. But even the application of the separation of church and state in the U.S. does not impose silence on public figures in that country in the expression of public views. On the contrary, it is argued that the doctrine itself has cleared the way for the flourishing practice of American politicians freely expressing religious views.

Canadian silence does not come from doctrine, nor from the court; it comes from prudence gained from experience. We have to run a country. Practising such prudence has allowed Canadian political parties to perform the essential roles of accommodation and conciliation. Canadian political parties have not made the same mistakes that those in the

United States have made, such as the contest on abortion between the Democrats and the Republicans, which is a source of great difficulty and reduces voter choice at election time. We have dealt with these issues in the Canadian Parliament by consensus. Parliament has developed its own way of dealing with sensitive and divisive moral issues through free votes, thus avoiding party positions and permitting individual members of parliament to give full expression to their core beliefs. That practice comes from prudence, and not from any Canadian doctrine. Of course, abortion and capital punishment issues fell into the category of free votes not because they had moral content, but because they were divisive. Parties did not take positions on these issues because they said, "the individual conscience of the individual member or senator will reign supreme." Having said this, it would be a mistake to conclude that legislative measures not dealt with by free votes lack moral content. Quite the contrary, much of our legislation gives expression to moral values founded at times upon religious convictions. Moral values, though often unstated, enter into the complex collection of considerations that enter into legislative policy.[2]

I am going to pick up one theme John English asked me to deal with: Social Catholicism, a form of Catholicism that emphasizes social justice, changing the world, and making things better. On February 20, 2003, I joined Roy Romanow at the annual Allan J. MacEachen Lecture on Politics at St. Francis Xavier University. Mr. Romanow dealt with the recommendations of his commission on health care and the steps taken in the federal budget towards implementation. It seemed appropriate for me to relate my role as minister of national health and welfare, and as legislator of the Medical Care Act, to the orientation I received as a student and professor at St. Francis Xavier. I recounted how, after the 1965 election, Mr. Pearson summoned me to his Caribbean retreat and asked me to become minister of national health and welfare to legislate medicare. I described to the audience how I approached this challenging task, which I took on with enthusiasm and conviction. This conviction was formed from my association with the leaders of the Antigonish movement as a student and professor at St. Francis Xavier. There I became an advocate of a socially directed system of providing health services.

The eloquent and tireless exponent of the principles of the Antigonish movement on the campus was a Catholic priest, Dr. Moses Coady. He envisioned a restructured economy brought about through adult education and co-operative ownership change. Social justice themes dominated his thinking, born from actual experience in Europe and North America and from many writings on social issues. His liberating influence taught me that social change was possible and that poverty and deprivation were not the inevitable companions of people on earth. To a young man like me, exposed to the limitations of life in a coal-mining town in Cape Breton in the 1930s, the philosophy I learned at St. Francis Xavier University was a profound insight and became a guiding principle of my future political life.

I am not alone in bringing such orientations to Parliament or to politics. Jean Marchand once said to me, "How is it you and I think alike so often on issues that come before cabinet?" I did not give an opinion at the time as it took me unawares, but now I believe the common elements of our approach came from our mentors, Dr. Coady in my case and Father Lévesque of l'Université Laval in Jean Marchand's case. Both teachers were advocates of social justice, of social Catholicism. I called Jacques Hébert to confirm that Marchand had studied under Father Lévesque, and Hébert explained that Fr. Lévesque had had a great influence on Marchand and on other prominent Quebeckers, including Maurice Lamontagne. Maurice and I worked in Pearson's office, and the contribution that Maurice made to Canadian public life has never been fully emphasized. I remember him writing long memoranda in longhand on all the Quebec issues, on public service unions, on regional development. Maurice kept in close touch with Father Lévesque.

When I talked to Jacques Hébert, our conversation naturally turned to Mr. Trudeau. Jacques was a lifelong close friend of Mr. Trudeau's, and I asked if he and Mr. Trudeau ever spoke about religious subjects. He replied, "No, there was no discussion. Mr. Trudeau was discreet on these matters." Jacques did share with me a single exception to Mr. Trudeau's practice of discretion, and I now share it with you. He and Pierre regularly had lunch together at a Chinese restaurant in Montreal. As Mr. Trudeau was becoming frailer over time, it became Jacques' habit to walk him back to his office. Normally Jacques left him at the door, but on this occasion Mr. Trudeau said, "Come to my office. I have something for you." Jacques found this unusual; after all, they had been together for two hours. The something he gave to Jacques was a passage from Teilhard de Chardin on God and death. De Chardin, in whom Mr. Trudeau apparently had a great interest, is variously described as a scientist, theologian, and mystic. Jacques was touched and surprised, and then he went on to offer a possible explanation. "Pierre, possibly feeling death coming upon him and sensing that I, though a Catholic, was a bit superficial, thought I ought to reflect on such matters."

Faith and Personal Experience

Tom Axworthy

In reflecting on this theme of Pierre Trudeau's faith and his immersion in Catholic philosophy, I went back to my notes of one of my first sessions as a member of the Prime Minister's Office (PMO) with Mr. Trudeau. Jim Coutts hired me for the PMO to write speeches and to advise on policy. In one of the first meetings after I was in the PMO, Mr. Trudeau called a speechwriters' meeting. Jim called me up and said, "You should go meet him – you will enjoy it." So off I went, and Mr. Trudeau was there with a very distinguished Jean Le Moyne who was on our speechwriting team. Mr. Le Moyne had been one of Quebec's most noted thinkers, and had won a Governor General's award. My degree from Queen's University did not quite measure up to his many attributes, and I quietly slipped into the office where Mr. Trudeau and Mr. Le Moyne very happily discussed Teilhard de Chardin, Jacques Maritain, and Emmanuel Mounier for about forty-five minutes. All of this discussion was in French, not my first language. It was all about Catholic philosophy, not my Methodist religion. At the end of it, Mr. Trudeau just looked at me and said, "Do you have anything to add?" I said, "No." Consequently, for the next four years he did not know my name, and when he finally learned it he called me Lloyd – so my entrée into this matter of faith and experience was less than auspicious.

I did learn from that first meeting, and I have some of the notes here, that if one was to work for Pierre Trudeau, at least in the domain that I did – speeches and ideas and policy – you had better learn his framework and try to understand where he was coming from, the intellectual axis that motivated this man. If there was one fundamental truth about Pierre

Trudeau, and many differing ideas are found in this book, it was that he was an intellectual, a man of ideas. There are many politicians who are well read. John Turner and Allan MacEachen are themselves learned individuals. But an intellectual, when approached with an issue, begins first to frame it within a world of concepts, a world of philosophy. There is a value frame through which an intellectual looks at issues that is rare in the world of power. Most (but not all) politicians I know, when faced with any given issue, begin to think about the substance, but also about public opinion, regional implications, and personal advantage in it. We all have value frames and frameworks. Trudeau's was an explicitly intellectual one. He always loved the world of ideas. His intellectual framework was enormously well developed and fleshed out by the time he went into politics in his late forties. He had spent all his life studying and working and thinking. He had a well-articulated philosophy, as Allan MacEachen has reminded us, through which he sifted the complex world of politics and governing Canada. But in many of its essentials, in my view, it did not change. This did not mean that every policy reflected exactly his philosophy. On many things, as any prime minister does, he would defer to the relevant minister, whatever his personal views were on an issue. This was necessary to keep the cabinet, the party, and the caucus together. But he always had a well-developed view on most things.

On the question of faith and spirituality, my impression of this intellectual man is that this was an aspect of his life, but it was not – in my experience – *the* aspect of his life. He knew Catholic philosophy and the Bible well, just as he knew English literature well, just as he knew Mayan architecture well, just as he knew music quite well. I am not here to give a hagiography about Mr. Trudeau, but the depth of his learning in a wide variety of fields was remarkable. You could raise subject after subject that he had studied at one time or personally experienced on his travels. He had an enormous breadth of interests, of which philosophy was certainly one, and which theology or Catholic theology was also one. But it was not the only one, and I do not think the main one.

By contrast, while working for him I had the chance to meet President Jimmy Carter. You do not need to spend very long with Jimmy Carter before you understand that a Christian theology informs his approach to a wide variety of issues. The same appears to be true of President George W. Bush. David Frum, in his book *The Right Man*, talks about his very first entrée into the Bush White House. The first thing that was said to him was, "Missed you at Bible class this morning." I have not been to the Bush White House, but from many accounts it is clear that theology is a very important aspect of the whole atmosphere. I never detected, in my years with Mr. Trudeau, that spirituality or theology was the overwhelming *Weltanschauung* of our office. Ideas were, Liberal philosophy was, but not necessarily spirituality or theology.

But I took one thing away from that first meeting with Trudeau: amidst the discussion of the various philosophers and theologians, I realized that I had to catch up rather quickly in areas where I did not know the individuals to whom they were referring, and the background with which Trudeau was so obviously conversant.

I worked my way through two Catholic intellectuals who I think had an enormous influence on Pierre Trudeau, both from the nineteenth century: Lord Acton and Cardinal Newman. I want to make some very brief references to Newman and his approach to knowledge and to ideas because I think that they were reflected in Trudeau's own approach. He would often comment on Acton in speech and in his writings, and often commented to me on Cardinal Newman's style and his approach to ideas.

As I read the *Apologia* and *Idea of the University*, I took three concepts out of Newman that I thought influenced Mr. Trudeau and that, in retrospect, I think have some continuing validity. The first is that Newman writes, in *Idea of the University*, that knowledge should not be examined as a series of specialties, but as a conceptual whole – that there is a unity in knowledge for which an educated person should strive. His ideal of a university maintained a broad base of knowledge: an ideal that we have wandered from in modern universities, where we have not only specializations between faculties but minute specialties within faculties. That was not the Newman view, which held that there was a broad synthesis for which one should try to aim. I think that this was very much Trudeau's approach. I repeat that he had a wide knowledge in a host of areas. In his retirement, for example, I remember meeting him and asking what he had been reading lately. I was not exactly expecting the latest novelist, but was taken aback when he told me he was rereading Marcel Proust's *A Remembrance of Things Past* because he had not looked at Proust for twenty-five years or so. By the next time I had lunch with him, he had pretty much finished it. He would take bodies of work – such as Russian literature and French novelists – and go through them very systematically, in a wide range of fields. The broadening aspect of knowledge was obviously something that attracted him.

Second, Newman made the point that knowledge should be appreciated on its own terms. There is a beauty and sensitivity to understanding knowledge and truth and one should not just look at understanding as useful; there is an intrinsic worth to the subjects themselves, and the use of the intellect can be a tremendous key to opening up life's possibilities. If there was one essential aspect of Pierre Trudeau, it was his wonderful belief in logic and his ability as a logician. He was a man who truly did believe in reason, who relished debate, who appreciated anybody who could contend with him, and who was devoted to what debate could bring in terms of clarity through the use of one's faculties. This was also the essence of Newman's argument regarding what a university should be about, and this was certainly my experience working with Trudeau himself. In some ways I think that among some of his colleagues he could be almost a fearsome, calculating machine when his logic began to flow, and he could be fierce in debate. But that is where he started from: this tremendous belief that assumptions should be debated, that contradictions should be raised, that the logic of a given position should be taken to its extreme. In these respects, I think he was very much a part of the Newman philosophy.

Third and lastly (and this may be more conjectural, because I do not remember ever speaking to Trudeau precisely about this point), Newman also argued that the idea of a university, the idea of broad knowledge, and the use of reason and knowledge on their own could inform faith. There was not a dichotomy or a division between reason and faith; an understanding of theology – which Newman argued had to be an essential part of one's university teaching – would bring an integrity to the intellectual exercise. Through faith, combined with knowledge, one would have a better moral sense of how to carry out one's life, and one's faith would itself be strengthened by reason. Newman has a famous phrase that there should be a stronger basis to belief than prejudice or tradition; reason, theology, and knowledge of the scriptures should add to that essential belief in revealed truth. Logic and reason were a companion of belief, and out of this understanding one became a stronger and better person.

I think that this, ultimately, was the element of spirituality that was part of Mr. Trudeau. He never wore his religion on his sleeve, as John Turner said. We never had prayer breakfasts; Reverend Jesse Jackson was never invited to come and talk (at least not about religion, although we might have invited him to discuss war and peace at some point). There was no public display. But I think that, in his own understanding of life, faith continued to be important to this supreme man of reason because he believed, like Newman, that reason supplemented his faith. He used his natural faculties to think through issues, to think through the questions of faith and those essential moral issues; this road was a twinned highway as opposed to a crossroads. And I think this was an aspect of

Newman that lay behind Mr. Trudeau's use of intellect, combined with his quiet belief in faith.

My notes from *Idea of the University*, in which Newman talked about that ideal, state that the first step in intellectual training is to impress upon a boy's mind the idea of science, method, order, principle and system of rule, richness, and harmony. Pierre Trudeau, a lifelong disciple of Cardinal Newman, carried out that ideal.

Faith and Public Life: Personal Experiences

Michael Valpy

Canadians do not feel comfortable talking publicly about religion. We may close our public schools and government offices on Good Friday and Easter Monday just as we did in the time of Sir John A. – and not for much longer, I feel confident in predicting. But we have no idiom of faith and spirituality for the public square. We have privatized religion, or, more accurately, to quote Roger Hutchinson, professor of Church and Society at University of Toronto's Emmanuel College, we have privatized piety, the display of reverence for God. And it is the wish of most Canadians that this should be so.

As University of Montreal theologian Solange Lefebvre noted, to be a Christian in this country – which more than 75 per cent of Canadians still nominally claim to be – is to be "discreet."

The newest census data reinforce the fact that Canada is part of what some sociologists call the "religion cold belt" of atrophied faith practice, stretching across Western Europe and, on this side of the Atlantic, north of the 49th parallel (with pious hot spots, like holes in the ozone layer, in Atlantic Canada, northern Ontario, and parts of the prairies).

Canadians are jarred by preachers, priests, rabbis, and imams who "get political."

Canadians prefer not to know much about the religious and spiritual inclinations of their political leaders – with two exceptions, and for two very different reasons: William Lyon Mackenzie King and Pierre Trudeau. Who knows what R.B. Bennett or Robert Borden thought about God? Or Louis St. Laurent or Joe Clark or Brian Mulroney? Or the four prime ministers no one can name between John A. Macdonald's second administration and

Wilfrid Laurier? We did know about Stockwell Day, and once the corporate media's early adoration of him had gone its way, he became an object of cruel and un-Canadian journalistic ridicule for his beliefs.

Should you want to look into Canada's religious or pious future through the prism of generational succession – the social science theory that the values of the generation in its twenties inevitably become the dominant values of the society – one of the most significant characteristics of today's Canadians in their twenties is their disconnect from religion. In fact, while attendance at regular religious services is marginally increasing in Canada because of immigration, one of the first steps young immigrants take in integrating themselves into Canadian life is to distance themselves from active participation in the faith of their parents.

This is something that fascinates me. The country is a far more interesting social laboratory – and getting more interesting by the year – than we have become used to thinking.

Here are Canadians in their twenties who have grown up immersed – drowned – in American culture but who nonchalantly show no sign – far less than their comparable American demographic – of buying into American religiosity, one of the many seminal elements of this generation's marked divergence from American cultural values.

Here are Canadians in their twenties who nonetheless overwhelmingly tell pollsters they believe in God and possess something called spirituality.

And here are Canadians in their twenties whom political and social scientists define as a highly moralistic generation passionately concerned with social justice, and who are amazingly, *amazingly*, socially inclusive and embracing of difference, and who speak of a search for – and here again the language is difficult – a search for harmony in the universe and harmony in their lives.

These are all notions that can fall under the rubric of "religion." Where are they getting it from? It's a question I often ask myself.

It struck me a few years ago, as a parent and a journalist – and this is something else Dr. Lefebvre referred to – that I can no longer work allusions from the Bible or the Anglican Book of Common Prayer into what I say or write – and I was taught both in high school English as literature – because no one under the age of forty understands what I am talking about. So where are they getting it from?

It is not from the Bible, which is going the way of the *Iliad*, and it's not from the Koran or Talmud or Midrash – or, if it is, it's by some osmotic or, more likely, Internet process that no one yet to my knowledge has adequately defined. What we know is that this is a generation of religious illiteracy.

Tom Axworthy observed that the source of moralism and social justice did not necessarily need to be faith-based, that it could well be the outgrowth of humanism. That's certainly possible, of course, but, with respect to Tom, I do not really think it's the prime answer; I think the prime answer is something deeper and as yet not fully formed...or voiced.

A spirituality outside comfortable definition.

Look at this book.

Here is Michael Higgins tracing the influences on Pierre Trudeau of Jesuit, Dominican, and Benedictine intellectuals. Here is Jesuit educator Jacques Monet explaining what a young Pierre Trudeau would have learned at Montreal's Jesuit Collège Jean-de-Brébeuf.

Here are other scholars assessing the shaping of Mr. Trudeau's thoughts by Catholic scholars Lord Acton, Cardinal John Henry Newman, and the French Catholic philosopher Gabriel Marcel and his notions of Christian Personalism emphasizing the value and dignity of each individual, the importance of dialogue and the notion of human solidarity.

What I have found so striking is the degree to which Mr. Trudeau and other politicians of the era kept private their piety, although religious thinking shaped so many of their ideas of public life. Many in his cabinet, such as Jean Marchand, had had as mentor the Dominican sociologist Georges-Henri Lévesque at Laval University. Allan MacEachen was a product of the liberal Catholicism of the Antigonish Movement that developed socio-economic programs for impoverished fishing families. John Turner's faith shaped his political life to a depth we catch only glimmers of but know to be profound. Social Gospel, the application of Christian teaching to the ills of an industrial society, had an enormous influence on leading members of Parliament such as Tommy Douglas.

Yet Mr. MacEachen has strongly cautioned us against assuming a connection between Mr. Trudeau's spirituality and his government's policies. The prime minister was a fish in the ocean, but the ocean was also in the fish, said Stephen Clarkson – meaning that Mr. Trudeau, regardless of his ideas and beliefs, governed according to the times. Mr. MacEachen read an excerpt from Trudeau-era minister Monique Bégin's autobiography, in which she said that the only time she ever heard religion mentioned in cabinet was in 1971 when the minister responsible for Statistics Canada announced that Catholicism had become Canada's largest religious denomination. In all their years together, added Mr. MacEachen, he had never had a conversation with Mr. Trudeau about religion and God.

I recall a conversation I once had with Mr. Trudeau, years after he left formal political life. I quoted something that I said was from the Christian New Testament's Epistle to the Corinthians. Mr. Trudeau corrected me, saying it was from the Epistle to the Romans. I can't remember the quote, although I can remember we were eating spaghetti – but until that moment, I had no idea he thought about such things.

Stephen Clarkson has suggested that Canadian politicians are discreet about religion because of the country's nineteenth- and early twentieth-century history of Catholics and Protestants politically savaging each other. Religious discretion, he says, may be a Canadian survival technique. Perhaps.

The contrast, nonetheless, to contemporary U.S. public life is stark. George W. Bush, as governor of Texas, declared a statewide Jesus Day; Al Gore, his Democratic Party opponent in the presidential election, said that he makes important decisions by asking himself: "WWJD?" (What would Jesus do?). John Ashcroft, the U.S. Attorney-General, told a university graduating class: "We have no king but Jesus."

And in Pierre Trudeau, Canadians clearly saw a spiritual man. Let me try to define this, as always with the caveat that the language is difficult and with the added disclaimer that I am a journalist, not a theologian.

Three or four years ago, I asked Environics president Michael Adams what great events lay ahead for Canadians, and he replied: "Canadians are not going to be prepared for Pierre Trudeau's death."

Prepared for what, precisely?

Mr. Trudeau was – is – our one truly mythological prime minister. Mythology is the delivery of idea and image at the same time. It is the simultaneous cultural message delivered both to the mind and to what Carl Jung calls the mind-below-the-mind, and others might call the soul. It reveals the deep patterns of meaning and coherence in a culture, of the harmony in the universe. It shows us who we dream ourselves to be.

In those deep patterns of meaning and coherence, as Jung said, lie the sacred in life. And in the comprehension of those patterns of meaning and coherence and their origin, a society approaches the sacred and the word *God*.

The things about Pierre Trudeau that touched Canadians most deeply were things bound to his spirituality – his affinity with nature, for example, and the ideas he took from Christian Personalism: the dignity of the individual, the will to human solidarity.

Those matters of Mr. Trudeau's soul bound him to the souls of Canadians, to what we know are Canadians' deep mythological attachments to the beauty of their land; to the Charter of Rights and Freedoms; to collective equity, fairness, justice. It was that loss to their spiritual souls by his death that Canadians were not prepared for. It is that loss, perhaps, that has brought us here, questing for spiritual understanding of him.

"There Is Always a Moment"

John Godfrey

I cannot claim to have known Pierre Trudeau well. My only qualification is to have spent time – two weeks – with him (and six others) on a canoe trip in the Northwest Territories in the summer of 1979. I saw him on and off afterwards in a variety of conditions, and in 1996 a group of us, including Pierre and my friend Ted Johnson, had a long-weekend canoe trip on the Petawawa.

In July 1979 when we landed in Yellowknife, in preparation for a trip down the Hanbury-Thelon Rivers, Pierre was fifty-nine years old. He had just lost an election; as leader of the opposition he was now able to take his first long canoe trip since he had become prime minister in 1968.

Pierre's view of canoeing is well known from his 1944 essay "The Ascetic in a Canoe," which describes the thousand-mile trip he took with some friends in the summer of 1941 from Montreal to James Bay. In 1941 Pierre Trudeau was twenty-one years old, subsisting during this trip on pretty basic meals of salt pork, fish, and venison. Free of what he called "useless material baggage," Trudeau describes three great things he derived from that canoe trip: "What fabulous and underdeveloped mines are to be found in nature, friendship and oneself?"

Nature, friendship, and oneself: three sources of pleasure that allow an alternation between solitude and companionship but always in the presence of nature. Of course, as we think of Pierre's life journey we can reflect on the difference between canoe trips when you are twenty-one, when you are fifty-nine, and when you are seventy-six. Nature and solitude are a constant, but the nature of companionship changes. In

1979 the only member of the group Pierre knew really well was Jean Pelletier, son of his oldest and best friend, Gérard Pelletier. Pierre and Jean canoed together (Pierre absolutely the steersman) and tented together. As for the rest of us, though we were a group not altogether without ego, here was a man who had been prime minister for eleven years and we were all a little awestruck. My own particular hangup arose from the fact that I had decided generally to speak to Trudeau in French. Would that be, "Pierre, *tu*?" or "Pierre, *vous*?" Many were the complex constructions, including "*on*," until he finally "*tu-toie*d" me. Another of our party, John Gow, suffered a worse fate, since Pierre called him Don for three days, until I finally got up enough nerve to take him aside and correct him.

On this canoe trip, Pierre was discovering that things had changed since 1941. He may have thought those who took trains were brutes, those who bicycled remained bourgeoisie, and those who paddled were children of nature, but these particular children were gourmets, if not gourmands, determined to eat and drink as well and as much as possible. Of the eight of us, there were three permanent chefs, and five rotating dishwashers, including Pierre. Halfway through the trip we camped at a place called Helen Falls, which is a very beautiful location with an absolutely spectacular waterfall. At the top of the portage, there is a cairn with a can in which travellers leave notes. Some bright soul, long after our trip, decided to take out the can, copy all the notes and, I hope, put it all back. Here is our cairn note of that trip, which I think conveys – quite literally – the flavour of the trip:

4 August 1979

This sturdy group of 8 fellows is travelling from Sifton Lake to Hornby's Cabin. Poor Hornby, we keep reflecting as we munch our way through baked stuffed fish, lamb kabobs, cheese fondue, complete with two bottles of Mouton Cadet. Let this diary record that our last member may well expire from over-eating; "*La grande bouffe en canoe.*" But enough of this idle chit-chat. No, we are not going to offer you metaphysical reflections on the mysteries of male bonding, or the Great Outdoors as Salvation of the Human Soul. For this the reader would be well advised to turn to other notes in this can or David Silcox's book *The Silence and the Storm* (not yet available in paperback). Down to the nitty-gritty. First, who are we? Well, we certainly are gritty (make that Gritty). Peter Stollery, MP Toronto-Spadina; Pierre Trudeau, MP, etc., Ottawa; John Gow; Craig Oliver from CTV News; Jean

Pelletier from *La Presse*; Tim Kotcheff, CTV News; David Silcox, Arts Magnate; John Godfrey, King's College. The weather was cold and blowy until today, the bugs were minimal (one of Mother Nature's little trade-offs), the coffee was always excellent owing to Peter Stollery, Esq., and nobody dumped. For further documentation you may consult *The Hanbury: Fat City* (in press, with recipes, meals and photos by Silcox and Kotcheff), or see John Gow's forthcoming cine-epic, *Rocks*. The more literary minded may care to turn to *Godfrey: The Diaries, volume 5*.

Your humble scribe,
John Godfrey

It is interesting that Pierre reflected back on this trip as a time of space, when he was making important decisions in his life. In his reflections he does not mention the lamb kabobs or the Mouton Cadet because I do not think this would have fit Pierre's storyline, his self-image, the public projection of his persona. What was he like on the trip? First, he was companionable and easy to get along with; since he had joined a group that had been canoeing together for several years, he did not attempt to assert himself or take a leadership role. He was the ultimate "go along" guy. In his 1941 essay he wrote, "The canoe is a school of friendship, you learn that your best friend is not a rifle, but someone who shares a night's sleep with you after ten hours of paddling at the other end of the canoe." He also pitched in on dishwashing and other duties. His special talent was making fireplaces out of flat rocks every evening as we set up camp. He was painstaking, meticulous, even Cartesian in this time-consuming activity. Happy hour, which consisted of over-proof rum daiquiris, went on longer than usual on the trip as we waited for Pierre to complete each masterpiece, with perhaps a commensurate increase in spirited if not spiritual conviviality. And, of course, all around us all the time was nature; the magnificent, rolling barren lands of the Arctic, the long, lingering summer days of those latitudes. Pierre frequently wandered off by himself after we had set up camp, along the river back into the hills, contemplating nature as he walked, thinking also no doubt about his political future and the rest of his life. Who knows what a man thinks as he walks alone? Certainly none of us asked him and we let him wander without disturbance.

Generally, the trip worked its magic, and all of us relaxed, calmed down, grew a little more silent ourselves perhaps, overwhelmed by the constant, harsh beauty around us. We also became more physical beings, indeed fitter beings: there was a restoration of the necessary balance between mind and body. Pierre clearly enjoyed his body, was aware of his body, and even showed off his body. In 1944 he wrote,

> How does the trip affect your personality? Allow me to make a fine distinction and I would say that you return not so much a man who reasons more, but a more reasonable man. For, throughout this time, your mind has learned to exercise itself in working conditions which nature intended. Its primordial role has been to sustain the body in the struggle against a powerful universe. A good camper knows that it is more important to be ingenious than to be a genius. And conversely, the body, by demonstrating the true meaning of sensual pleasure, has been of service to the mind. You feel the beauty of animal pleasure when you draw a deep breath of rich morning air, right through your body, which has been carried by the cold night, curled up like an unborn child. How can you describe the feeling which wells up in the heart and stomach as the canoe finally rides up on the shore of the campsite after a long day of plunging your paddle into rain-swept waters? Purely physical is the joy which the fire spreads through the palms of your hands and the soles of your feet while your chattering mouth belches the poisonous cold. The pleasurable torpor of such a moment is perhaps not too different from what the mystics of the East are seeking. At least, it has allowed me to taste what one respected gentleman used to call the joys of hard living.

In 1979 he was still in great shape, truly revelling in the physicality of canoeing. In 1996, on the last canoe trip on which I saw him, Pierre's body was letting him down. He was weak and moved slowly. His canoeing partner, Wally Shaber from Trailhead in Ottawa, did all the heavy work in the rapids and on the portage. Pierre was even more silent and inward on that trip. But he was also philosophical about his diminished physicality. He told me that though he had not changed his diet, he had lost about fifteen pounds. He told me that he still swam the same distance in his pool in Montreal but that it took him twice as long. All this was said with calm, stoicism and grace, more with mild surprise than regret or bitterness.

As the trip neared its end, we reached the ruins of Hornby's Cabin on the Thelon. John Hornby was an English remittance man who travelled down the Thelon in 1926 with his young nephew, Edgar Christian, and a third man, and decided unwisely to try to winter over. They built a cabin and disaster struck. The fish, caribou, and birds they had counted on to sustain them failed to appear, and they all starved to death. Edgar Christian was the last to die, in May 1927; he kept a diary, which survived him. As you may recall from my cairn note, there was something of a contrast between the pitiful state of the Hornby expedition and our own fat-cat existence. A bit of that spirit showed itself as we walked around the remnants of the cabin and the grave sites. Pierre was deeply moved but said nothing.

That night, our last in camp before the planes would arrive early the next morning to take us out, Pierre, who had been cordial, pleasantly funny but reserved throughout the trip, suddenly opened up. It was almost as if knowing he was leaving at dawn, never to be as intimate with us again, he felt he could let himself go. He proposed a toast to the brave men who had died with Hornby. Because I had been teaching a course on modern French intellectual history, I had been reading Emmanuel Mounier and we had a long talk about Personalism. Since our last-night revelries went long into the night, I am afraid I cannot now recall, nor could I probably have done so the next morning, much of the details of our conversation. I can only tell you it was marvellous, that we were in "the zone" like a great tennis game.

Something I do recall was our discussion of Mounier's formulation *voir, juger, agir*: to see, to judge, to act. Looking back on Trudeau's life I have often reflected on how apt this triad of verbs is in explaining the way in which he made his crucial political decisions. It is the perfect formulation for the engaged intellectual, the intellectual in politics. It is, as Tom Axworthy said, the frame, the formula for decision. Stephen Clarkson and Christina McCall speak of Personalism as a philosophical alternative to existentialism in post–World War II France, yet later refer to Mounier, the leading Personalist thinker of his day, as an existentialist. I will leave it to others to sort out which is the appropriate conclusion. I do know that Pierre, like all of us, faced a number of true existential choices in his life. Compared to the rest of us, however, the stakes were a lot higher in his choices, as was the case with the Québec referendum or the War Measures Act.

To see, to judge, to act: the Trudeau approach to existential choices. One day, in the middle of the 1979 trip, we came to a short but nasty S-shaped rapid. There was an easy portage of a few hundred feet and most of us elected to take it. John Gow, however – still smarting at having been called "Don" for three days – decided in typically boastful summer-camp diary fashion to challenge Pierre: "I don't know about you, Pierre, but I think I am going to run this empty canoe." Note that he did not say, "I don't know about you, Godfrey," because I would have said, "Enjoy!"

Not that Pierre's having been prime minister could have had anything to do with this, of course. For those of you who know Pierre, you can guess the result. Whether it was a weakness or a strength, Pierre could not have resisted a challenge like that from a young buck. On a canoe trip, we are all sixteen years old again. But Pierre was also the master of the calculated risk: *voir, juger, agir*. I don't know how many times he walked up and down that bloody rapid, looking and judging. John Gow, in his early thirties, was the first to go. A mountain guy, he was actually deficient on one side to the tune of one half of a foot, and the other side to the tune of one half of a leg, but he does better without those things than most of us do with them. He was extremely fit, he had done a lot of canoeing, and he shot down that "S" as if nothing was involved. As Pierre prepared to go, most of the others, especially the journalists, rushed to the top of the bluff, telephoto lenses at the ready, prepared to document the death of the former prime minister. Since my camera was not that good, I decided it might be more helpful to be at the foot of the bluff to lend a hand if anything went wrong. Pierre came shooting down. It was not going well, and he was coming straight at the wall of the cliff. Since I was level with him I could see what the others could not: his eyes. At one moment I saw a look of horror as he thought he was going to crash, and then he took a mighty swipe with his paddle and in a raggedy fashion saved himself. *Voir, juger, agir*. At the bottom of the rapid, as we reloaded the canoes, everyone congratulated him on his successful run. Afterward I said to him, aside, "That was pretty good, but I was watching you and there was a moment." He turned to me and said simply, "There is always a moment."

Discussion

John Fraser: I find it really moving and touching that some of the conference presenters are slightly uncomfortable at getting into the world of the relationships that they had with Pierre Trudeau. I think it was typical of him to trust that a relationship would not be betrayed. I remember when he would stay at Massey College when he came to Toronto to see his daughter, and he stayed in one of the college's senior suites, which had a fireplace because he liked to have a fire going in the wintertime. One time I came up and he was lost in thought before the fire, and I felt like the greatest intruder on his world. I probably was, actually. I did have this sense that he was completely disconnected from ordinary concerns towards the end of his life, and I do not think he gave two hoots about what we thought of him or whether we were analyzing what was going on in his mind. I thought that his *Memoirs* was a rather cynical exercise that was kind of the testimony.[1] Is it necessary to probe so deeply in front of his soul, as his soul was manifested through his being, his life, his legislation, and his actions?

Nancy Southam: I would say yes and no. I did not know him all the way through his political life; I met him during the latter bit. I think he was an intensely private man, and I am sure that Jim Coutts would say that, too. I think that if he trusted you then a lot of stuff came out. Sometimes you had to push him to open up, but I think that more often than not he would answer any questions I had.

John Fraser: How did an intensely private man cope with the fact that his life was splattered all over the country, everything from the troubles with Margaret to the relationship with his boys? There was the media all around doing it, but he kept up this amazing dignity and we all admired him for that. Yet, for an intensely private man, he chose a way of life that splattered his life all over the place.

B.W. Powe: I can share an anecdote that I do not think he would mind me talking about. Sometimes he did not really seem to be as aware of how public he was as you may think. When I went to see him at one point I was going through a divorce and custody conflict. My ex-wife had often gone with me to lunch with him, and he asked, "Where is she? Is she not going to join us today?" I replied, "No, I am sorry to say, sir, that we are in the throes of separation." He slumped in his chair and looked very sympathetic, and said, "That is too bad. You know I have been through that, too." I almost said, "No kidding. I might have been out of the country when that happened." But what startled me about the remark was that it was not delivered in a witty way – it was utterly sincere and very sympathetic. Then he sort of shrugged and said, "Well, you know these things happen and one goes on," which is very much the way he dealt with things. Nevertheless, I had a sense of this insularity – that he was not aware of the implications of his actions in public. But that is not quite what I meant here. I was trying to get at the consistency, commitment, and engagement that revealed the sharpness of his soul, and that that is as much theology as we need to know.

Ron Graham: Pierre Trudeau genuinely liked solitude. He was perfectly happy to be alone reading a book or thinking; he was used to it. I think that is probably a difficult thing for many people, and certainly a difficult thing for most politicians. Politicians like to be with other people. It is very much a people-oriented business – lots of company and anecdotes and gossip. Journalism is much the same way. Mr. Trudeau could be by himself for hours or days and be perfectly content; not feeling upset, not asking "Why is someone not calling me?" He would think and he would read, and he was not to be pitied because he was used to solitude and enjoyed it. If the schedule was too busy, he would insist on time by himself: to walk, to read, to do other things. So solitude was a part of his life.

Play-acting was another aspect that we should not underestimate. Among his many gifts was a theatrical sense, in which he knew what he was doing. It was either instinctual, or he could play for the crowd.

When he went to the Grey Cup, in that enormous hat and grey cape pictured on the cover of Richard Gwyn's book, that was an effect of the Northern Magus. It did not just happen that he was at the Grey Cup in a cape; whatever was going through his mind that day, that outfit was for an effect. Or when we had a canoeing event for some anniversary in Ottawa and he arrived in his buckskins looking like Davy Crockett – that was theatre. He knew the world that he was in was theatre. He had these amazing compartments. I have often thought that no one knows all of Trudeau; maybe Pelletier was the closest. There were so many different aspects of him and different parts would be revealed, but I do not think he ever revealed the whole thing to anybody, maybe not even himself.

Richard Gwyn: I have a question based on the comments made by Tom Axworthy and by Bruce Powe, which are divergent. Tom, you said that his faith was an aspect of him but it was not by any means *the* aspect, and you cited others, such as literature and music. Bruce, you reminded us that his discourses and actions were suffused with an appreciation or expression of the importance of rights and values. I think that the reason why Trudeau has made such a mark – other than being sexy and glamorous – is that the public thinks of him as a politician of rights and values, which is most unusual. Could he have been the kind of politician he was, a politician who seemed to be one of rights and values, if he had not been a person of faith and if he had not been a person of examined faith?

Tom Axworthy: I think so, Richard. One can be a humanist and have the greatest possible belief in individual dignity and not in any way ascribe it to the divine. I think that, theoretically, the devotion to human dignity does not have to have a supernatural or spiritual connotation. It can have it, but it does not have to be that way. Therefore, I think that the wellsprings to whom I heard Trudeau refer most often were Acton and Jefferson. I once asked him about a style he admired, and he sent me to Newman because it was a style of essay he liked. He was a man of the book and writing was very important to him. If he ever attached his name to anything, he would be the most precise editor in the world. The comma had to be exactly right, because it was very important. Pelletier used to tell stories about him with *Cité libre*, racing to the publisher with hours to go because he had found one typo that had to be corrected, and he would try to hold up the press. Words were very important to him – I think much more than his television comments were. As Nancy said, he was a private individual; he would virtually never talk about his family or a whole host of things except philosophically. In those sets of meetings with Jean Le Moyne and others, you would get a good sense of where he was coming from – on the value frame – because the words would be very important to him. Speeches were important to Trudeau, and he most liked the speeches in which you gave him suggestions but he would deliver them in his own way. He sometimes would ramble a lot in those speeches, but those were the ones he really liked. He disliked reading other people's words, and he particularly disliked the correspondence machine. He hated if his name was attached to something that he had not actually looked at. Therefore, some of the best sessions of exchanges I had with him were on the speeches, where we would talk about books and personal experience, almost all of which were philosophical and never theological.

B.W. Powe: I agree with Tom's first remark about the humanist's upholding human dignity. Of course, I will stick to my thesis and say that I do not think that Trudeau would be the same man without those convictions and faith.

VI

Concluding Reflections

Soul's Flow:
Pierre Trudeau's Hidden Current

B.W. Powe

Stephen Clarkson referred to the Zen statement that the fish is in the water, and the water is in the fish. I won't try to interpret this enigmatic koan, except to add a McLuhanesque twist: a fish is not (usually) aware of the water in which it lives. In short, our environments are mostly invisible to us.

* * *

I will look at the mythopoetic aspects of Trudeau's time – the mythic impact he made on Canada, and on me. The word "myth," in this context, I take to mean narrative, symbol, allegory, the wedding of image and word, the crystallization of quintessential story, the poetry of exist-ence, our intimations and intuitions of what may be transcendent. I want to respond as a reader of Trudeau's life – and I'll be speaking as odd man (person?) out: I am not a theologian, a politician, a political scientist, an economist, a psychologist, a sociologist, or a Catholic.

* * *

It is in Pierre Trudeau's *Against the Current: Selected Writings 1939–1996* that we find one of his rare acknowledgments of spirituality. It is the passage the organizers of this conference chose for their epigraph. He responds to the query "Are you a believer?" with a simple "Yes." Then: "Let's say...I remain...a believer." Nothing more. What surrounds this fragment, almost elusive enough to be something from Pascal's note-books, is enigmatic space. We do not find much anywhere else on soul, or faith – on metaphysics or mysticism. On this Trudeau remained rigorously evasive. A whole conference, then, based on a fragment – an elliptical inference, the hidden: what he chose to keep from us. Yet Trudeau's orations, his contrary style, his articulation of Canada's destiny, his agenda of difference and otherness (through minority rights, and the politics and culture of the Charter), his conflicts with fellow charismatic figures like René Lévesque and Lucien Bouchard, indeed his own courage and self-discipline, appear steeped in cosmic drama, the language of vision. When he died in September 2000, critics said he was original, a rare creature of conviction. *Necessity, urgency, greatness, limitless potential, first principles of rights and values*: these words fired his speech, and inflamed us.

The soul's flow – the other current in Trudeau – can't be entirely invisible because, I submit, this is what moved him, and sometimes moved us. I'll also confess: it is what continues to move me, in part, about him, and his legacy, his memory.

I confess, too, that I find this subject hard to address. How does one talk about what is so private – as it was to Pierre – and yet so essential to how some of us endure? Spirituality, mysticism. One blunders onto those frontiers with hesitations. I'll address why one can be skeptically hesitant in a moment. But if one believes that we are as much spirit and soul, or in a perpetual communion of mystery and mind, as we are body and matter, then a host of ideas and approaches must follow. Sometimes we're driven to say what may be unsayable, or to do what we sense must be done, at risk of appearing foolish.

I wander, then, into esoteric areas that nevertheless shake, inspire, confound, and reform the realms of political engagement. And so I'll try to describe Trudeau's soul current, and why it matters to speculate about it.

I'll address this premise: There is, continuing in contemporary discourse and debate, an identification of all religious discussion with political reaction and extremism, and yet if one looks closely at political progressives, many who did not turn to Marxism were in fact spiritually engaged, moved by inner necessity, the higher voice, so it's been called. Many of the most formidable critiques of inauthenticity, reaction, repression (both political and psychological), authoritarianism, social inertia, racism, vicious intolerance, deadening convention and rote, and blatant inequality, have been spiritual writers and thinkers. John Locke, Martin Luther King Jr., Mahatma Gandhi, Rousseau, Jefferson,

Thomas Merton; visionary poets, from Milton through to Blake, Shelley, Rimbaud, Emerson, Thoreau, and Whitman: for them, liberty itself was God's destiny for creation. Liberty, rights leading to justice, were self-evident values. Any first-year political science student will tell you this is not a logical argument; a self-evident, or so-called common sense, premise seems barely rational. Yet this intuitive knowledge thrived at the core of the missions, visions, declarations, and rebellions of those people who inspired us to imagine how we could live, and why we should be committed to (yes, devoted to) transforming our hearts and minds, intensifying and illuminating consciousness.

As someone once quipped, we haven't had much of a need for revolutionary politics in Canada because we have had Tommy Douglas and his faith, and Pierre Trudeau and his.

And on a digressive but apposite note, I'll add that the visionary company of Blake and Emerson was continued in Canada by the two mystics who shaped the Canadian imaginative, intellectual sphere: Northrop Frye and Marshall McLuhan.

* * *

I'll speak personally now, on knowing Trudeau, politics today, spiritual crises, and gulfs of meaning in the recently fought Gulf War II, bringing out my hesitations about our subject, the current of spirituality.

In the years I knew Trudeau, when we talked on the phone, had lunches or coffee together, or when we walked around Montreal, only once did the subject of his faith come up. I wish I could say that I have some inside track on his beliefs because of our fifteen years' worth of conversations. Only once, I said. He talked in September 1999, about the line-up of speakers for The Trudeau Era Conference I helped to direct that autumn in Toronto. Noting the inclusion of Michael Higgins' discussion of Trudeau's Catholic faith in politics, Pierre himself, over lunch, sat back and said, vehemently,

"At last."

As if no one had thought before to inquire into the importance of his devout priorities, his first principles. I was startled into recognizing that this was a significant opening. I also thought I knew him well enough not to invade his inner contemplations. He'd tell me what he wanted to, I'd found; and when you left him alone, when you didn't badger or probe, he often intimated a lot between the lines. He didn't offer anything more, however. Still, I intuited how much spirituality meant to him.

But surely he knew, as I know, that to raise the soul, raise sacredness or divinity, raise love and justice – the hidden words of the cosmos, according to Thomas Merton – raise the challenge of spiritual destiny, raise the issue of liberty being our soul's gift, raise the idea that the cosmos attends to our minds and actions, and you could sound like you are about to join a Pat Robertson crusade. Bring religion into the discussion, and you may sound maddened, like a zealot with a penchant for medieval martyrdom and a contempt for pluralism, the division of powers between state and church, rights for gays and minorities, and a horror for the libertine edge of sex, art, and intoxicants that are part of modernity's heritage. (I did talk to Pierre a great deal about poetry: the poets we turned to tended to be the gnostic adventurers – Baudelaire, Rimbaud, Yeats, and Cohen – none of whom are known for their pure, uneventful private lives.)

Further, invest political debate with spirituality, and you could sound like a member of President George W. Bush's morning Bible meetings at the White House. Recently, at my church – Christchurch Anglican, which my children and I more or less regularly attend – in my small town of Stouffville, my parish priest advocated adding a prayer to our service for the victims of Gulf War II. He meant the babies shredded by cluster bombs. Yes, a few of the parishioners said, but only if we also include a prayer for Bush's plan to trigger Armageddon in the Middle East, following the prophecies of "The Book of Daniel," of which the President is especially fond, thus fulfilling the messianic message of apocalypse in Jerusalem. Our parish priest politely demurred. (And I hope President Bush's readings move to Ecclesiastes soon. Proverbs will do.)

I may be making light of this, but the issues are vast, serious. Enter the arena of religion, cross into issues of revelation, revive ideas of mission and destiny, introduce the language of God and soul, and you could be identified with fundamentalist extremism or literalist evangelism, the dulling platitudes of mainstream churches or the excluding paranoia of cults. Perhaps worse for a writer, you will likely be called anti-intellectual, regressive, an upholder of oppressive power structures (Michel Foucault), a faddish follower of New Age; some will deconstruct your work (if they take you that seriously) into ironic oblivion. It goes without saying that neo-Marxist theorists (the academies abound with them) will be antagonistic. Secular-minded friends, and family members, will become grim. All of this counsels one to side with Pierre's near-silence on the subject.

Yet enter the arena I feel I must. George Steiner, essayist and novelist, has said it is almost impossible to comprehend certain figures without reference to the transcendental. It is notable how certain of the most illustrious liberal thinkers, such as Locke and Jefferson – I use the word "liberal" in its radical Latin source, that of *libera*, the free self, who can and must choose – were inclined to the spiritual. Nietzsche, that rigorous non-theist, called John Stuart Mill "a blockhead" because he wanted a good society, a just social order with liberty, freedom of conscience, and protection of the citizen's right to economic fairness, without transcendental justification or reference: in short, to have a Christian soul-based society without Christ or the soul. Nietzsche's furious honesty about Mill (who is one of my political heroes) brings me up short. Many cloak their spirituality for fear of ridicule or fear of incomprehension. Some drop spirituality from all references because they wish to elude the implications of including it.

If one looks closely at Trudeau's language, actions, style, and determination – his references to greatness and destiny – one cannot avoid recognizing that here was a statesman drenched in the spirituality of confirming the potential of personhood through the Charter of Rights, of witnessing history through full existential engagement, of seeing Canada to be an alternative current in the wake of globalization, of demanding that we pursue what is best and true in us, of understanding that our soul dramas are packed with meaning, that speech and silence, words and gestures, carry weights of intention and allusion (indeed, persuasion and argument are parts of the calling to serve), of seeking what is the good and of necessity in our lives, beyond irony and cynical detachment, of finding unity in our engagements, thus to fight at every turn the alienating agonies of separation. The word "cosmos" inhabits one of Trudeau's favourite words, "cosmopolitan." Canada for him was a microcosm of the universal concerns, which are liberty, rights, justice, truth for both self and community, the just use of resources and materials, opportunity, protection of the inward way and of difference (this is pluralism; if we are each invested with soul and consciousness, then that conscious soul must be unique, our indelible property), the importance and role of government, and the profound limitations of the state.

Hemingway described in *A Farewell to Arms* how soldiers were suspicious of bloated terms like "justice." Too many were butchered in the name of higher truth. After Gulf War II, we are apt to be suspicious of the words "liberty" or "liberal," because of the gulfs of meaning we perceive among those using them in alarmingly divergent ways. Never in my years of talking to Pierre did I sense that he thought these words were mere campaign slogans. Points of ambiguity, open to interpretation, surely. But the experiencing of those words, and the need to persuade us of their importance, carried him, and sometimes transported us, into believing that we could be in Canada greater than we have been, or are. That our destiny is not merely to waffle or welcome every initiative that comes from elsewhere, but to reason out, constantly and clearly, how we may differ.

This is why for Pierre, Canada remained beautiful, despite the grabbing and sprawl, the confusions and mistakes, the weaknesses and flaws, the errors and overreaching, the caution and caustic exchanges of a political life where disappointment is inevitable and policy is transitory. Someone with a spiritual frame of reference knows that "beauty" is not a term to use flippantly. Beauty is attached to the ideal of harmony, which is another way of comprehending justice and of seeing life in its sublime potency and radiance. We find harmonies in the shapely cut of a sentence, in the way water ripples behind a gliding canoe. The recognition of beauty is part of the soul's flow.

* * *

Consider more: We must see that Trudeau was a creature of the 1960s, a period when electric mass media and progressive politics, when technology and affluence, converged. There was a search for alternatives, for authenticity. Spiritual shifts surrounded us. I was too young for Woodstock, but old enough to be impressed. There was to Trudeau in 1967 and '68 something of the heretical youth, a role he eventually shed, like a worn-out mask, to become the mentor or elder for a constitutionally renewed nation. There can be no reform without a vision of form. Early I sensed, with others, that here was a chance, with him, for Canada to evolve into a place shaped for the dawning planetization of culture and technology that McLuhan had described and evoked. Canada: multicultural, multilingual, free and multiform, capable of metamorphosis.

Events of our youth forever guide us. I bumped into Trudeau on the packed floor of the Liberal convention in Ottawa in 1968; he was hustling by, after he'd given his speech, with his aides. My father had taken me; he often did to important occasions. (Powe Sr., by the way, worked for John Turner; over those days, I had to secretly pin my Trudeau buttons on the inside of my jacket.) I had a sense of opened doors: some fresh spirit. But violence shadowed Trudeau's victory. Martin Luther King Jr. had been gunned down; American cities smouldered. Weeks later, Robert Kennedy was cut down in the kitchen of an L.A. hotel. Weeks after that, Trudeau, pelted by bottles and trash, sat still during the St-Jean Baptiste Day rally in Montreal. The sixties summoned dreams and looming cruel forces. The romanticism of that time – so much a period when the renewing spirits of Blake, Shelley, and Whitman presided in the air – quickly dissolved. Pragmatism and manoeuvring, reaction to unruliness, and fear of liberty soon prevailed. The blasting out of conventions, the feel of social mobility, the expansion of imagination, the incendiary dialogues of change and rights rolled back like winds suddenly blocked by massive walls.

Tom Axworthy once told me that he thought it unlikely that a politician like Trudeau could have been elected after 1972. Frankly, I doubt if Pierre would be elected in any coming election anywhere today. Nor could I imagine anyone in the United States electing the introspective Jefferson. Many of our public figures have religious convictions, but their unease with the language and form of their faiths often limits their call to transcendent vision. A notable article by Doug Saunders in the *Globe & Mail* (May 3, 2003) stated that Canadians prefer our leaders to be bland – it's less troubling, more a sign that they are capable and steady rather than followers of an inner beat and rhyme. I believe charisma and metaphysics are linked. Inner intensity and conviction become audacity and inspiration in the political arena. Do we have something to fear in such intensities? Is that why we steer away from them? Susan Sontag's remark, "The problem with socialism is that it is too dull; the problem with fascism is that it is too exciting," is an especially relevant reply. And yet when this appeal to what is greater than us is absent, we feel the void.

And Mystery reels around us, searing into our nerves and senses.

Images from Gulf War II harrowed us in past weeks. E-media haunt and cling with pictures and sounds bites. This communications' realm appears unbridled – incited with mystique, reminding us of our connection to others, of our liberty to murder and make, showing us individual sorrow and ecstasy, reminding us of our power, which from our screens every day we can see is enormous, as great as any higher power, recalling at every moment the world's beauty and pain. What we see looks unmoored, anarchic. Simultaneously, institutional authority has never seemed so successful and codified, huge and remote from the touch of citizens. Government, corporations, universities, Big Media rule more by system, code, law, structure, than by exciting heresy, so it often appears. Military mobilization can be another form of repression. Canadians live beside a bruised, enraged Rome. My students often acknowledge how troubled they are by institutions and forces that seem immune to their longings. How open is the system? How can each be treated according to one's own? (If you doubt the truth of what I say, I invite those here who aren't teachers to see the size of the average class.) Even the prevailing philosophies of the academy sometimes state it is better to be dismissive and scornful of metaphysical meaning. It is indeed hard to imagine how a Trudeau could rise, given such conditions.

Part of the message that I try to convey comes from what I learned from talking to Pierre, and from following the twists and turns of his political life. Drain the debate about why we're here from glimmers of the transcendental, and you could reduce it all to play (which may not be that bad) or to mechanics, the politics of accounting; you could replace metaphysics with messianic ideology, the ghastly results of which we have seen in the last century. But in the privacy of one's mind, engaging the spirit that sometimes comes in flashes of illumination, we may be aware, suddenly, that there is more to what we are, and because each of us has that dormant potential, we can honour the spark. I try to talk about connection, journeying, meaning, the strangeness of existence, the choices we will have to make, about the search for depth and continuity, for contact with other souls and their fire. Canada is one of the many places in the world where the spark still has ethical implications for the entire system, where there is solitude and time to review our actions and choices. A spiritual purpose recalls the cord that links our minds to the stars.

I doubt if it's merely romanticism, or mythologizing, to say Trudeau kept his spirituality private because his actions and words revealed his heart. He didn't have to express directly what was obvious in the drama he enkindled in Canada. To our motto of "peace, order, and good government," with its Hobbesian overtones of repression, subjugation, efficiency, and prohibition, he added the Charter's emphasis on individual rights, therefore on liberty. (In this reading of him, we may understand the War Measures Act, and its abiding controversy, in terms of protection of our rights against violent extremism; the application of the Act, often indiscriminately punitive to the wrong people, is another question.) He confirmed and affirmed his connection with the line of visionaries who articulated that the soul must flow. Our most private of prime ministers allowed his soul to be transparent.

* * *

And so how does one air what is spiritually essential – and private – in the communications' arena, where there is no privacy? What does an ethical grounding of first principles mean to one (such as myself), even if all this, as it was for Trudeau, is left implicit, unspoken, sometimes shrouded in elliptical or evasive terms? I suggest something like the following: it means to make something of what we are, to mould life as we were moulded, to know that our names have individual shape and possibly a destiny (not just a fate), to remember how powerful we are and can be (for good or ill), to love the world, which is our paradise, to remind one another that we are of value (even when that seems most unlikely), to listen for the traces of obscured harmonies (Shakespeare reminded us that this was the fabled music of the spheres), to know, as Trudeau knew, that we are engaged with what is here because we must be, to sketch our selves back into the outline of the cosmic Soul, the great Mind, that encompasses – indeed, compasses – our minds and souls, giving us hope.

Afterword

When I commented to Richard Gwyn on the occasion of his appointment to the chancellor's position at St. Jerome's University that religion had a minor part in his biography of Trudeau, he immediately suggested a conference. Without a second's hesitation, President Michael Higgins agreed. As an historian who needs evidence for assertions, there was, for me, scant evidence in the public realm upon which to build the foundations of a paper, much less a conference. In his memoirs, Trudeau acknowledges the influence of his religious education but remains very reticent in his discussion of the character and depth of his faith. He made his most explicit statement about religious belief to the editor of the United Church *Observer*. Although Trudeau refused to talk about "questions" and "meanings," he said, simply, that "I remained – I remain – a believer." But belief is never simple, especially with Pierre Trudeau.

As Richard Gwyn pointed out in the prologue, Trudeau's reticence reflected his political times. The determined secularism of the 1960s and '70s in Canada swept away formal and informal expressions of religious faith in public life. The "swinging" bachelor who became prime minister in 1968 embodied for Canadians their new liberal ways that broke distinctly with their conservative social values of the past. The reticence had two foundations. The first was the sense that religion in politics had been a divisive and largely negative force. For Canadians in the 1960s, being modern meant leaving the old sectarian quarrels behind. The second foundation was a belief that one's religious beliefs should not directly influence a political leader's public actions. Here the text came from John Kennedy's famous declaration that his Roman Catholic faith would not influence his political decisions. Pierre Trudeau followed that text closely.

Trudeau's famous declaration that the state had no place in the bedrooms of the nation responded to the secularism of the '60s and reflected Kennedy's separation between personal belief and political action. Moreover, Trudeau's antipathy to the twentieth-century role of the Catholic Church in politics in Quebec was well known to readers of *Cité libre* and of his other essays. While he wrote about the Church as a political actor, Trudeau was curiously silent in philosophical debates about religion or even about the role of a Catholic in society. While other young francophone Catholics became activists through the *Jeunesse Étudiante Catholique*, Trudeau, as Marc Nadeau said, stood aside.

Much later, when Allan MacEachen or Otto Lang, devout and practising Catholics, worked closely with Trudeau on many topics that were controversial within the Catholic Church, Trudeau apparently did not discuss the religious debates with them. John Turner's account of the change in Canada's abortion law also does not report any discussion with Trudeau about Trudeau's own personal opposition to abortion. As MacEachen argues, the "bargain" of Canadian politics meant that matters of faith were private and that public policy debate took place without reference to those private beliefs. Sometimes the tension was great, as in the case of Otto Lang during the cabinet debate about abortion. Nevertheless, during the Trudeau years this Canadian concordat held.

Because of his personal style, which certainly offended many Catholics, and the legislation that he introduced as justice minister and then as prime minister, most Canadians assumed that Trudeau was not a devout Roman Catholic. Those who knew Quebec realized that Trudeau had studied at strongly Catholic institutions, notably at Brébeuf and the Université de Montréal. Such background proved little about one's future: many other Brébeuf and Montréal students had similar educations but had closed the door on their religious past as they embraced mid-century secularism. Others were devout and participated vigorously in debates about religion and society. Claude Ryan and even Trudeau's close friend Gérard Pelletier openly professed their faith and, in their writings, based arguments upon those principles. Trudeau, however, long kept his silence.

Trudeau's remark to Bruce Powe – "at last" – when told that Michael Higgins was presenting a paper on Trudeau's religious faith, suggests that Trudeau himself recognized how fundamental that faith was to his development and character. What Higgins has discovered is the varieties of Trudeau's Catholic religious experiences and how actively Trudeau participated in retreats, services, and personal discussions about his faith. Jean-Philippe Warren and David Seljak place Trudeau's beliefs and development within the context of Quebec Catholicism and the debates about Personalism that so deeply influenced French Catholicism as well as Trudeau himself.

In his biography of Trudeau, Michel Vastel chose to focus on Trudeau "le Québécois," an aspect he believed other biographers have overlooked.[1] He demonstrated how, in his youth and adolescence, the bilingual and bicultural Trudeau chose the French or the "Quebec" path, as in his choice of Université de Montréal over McGill. Vastel's insight is important and Trudeau's own papers reveal how that choice derived in part from his deep immersion in the experience of Quebec Catholicism in the 1930s and 1940s.

What Trudeau's papers reveal is a young man deeply enmeshed in Quebec Catholicism, active in its debates and attentive to the subtlety of theological difference. His courses and marks at Brébeuf and, to a lesser extent, the Université de Montréal reflect his profound interest in theology, philosophy, and the traditions of the Quebec Church. He even learned his history from Abbé Groulx in 1940 and appears to have become sympathetic to Groulx's nationalism based upon the identification of the Church with the Quebec nation. As Vastel recognized, Trudeau's youth gained its definition through his participation in Quebec political debates and Catholic experience. A recent biography of the Quebec liberal Jean-Charles Harvey complains that Gérard Pelletier dismissed Harvey in his memoirs even though Harvey had been arguing for the separation of church and state and against clerical nationalism as Pelletier and Trudeau did in the 1950s. Harvey and other liberals such as Jean-Louis Gagnon, however, made their arguments against the Church; Trudeau and Pelletier before the 1960s made their arguments within the Church.[2]

In the 1940s Trudeau pored over religious texts, debated furiously about theological matters, and even broke up with a girlfriend as she moved towards agnosticism and he remained, as he wrote, forever within the Church. There he took his stand, elusive, paradoxical, yet emblematic. A man of his people and his age.

John English

Notes

Editor's Note

1   George Radwanski, *Trudeau* (Toronto: Macmillan, 1978), 26.

2   Claire Hoy, *Margin of Error* (1988), quoted in John Robert Colombo, *The Dictionary of Canadian Quotations* (Toronto: Stoddart, 1991), 580.

PART I

Defined by Spirituality?

1   "In His Prime," *The Globe and Mail*, 3 May 2003.

2   *Sojourners* (November–December, 2000)

3   *The Globe and Mail*, 26 April 2003.

4   Edith Iglauer, *The Strangers Next Door* (Madeira Park, BC: Harbour Publishing, 1991), 175.

5   "Christians in Public Life," 2000 John Wintermeyer Lecture, St. Jerome's University, Waterloo, Ontario.

6   *Trudeau's Shadow: The Life and Legacy of Pierre Elliott Trudeau*, eds. Andrew Cohen and J.L. Granatstein (Toronto: Vintage Canada, 1999), 283–294.

7   Michael W. Higgins and Douglas R. Letson, *The Jesuit Mystique* (Toronto: Macmillan, 1995), 73.

8   Private correspondence, 10 April 2003.

9   Ronald J. Zawilla, "Dominican Spirituality," *The New Dictionary of Catholic Spirituality* (1993), 293. (Author's comments in brackets.)

10   "Freedom and Responsibility: Towards a Spirituality of Government," *Sing a New Song: The Christian Vocation* (1999), 82–83.

11   "Monasticism as Rebellion," CBC *Ideas*, 1986.

12   "Monasticism as Rebellion."

Discussion

1   See Samuel P. Huntington, "The Clash of Civilizations," *Foreign Affairs* 72/3 (Summer 1993), 22–49, and *The Clash of Civilizations and the Remaking of World Order* (New York: Simon & Schuster, 1996).

PART II

Trudeau and the Privatization of Religion: The Quebec Context

1   www.globeandmail.com/series/trudeau/homily.html (accessed 23 April 2004).

2   A. Breton et al. "Pour une politique fonctionelle," *Cité libre* 15/67 (mai 1964), 11–17.

3   José Casanova, *Public Religions in the Modern World* (Chicago: University of Chicago Press, 1994), 38.

4   For classic statements of this theory see Peter Berger, *The Sacred Canopy* (New York: Doubleday, 1967) and Bryan Wilson, *Religion in Secular Society* (London: Pelican, 1969).

5   Casanova argues that the first human right is the right of freedom of religion. Without freedom of conscience the other civil liberties (e.g., freedoms of expression, assembly) are pointless. See *Public Religions*, 40.

6   See, for example, *The Secularization Debate,* ed. William Swatos, Jr. and Daniel Olson (Lanham, MD: Rowman and Littlefield, 2000).

7   E.-Martin Meunier and Jean-Philippe Warren, *Sortir de la « Grande noirceur ». L'horizon «personaliste» de la révolution tranquille,* (Québec: Éditions du Septentrion, 2002).

8   Quebec historians and sociologists no longer accept this model of Quebec in the 1950s. Most French Canadians lived in cities, not the countryside, and worked in factories, not on farms. For an example of Quebec history that takes this modernization seriously, see Paul-André Linteau et al., *Quebec since 1930,* trans. Robert Chodos and Ellen Garmaise (Toronto: Lorimer, 1991).

9   Pierre Elliott Trudeau, "The province of Quebec at the time of the strike," *The Asbestos Strike,* ed. P. Trudeau, trans. J. Boake (Toronto: James Lewis and Samuel, 1974), 1–81.

10   P.E. Trudeau, « La nouvelle trahison des clercs, » *Cité libre* 13/46 (avril 1962), 15. My translation of: « Certes ces valeurs sont plus privés que publiques, plus introverties qu'extroverties, plus instinctives et sauvages qu'intelligentes et civilisées, plus narcissistes et passionnées que généreuses et raisonnées. »

11   Political philosophers such as Will Kymlicka and Charles Taylor (who was also a committed Catholic and friend of Trudeau) have challenged the desirability or even possibility of such a rational, "culture-neutral" politics. See Kymlicka's *Politics in the Vernacular: Nationalism, Multiculturalism, and Citizenship* (Oxford: Oxford University Press, 2001), Taylor's *Reconciling the Solitudes: Essays on Canadian Federalism and Nationalism* (Montreal: McGill-Queen's University Press, 1993) and *Multiculturalism and "The Politics of Recognition": An Essay* (Princeton, NJ: Princeton University Press, 1992).

12   See Casanova, *Public Religions,* 216–218.

13   Naturally, these categories are over-generalizations, what sociologist Max Weber would call "ideal types." For an interesting discussion on the liberal division of society as it pertains to gender, see Jean Bethke Elshtain, *Public Man, Private Woman: Women in Social and Political Thought* (Princeton, NJ: Princeton University Press, 1981).

14   See my "Catholicism's 'Quiet Revolution': *Maintenant* and the New Public Catholicism in Quebec after 1960," in *Religion and Public Life in Canada: Historical and Comparative Perspectives,* ed. Marguerite Van Die (Toronto: University of Toronto Press, 2001) and "Resisting the 'No Man's Land' of Private Religion: The Catholic Church and Public Politics in Quebec," in *Rethinking Church, State, and Modernity: Canada Between Europe and America,* ed. David Lyon and Marguerite Van Die (Toronto: University of Toronto Press, 2000), 131–148.

15   The letter and commentary on it can be found in *Ethics and Economics: Canada's Catholic Bishops on the Economic Crisis* (Toronto: James Lorimer and Company, 1984), also reproduced in *Do Justice!: The Social Teaching of the Canadian Catholic Bishops (1945–1986),* ed. E.F. Sheridan (Sherbrooke and Toronto: Éditions Pauline/Jesuit Centre for Social Faith and Justice, 1987).

16   Victor Malarek, "Bishops in Quebec Back Call for Reform," *The Globe and Mail,* 8 January 1983, A1–A2.

17   *La justice sociale comme bonne nouvelle: Messages sociaux, économiques et politiques des évêques du Québec, 1972–1980,* dir. Gérared Rochais (Montréal: Éditions Bellarmin, 1984).

18   Casanova, *Public Religions,* 167–207.

19   It should be noted that even on these issues the Quebec bishops are the most progressive in the Canadian Church. See Jean Hamelin et Nicole Gagnon, *Histoire du catholicisme québécois, Tome 2: De 1940 à nos jours,* tome 2 (Montreal: Boréal Express, 1984).

20   Casanova, *Public Religions,* 221–222.

Politics and Religion in Quebec:
Theological Issues and the Generation Factor

1   Translation of P.E. Trudeau, « La province de Québec au moment de la grève » [The province of Quebec at the time of the strike], in *La grève de l'amiante* [The Asbestos Strike] ed. P.E. Trudeau (Montreal: Les éditions Cité libre, 1956), 21.

2   See *Vatican II, Les seize documents conciliaires* [Vatican II: The sixteen conciliar documents] (Montreal: Fides, 1966), and especially the commentaries on the conciliar texts published by Mame, Paris, in the collection « *Vivre le Concile* »: *Vatican II, L'Eglise dans le monde de ce temps* ["Living the Council": The Church in the Modern World] (1968); *L'Apostolat des Laïcs* [The Apostolate of Lay People] (1966), text, notes and commentaries by a team of lay people and priests.

3   See S. Lefebvre, « *Générations contemporaines, itinéraires et solidarités* » [Today's generations, their paths, their ties], in *Le défi des générations* [The challenge of the generations], eds. Lise Baroni and coll. (Montreal: Fides, 1995), 89–181; also « *Rapports des générations. Une conjoncture socio-économique et culturelle* » [Intergenerational relations. A socio-economic and cultural portrait], *Cahiers internationaux de sociologie,* vol. CII (1997), 183–198.

4   See also Wade Clark Roof, Jackson W. Carroll and David A. Roozen, eds., *The Post-War Generation and Establishment Religion: Cross-Cultural Perspectives* (Boulder/San Francisco/Oxford: Westview, 1995).

5   See, for example, Roland Campiche, ed., *Cultures jeunes et religions en Europe* [Religions and youth cultures in Europe] (Paris: Cerf, 1997).

6   On this subject, see Mikhaël Elbaz, Andrée Fortin and Guy Laforest, eds., *Les frontières de l'identité : Modernité et postmodernisme au Quebec* [The boundaries of identity: Modernity and postmodernism in Quebec] (Sainte-Foy/Paris: PUL/L'Harmattan, 1996). This work brings into question the split between tradition and modernity, a linear vision of progress, which shaped many rereadings of Quebec history, making it possible to examine the dynamic tensions between tradition and modernity in the past as well as in the present.

Let the Jesuits and the Dominicans Quarrel: A French-Canadian Debate of the Fifties

1   Marcel Rioux, *Quebec in Question* (Toronto: James Lewis & Samuel, 1971), 69.

2   Maurice Tremblay, *La Pensée sociale au Canada français*, quoted in Rioux, *Quebec in Question*, 68–69.

3   See, for example, Jean-Philippe Warren et E.-Martin Meunier, *Sortir de la « Grande Noirceur ». L'horizon personnaliste de la révolution tranquille* (Québec: Septentrion, 2002) and Jean-Philippe Warren, « Gérard Pelletier et *Cité libre*: la mystique personnaliste de la Révolution tranquille, » *Société* 20–21 (Summer 1999), 313–346.

4   Quoted in George Radwanski, *Trudeau* (Toronto: Macmillan, 1978), 57.

5   Esther Delisle, *Essais sur l'imprégnation fasciste au Québec* (Montreal: Varia, 2003), 40–49.

6   Pierre Elliott Trudeau, « Finie la flèche du conquérant, vive le drapeau de la liberté (M. P. Trudeau) », *Le Devoir*, 26 novembre 1942, 3, 8.

7   Gérard Pelletier et Pierre Elliott Trudeau, « Pelletier et Trudeau s'expliquent, » *Cité libre* no 80 (octobre 1965), 4.

8   Quoted in Radwanski, *Trudeau*, 77.

Pierre Elliott Trudeau and the *JÉC*

1   Stephen Clarkson and Christina McCall, *Trudeau and Our Times: The Magnificent Obsession, vol. 1* (Toronto: McClelland & Stewart, 1990), 404.

2   André J. Bélanger, *Ruptures et constantes: Quatre idéologies du Québec en éclatement* [Change and Continuity: Four Ideologies in a Quebec in Turmoil]: *La Relève, La JEC, Cité Libre, Partis Pris* (Montreal: Hurtubise HMH, 1977), 55. My translation.

3   Clarkson and McCall, *Trudeau*, 61.

4   Translation of Bélanger, *Ruptures*, 44.

5   Ibid., 57.

6   Translation of quote in ibid., 57.

7   Ibid., 61.

8   Translation, ibid.

9   Clarkson and McCall, *Trudeau*, 63. Translator's note: I took into account the phrase used in the book quoted: "his old Jéciste colleagues."

10   Translation of Bélanger, *Ruptures*, 59.

11   Ibid., 48.

12   Translation of ibid., 49.

13   Translation of Pierre Trudeau, « *L'ascétisme en canot* » [The asceticism of the canoe trip], *JÉC* (June 1944), 5.

14   Translation of Pierre Juneau, « *Culture 'Plutardiste'* » ['Someday' Culture], *JÉC* (October 1944), 2.

15   Translation of Juneau, « *Présence Chrétienne* » [Christian presence], *JÉC* (December 1946), 11.

16   Translation of Roméo LeBlanc, « Optique de vivants » [Through the Lens of the Living], *JÉC* (June 1949), 2.

17   Translation of ibid.

PART III

The Man's Formation in Faith

1   The theologian in me could be tempted to go on about the Trinitarian quality of this purpose: God the creator is sought in all things; Jesus Christ, as the person who has "divinized" human beings is the model; and the Holy Spirit inspires and empowers leadership in service. But I will not give in.

2   Gérard Pelletier, *Les années d'impatience* (Montréal: Stanké, 1983), 35.

3   Pierre Elliott Trudeau, *Memoirs* (Toronto: McClelland and Stewart, 1993), 23.

4   Ibid., 25.

5   Quoted in Hugh Trevor-Roper, "Introduction," *Lord Acton: Lectures in Modern History* (London: Collins, 1960), 11.

6   Donald Wolf, "Mounier, Emmanuel" in *New Catholic Encyclopedia* vol. 10 (Toronto: McGraw Hill, 1966), 43–44.

7   Trudeau, *Memoirs*, 22.

8   Ibid., 40.

9   Citing the stifling atmosphere of Quebec, the "intellectual immaturity" of its people, and the lack of freedom of expression in the province, he decided to remain in Paris, where for the next quarter century he published more novels, more books of increasingly dark philosophy, and poetry. In the late 1960s, long past Personalism, he returned to Quebec as a flaming separatist.

10   Quoted in Mark Schoof, O.P., *A Survey of Catholic Theology, 1800–1970* (New York, 1970), 99.

11   Pelletier, *Années*, 145.

12   Trudeau, *Memoirs*, 47.

PART IV

Faith and Politics

1   Our firm did not represent him at the time, as we do now as counsel to the Archdiocese of Toronto.

2   House of Commons, *Debates*, First Session, 28th Parliament, vol. VII (1969), 17 April 1969, 7633–35.

3   House of Commons, *Debates*, First Session, 28th Parliament, vol. VIII (1969), 12 May 1969, 8576–77.

Slow to Leave the Bedrooms of the Nation: Trudeau and the Modernizing of Canadian Law, 1967–1969

1   The phrase was originally coined by Martin O'Malley of the *Globe and Mail*; however, Trudeau has been given credit for it. Stephen Clarkson and Christina McCall, *Trudeau and Our Times: The Magnificent Obsession* vol. 1 (Toronto: McClelland & Stewart, 1990), 107.

2   Pierre Elliott Trudeau, *Memoirs* (Toronto: McClelland & Stewart, 1993), 83.

3   *Hansard*, House of Commons, Canada, December 4, 1967, 5014.

4   According to George Radwanski, Trudeau's handling of the reforms eventually "rocketed [him] toward the status of national hero." George Radwanski, *Trudeau* (Toronto: MacMillan of Canada, 1978), 96.

5   Jacques Hébert, "Legislating for Freedom," in *Towards a Just Society: The Trudeau Years,* eds. Thomas S. Axworthy and Pierre Elliott Trudeau (Markham, ON: Penguin Books Canada 1990), 134.

6   Clarkson and McCall, *Trudeau and Our Times* vol. 1, 38, 47. See also Radwanski, *Trudeau*, 119.

7   Pierre Elliott Trudeau, "Some Obstacles to Democracy in Quebec," in *Federalism and the French Canadians* (Toronto: Macmillan of Canada, 1968), 109.

8   Bernard E. Doering, *Jacques Maritain and the French Catholic Intellectuals* (Notre Dame, IN: University of Notre Dame Press, 1983), 68, 78; McCall and Clarkson, *Trudeau and Our Times* vol. 1, 48.

9   Clarkson and McCall, *Trudeau and Our Times* vol. 1, 58.

10   Trudeau, "Quebec and the Constitutional Problem," in *Federalism and the French Canadians*, 11.

11   Trudeau, "A Constitutional Declaration of Rights," in *Federalism and the French Canadians*, 54.

12   The three submissions were: (1) "Canadian Catholic Conference statement on Contraceptives presented to the House of Commons Standing Committee on Health and Welfare, 9 September 1996," *Proceedings of the House of Commons Standing Committee on Health and Welfare*, no. 18, 11 October 1966, 576–581; (2) Canadian Catholic Conference statement on divorce presented to the Special Joint Committee of the Senate and House of

Commons on Divorce, 6 April 1967, *Proceedings of the Special Joint Committee of the Senate and House of Commons on Divorce*, no. 24, 20 April 1967, 1510–1513; (3) "Canadian Catholic Conference pastoral statement on abortion published 7 February 1969. Canadian Catholic Conference witnesses appeared before the House of Commons Standing Committee on Health and Welfare, 5 March 1968," *Proceedings of the House of Commons Standing Committee on Health and Welfare*, no. 24, 5 March 1968, 860-863. The three submissions were later published together in a booklet entitled *Contraception, Divorce, Abortion: Three Statements by Canadian Catholic Conference; Discussion Outline by Canadian Catholic Conference Family Life Bureau* (Ottawa: August 1968).

[13]   *Contraception, Divorce, Abortion*, 10, 15.

[14]   Ibid., 17.

[15]   Ibid., 19.

[16]   Ibid., 20–1.

[17]   Ibid., 23.

[18]   Ibid., 24.

[19]   For a critical assessment of the federal government's involvement in family-planning programs, see Larry D. Collins, "The Politics of Abortion: Trends in Canadian Fertility Policy," *Atlantis*, vol. 7, no. 2 (1982), 1–18.

[20]   *Hansard*, House of Commons, Canada, 4 December 1967, 5015.

[21]   *Hansard*, 4 December 1967, 5014.

[22]   *Hansard*, 23 January 1969, 4723.

[23]   Trudeau, *Memoirs*, 83.

[24]   The *Omnibus Bill* of 1969 added sub-sections 4, 5, 6, and 7 to the existing abortion laws. According to article 6(d) of Section 251 of the *Criminal Code of Canada*, a "'therapeutic abortion committee' for any hospital means a committee, comprised of not less than three members each of whom is a qualified medical practitioner, appointed by the board of that hospital for the purpose of considering and determining questions relating to terminations of pregnancy within that hospital."

[25]   *Contraception, Divorce, Abortion*, 28.

[26]   Ibid., 30.

[27]   *Hansard*, 30 April 1969, 8177, 8186; *Hansard*, 5 May 1969, 8321.

[28]   *Hansard*, 5 May 1969, 8321. Humanism is defined as "a philosophy that usually rejects supernaturalism and stresses an individual's dignity and worth and capacity for self-realization through reason." *Webster's Ninth New Collegiate Dictionary* (Markham, ON: Merriam-Webster, 1987), 586.

[29]   Margaret Trudeau, *Beyond Reason* (New York: Paddington Press, 1979), 55.

[30]   *Hansard,* 23 January 1969, 4722.

[31]   Ed Broadbent, "The Liberal Rip-off: Trudeauism vs. The Politics of Equality" (Toronto: New Press, 1970), 3.

[32]   Department of National Health and Welfare, *Review of Abortion Legislation and Experience in Selected Countries, 1970: Research and Statistics Memo* (Ottawa: May 1971), 24–25.

33 *Roe v. Wade*, 410. US. 113 (1973).

34 *Doe v. Bolton*, 410. US. 179 (1973).

35 For a biography of Dr. Henry Morgentaler, see Catherine Dunphy, *Morgentaler: A Difficult Hero* (Toronto: Random House of Canada, 1996).

36 *Morgentaler v. R.* (1974) (Que.C.A.), 319, 494.

37 En Appel d'un jugement de la cour d'appel du Québec entre Dr. Henry Morgentaler et Sa Majeste la Reine, 25 avril 1974, 11.

38 Ibid., 5; see also Bernard M. Dickens, "The Morgentaler Case: Criminal Process and Abortion Law," *Osgoode Hall Law Journal*, vol. 14, no. 2 (October 1976), 235.

39 See Collins, "The Politics of Abortion."

40 Badgley Commission, *Report on the Committee on the Operation of the Abortion Law*, Submitted to the Honourable Ron Basford, Minister of Justice and Attorney-General of Canada (Ottawa, 1977), 20, 278.

41 Badgley, 31.

42 *Letter to the Honourable Ron Basford, Federal Minister of Justice from the Honourable Marc André Bédard, Minister of Justice for Quebec*, 8 December 1976.

43 Ibid., See also *Her Majesty the Queen v. Dr. Henry Morgentaler et al*, in the Supreme Court of Ontario (Court of Appeal), Respondent's Statement of Fact and Law Relating to Paragraphs III and IV in the Notice of Motion and Cross-Appeal, 29 March 1985, 71–75.

44 Badgley, 17.

45 *Hansard*, 9 June 1978, 6228.

46 "Cardinal Carter drops opposition to rights charter," *Globe and Mail*, 3 April 1981.

47 *Hansard*, 27 November 1981, 13438.

48 *Borowski v. Attorney-General of Canada and the Minister of Finance of Canada*, Canadian Criminal Cases, 8 C.C.C. (3d), 392.

49 Ibid., 401.

50 Ibid., 407.

51 His appeal was dismissed because of the 1988 Morgentaler decision. *Borowski v. Canada*, (1989), S.C.C. (20411), p. 343.

52 See *R. V. Morgentaler et al.* (1984), in the Supreme Court of Ontario, 1670–2.

53 *R. v. Morgentaler et al.* (1988), S.C.C. (19556), 37.

54 Mollie Dunsmuir, *Bill C-43: An Act Respecting Abortion: Legislative Summary*, Law and Government Division, Research Branch, Library of Parliament, 8 November 1989, 2.

55 Dunsmuir, *C-43*, 8.

Trudeau and the Bedrooms of the Nation:
The Canadian Bishops' Involvement

1   For more details, see Bernard M. Daly, *Remembering for Tomorrow: A History of the Canadian Conference of Catholic Bishops 1943–1993* (Ottawa: Concacan, 1995), 111–126.

2   See, for example, "Submission on Behalf of the Canadian Conference of Catholic Bishops to the Parliamentary Committee on Abortion," CCCB "For Your Information" Document no.1430, 31 January 1990, CCCB Archives.

3   Mary Jo Leddy, "Why Can't the Bishops Get Across Their Message on the Abortion Issue?" *Compass*, Toronto (May/June 1992), 22.

4   Pierre Trudeau, *Memoirs* (Toronto: McClelland & Stewart, 1993), 40.

5   See J. Hamelin in *Histoire du catholicisme québécois* v. III, ed. N. Voisine (Montréal: Boréal, 1984), 139.

6   Mark R. MacGuigan, "The Political Freedom of Catholics," in *Brief to the Bishops: Canadian Catholic Laymen Speak their Minds,* ed. Paul T. Harris (Toronto/Don Mills: Information Centre/ Longmans Canada, 1965), 18–25.

7   Trudeau, *Memoirs*, 186.

8   Trudeau, *Memoirs*, 39.

9   LG, 10.

10   LG, 30.

11   LG, 33.

12   GS, 43.

13   *Apostolicam Actuositatem*, 5.

14   AA, 6.

Part V

Reflections on Faith and Politics

1   There is a sequel to this story. Almost 25 years later, John Turner had a Liberal Caucus in Mont Orford in Quebec near Saint Benoît-du-Lac. I said, "Here is my first chance to respond to the many invitations I got from the abbot, especially after the grant was approved, to come to the monastery for meditation and prayer." On Sunday morning off we went: John Turner, Raymond Garneau, Jean Le Moyne and I went to mass at Saint Benoît-du-Lac. However, the abbot was ill in the infirmary and unavailable to meet me.

2   In my legislative career (probably because I am filled with Liberal arrogance!), I thought at times I was building the kingdom by supporting legislation with considerable moral values, Christian values.

"There Is Always a Moment"

1   This reminds me of the great story of Pierre and Dennis McDermott, the late leader of the Canadian Labour Congress, who apparently met at one point. For some bizarre reason Pierre insisted on calling him Bill. If you know Dennis McDermott, he also was not entirely without ego, and so he was beside himself and he thought of everything he could do to straighten this out without actually pointing it out. So he said, "Pierre, I was talking to his Holiness the Pope the other day, and he said to me, 'Dennis, Dennis, we gotta do something about those labour unions, Dennis!'" To which Pierre, as a sport, replied, "Gee, Bill, that's an interesting story."

Discussion

1   Later in the discussion Bruce Powe noted: "The one time I mentioned to him about writing his memoirs, he said he had no interest in writing a narrative autobiography; that if he wrote one – and this was before the somewhat shallow *Memoirs* came out – he would prefer to do something along the lines of Jean-Paul Sartre's *The Words*, which is an intellectual memoir. I regret that he never did it."

PART VI

Afterword

1   Michel Vastel, *Trudeau le Québécois*, nouvelle édition (Montréal, 2000), 9–10.

2   Yves Lavertu, *Jean-Charles Harvey: Le Combattant* (Montréal, 2000), 397.

Further Reading

On Pierre Elliott Trudeau

Axworthy, Thomas S. and Pierre Elliott Trudeau, eds. *Towards a Just Society: The Trudeau Years*. Markham, ON: Viking, 1990.

Bélanger, André-J. *Ruptures et constantes: quatre idéologies du Québec en éclatement: La Relève, la JÉC, Cité libre, Parti pris*. Montréal: Hurtubise HMH, 1977.

Bergeron, Gérard. *Notre miroir à deux faces: Trudeau-Lévesque*. Montreal: Québec/Amérique, 1985.

Brimelow, Peter. *The Patriot Game: National Dreams and Political Realities*. Toronto: Key Porter, 1986.

Brunelle, Dorval. *Les trois colombes: essai*. Montréal: VLB, 1985.

Butler, Rick and Jean-Guy Carrier, eds. *The Trudeau Decade*. Toronto: Doubleday Canada, 1979.

Chambers, Stuart. "Pierre Elliott Trudeau and Bill C-150: A Rational Approach to Homosexual Acts, 1967–1969." M.A. thesis, University of Ottawa, 2002.

Christiano, Kevin J. *Pierre Elliott Trudeau: Reason Before Passion*. Toronto: ECW Press, 1994.

Clarkson, Stephen and Christina McCall. *Trudeau and Our Times*. 2 vols. Toronto: McClelland & Stewart, 1990, 1994.

Cohen, Andrew and J.L. Granatstein, eds. *Trudeau's Shadow: The Life and Legacy of Pierre Elliott Trudeau*. Toronto: Vintage Canada, 1999.

Couture, Claude. *Paddling with the Current: Pierre Elliott Trudeau, Étienne Parent, Liberalism and Nationalism in Canada*. Trans. Vivien Bosley. Edmonton: University of Alberta Press, 1998. Also issued in the French as *La loyauté d'un laïc*.

Crenna, C. David, ed. *Pierre Trudeau: Lifting the Shadow of War*. Edmonton: Hurtig, 1987.

Egerton, G. "Trudeau, God, and the Canadian Constitution: Religion, Human Rights, and Government Authority in the Making of the 1982 Constitution," in *Rethinking Church, State, and Modernity: Canada Between Europe and America*, eds. David Lyon and Marguerite van Die. Toronto: University of Toronto Press, 2000. 90–112.

Gossage, Patrick. *Close to the Charisma: My Years Between the Press and Pierre Elliott Trudeau*. Toronto: McClelland & Stewart, 1986.

Graham, Ron, ed. *The Essential Trudeau*. Toronto: McClelland & Stewart, 1998. Also issued in French as *Trudeau: l'essentiel de sa pensée politique*.

___ *One-Eyed Kings: Promise and Illusion in Canadian Politics*. Toronto: Collins, 1986.

Granatstein, J.L. and Robert Bothwell. *Pirouette: Pierre Trudeau and Canadian Foreign Policy*. Toronto: University of Toronto Press, 1990.

Griffiths, Linda. *Maggie & Pierre: A Fantasy of Love, Politics and the Media: A Play*. Vancouver: Talonbooks, 1980.

Gwyn, Richard. *The Northern Magus: Pierre Trudeau and Canadians*. Edited by Sandra Gwyn. Toronto: McClelland & Stewart, 1980.

Harbron, John D. *This Is Trudeau*. Toronto: Longmans, 1968.

Johnston, Donald, ed. *With a Bang, Not a Whimper: Pierre Trudeau Speaks Out*. Toronto: Stoddart, 1988.

Laforest, Guy. *Trudeau and the End of a Canadian Dream*. Trans. Paul Leduc Browne and Michelle Weinroth. Montreal: McGill-Queen's University Press, 1995. Translation from the French *Trudeau et la fin d'un rêve canadien*.

Laxer, James and Robert Laxer. *The Liberal Idea of Canada: Pierre Trudeau and the Question of Canada's Survival*. Toronto: J. Lorimer, 1977.

Lynch, Charles. *Our Retiring Prime Minister*. Toronto: McClelland & Stewart/ Bantam, 1983.

McDonald, Kenneth. *His Pride, Our Fall: Recovering from the Trudeau Revolution*. Toronto: Key Porter Books, 1995.

McIlroy, Thad, ed. *A Rose Is a Rose: A Tribute to Pierre Elliott Trudeau in Cartoons and Quotes*. Toronto: Doubleday, 1984.

McRoberts, Kenneth. *Misconceiving Canada: The Struggle for National Unity.* Toronto: Oxford, 1997.

Our Last Farewell: Pierre Elliott Trudeau 1919–2000. Toronto: McClelland and Stewart, 2000.

Peterson, Roy. *Drawn & Quartered: The Trudeau Years.* Toronto: Key Porter Books, 1984.

Powe, B.W. *The Solitary Outlaw: Trudeau, Gould, McLuhan.* Toronto: Key Porter, 2002.

Radwanski, George. *Trudeau.* Toronto: Macmillan of Canada, 1978.

Simpson, Jeffrey. *Discipline of Power: The Conservative Interlude and the Liberal Restoration.* Toronto: Macmillan of Canada, 1984.

Smith, Denis. *Bleeding Hearts, Bleeding Country.* Edmonton: Hurtig, 1971.

Somerville, David. *Trudeau Revealed: By His Actions and Words.* Scarborough: BMG, 1978.

Stewart, Walter. *Shrug: Trudeau in Power.* Toronto: New Press, 1971.

Stuebing, Douglas et al. *Trudeau: A Man for Tomorrow.* Toronto: Clarke, Irwin & Co., 1968.

Trudeau: The Life, Times and Passing of Pierre Elliott Trudeau. Toronto: Key Porter, 2000.

Trudeau Albums. Toronto: Penguin Studio, 2000.

Trudeau, Margaret. *Beyond Reason.* New York: Paddington Press, 1979.

Trudeau, Pierre Elliott. *Against the Current: Selected Writings 1939–1996.* Toronto: McClelland & Stewart, 1996.

___ ed. *The Asbestos Strike.* Trans. James Boake. Toronto: James, Lewis and Samuel, 1974.

___ *A Canadian Charter of Human Rights.* Ottawa: Queen's Printer, 1968.

___ *Conversations with Canadians.* Toronto: University of Toronto Press, 1972.

___ "De l'inconvénient d'être catholique," *Cité libre* 35 (March 1961), 20–21.

___ *Federalism and the French Canadians.* Toronto: Macmillan of Canada, 1968.

___ *Memoirs.* Toronto: McClelland & Stewart, 1993. Also issued in French as *Mémoires politiques.*

___ "Note sur le parti cléricaliste," *Cité libre* 38 (June/July 1961), 23.

Vastel, Michel. *The Outsider: The Life of Pierre Elliott Trudeau*. Toronto: Macmillan of Canada, 1990. Translation from the French of *Trudeau, Le Québécois*.

Westell, Anthony. *Paradox: Trudeau as Prime Minister*. Scarborough, ON: Prentice-Hall, 1972.

Zink, Lubor. *Trudeaucracy*. Toronto: Toronto Sun Publishing, 1972.

Zolf, Larry. *Just Watch Me: Remembering Pierre Trudeau*. Toronto: Lorimer, 1984.

On the Catholic Church and Faith in Canadian Public Life

Abbott, Walter M., S.J. *The Documents of Vatican II*. Piscataway, NJ: New Century, 1966.

Audet, L.-P. *Histoire de l'enseignement au Québec 1840-1971*. 2 vols. Montréal: Holt, Rinehart and Winston, 1971.

Baum, Gregory. *The Church in Quebec*. Ottawa: Novalis, 1991.

Bibby, Reginald. *Fragmented Gods: The Poverty and Potential of Religion in Canada*. Toronto: Irwin, 1987.

Carter, Gerald Emmett. *The Catholic Public Schools of Quebec*. Toronto: W.J. Gage, 1957.

Caulier, Brigitte, dir. *Religion, sécularisation, modernité: les expériences francophones en Amérique du Nord*. Sainte-Foy: Presses de l'Université Laval, 1996.

Clément, G. *Histoire de l'Action catholique au Canada français*. Montréal: Fides, 1972.

Congar, Yves. *Lay People in the Church*. London: Geoffrey Chapman, 1985.

Croteau, Georges. *Les frères éducateurs, 1920–1965: promotion des études supérieures, modernisation de l'enseignement public*. LaSalle, QC: Hurtubise HMH, 1996.

Cuneo, Michael W. *Catholics Against the Church: Anti-Abortion Protest in Toronto, 1969-1985*. Toronto: University of Toronto Press, 1989.

Daly, Bernard M. *Remembering for Tomorrow: A History of the Canadian Catholic Conference of Bishops 1943–1993*. Ottawa: Concacan, 1995.

Di Giovanni, Caroline, ed. *The Philosophy of Catholic Education*. Ottawa: Novalis, 1992.

Fay, Terence J. *A History of Canadian Catholics: Gallicanism, Romanism, and Canadianism*. Montreal & Kingston: McGill-Queen's University Press, 2002.

Fox, Thomas C. *Sexuality and Catholicism*. New York: George Braziller, 1995.

Gould, Jean. *Des bons pères aux experts: les élites catholiques et la modernisation du système scolaire au Québec, 1940–1964*. Thèse (M.A.), Université Laval, 1999.

Graham, Ron. *God's Dominion: A Sceptic's Quest*. Toronto: McClelland & Stewart, 1990.

Grail: An Ecumenical Journal.

Gremilion, Joseph. *The Gospel of Peace and Justice: Catholic Society Teaching Since Pope John*. New York: Orbis, 1976.

Guindon, Hubert. *Quebec Society: Tradition, Modernity, and Nationhood*. Toronto: University of Toronto Press, 1988.

Hellman, John. *Emmanuel Mounier and the New Catholic Left, 1930–1950*. Toronto: University of Toronto Press, 1981.

Hertel, François. *Pour un ordre personnaliste*. Montréal: l'Arbre, 1942.

Higgins, Michael W. *The Muted Voice: Religion and the Media*. Ottawa: Novalis, 2000.

Higgins, Michael W. and Douglas R. Letson. *My Father's Business: A Biography of His Eminence G. Emmett Cardinal Carter*. Toronto: Macmillan, 1990.

____ *Portraits of Canadian Catholicism*. Toronto: Griffin House, 1986.

____ *Power and Peril: The Catholic Church at the Crossroads*. Toronto: HarperCollins, 2002.

____ *Women and the Church: A Sourcebook*. Toronto: Griffin House, 1986.

Higgins, Michael W. et al. *Catholic Education: Transforming Our World: A Canadian Perspective*. Ottawa: Novalis, 1991.

Lefebvre, Solange. *Religion et identités dans l'école québécoise: comment clarifier les enjeux*. Saint-Laurent, QC: Fides, 2000.

____ entrevue avec Jacques Grand'Maison. *Le défi des générations*. Sillery, QC: Revue Notre-Dame no 11, 1997.

Letson, Douglas R. and Michael W. Higgins. *The Jesuit Mystique*. Toronto: Macmillan, 1995.

Lévesque, Georges-Henri. « Le droit à l'éducation, » *Revue Dominicaine* (July/August 1958), 1–8.

Lyon, David and Marguerite van Die, eds. *Rethinking Church, State, and Modernity: Canada between Europe and America.* Toronto: University of Toronto Press, 2000.

Menendez, Albert J. *Church and State in Canada.* Amherst, NY: Prometheus Books, 1996.

Meunier, E.-Martin et Jean-Philippe Warren. *Sortir de la grande noirceur: l'horizon personnaliste de la Révolution tranquille.* Sillery, QC: Septentrion, 2002.

Mounier, Emmanuel. *Le personnalisme,* 17e éd. Paris: Presses universitaires de France, 1949 [2001].

Paul VI. *Of Human Life: Humanae Vitae.* Boston: St. Paul's Books & Media, 1968.

Pelletier, Gérard. "D'un proletariat spiritual," *Esprit* 20 (August/September 1952), 190–200.

Routhier, Gilles. *L'Église canadienne et Vatican II.* Saint-Laurent, QC: Fides, 1997.

Routhier, Gilles et Jean-Philippe Warren, dir. *Les Visages de la foi: figures marquantes du catholicisme québécois.* Saint-Laurent, QC: Fides, 2003.

Ryan, Claude. "L'Eglise Catholique et l'évolution spirituelle du Canada français," *Chronique sociale de France* 65 (15 September 1957), 443–57.

Seljak, David. "Why the Quiet Revolution was 'Quiet': The Catholic Church's Reaction to Secularization of Quebec after 1960," Canadian Catholic Historical Association *Historical Studies* 62 (1996), 109–24.

Sheridan, E.F., ed. *Love Kindness! The Social Teaching of the Canadian Catholic Bishops.* Toronto: Jesuit Centre for Social Faith and Justice, 1991.

Turcotte, Paul-André. *L'enseignement secondaire public des frères éducateurs, 1920–1970: utopie et modernité.* Montréal: Éditions Bellarmin, 1988.

Van Die, Margeurite, ed. *Religion and Public Life in Canada: Historical and Contemporary Perspectives.* Toronto: University of Toronto Press, 2001.

Voisine, Nive. *Histoire du catholicisme québécois.* Montréal: Boréal express, 1984.

On the Times

Astor, Howard and Tom Axworthy. *Searching for the New Liberalism: Perspectives, Policies, Prospects.* Oakville, ON: Mosaic Press, 2002.

Behiels, Michael D. *Prelude to Quebec's Quiet Revolution: Liberalism versus Neo-nationalism, 1945–1960.* Montreal and Kingston: McGill-Queen's University Press, 1985.

Black, Conrad. *Duplessis.* Toronto: McClelland and Stewart, 1977.

Bliss, Michael. *Right Honourable Men: The Descent of Canadian Politics from Macdonald to Chrétien.* Toronto: HarperPerennial Canada, 2004.

Bothwell, Robert, Ian Drummond, and John English. *Canada Since 1945*, rev. ed. Toronto: University of Toronto Press, 1989.

Cahill, Jack. *John Turner: The Long Run.* Toronto: McClelland and Stewart, 1984.

Coleman, William D. *The Independence Movement in Quebec, 1945–80.* Toronto: University of Toronto Press, 1984.

Cook, Ramsay, ed. *French Canadian Nationalism.* Toronto: Macmillan, 1969.

Gwyn, Richard J. *Nationalism Without Walls: The Unbearable Lightness of Being Canadian.* Toronto: McClelland & Stewart, 1996.

Lackenbauer, P. Whitney, ed. *An Inside Look at External Affairs During the Trudeau Years: The Memoirs of Mark MacGuigan.* Calgary: University of Calgary Press, 2002.

Leduc, Diane. *Notes on Bill C-150 – The Omnibus Bill.* Ottawa: Library of Parliament (Parliamentary Research Branch) 23 Nov. 2001. Press clippings.

MacDougall, Bruce. *Queer Judgments: Homosexuality, Expression, and the Courts in Canada.* Toronto: University of Toronto Press, 2000.

McCall-Newman, Christina. *Grits: An Intimate Portrait of the Liberal Party.* Toronto: Macmillan of Canada, 1982.

McRoberts, Kenneth. *Quebec: Social Change and Political Crisis*, 3rd ed. Toronto: McClelland and Stewart, 1993.

McWhinney, Edward. *Canada and the Constitution, 1979–1982: Patriation and the Charter of Rights.* Toronto: University of Toronto Press, 1981.

———. *Quebec and the Constitution, 1960–1978.* Toronto: Lorimer, 1978.

Ogilvie, M.H. *Religious Institutions and the Law in Canada.* Toronto: Irwin Law, 2003.

Pelletier, Gérard. *Years of Choice: 1960–1968*. Trans. Alan Brown. Toronto: Methuen, 1987.

———. *Years of Impatience: 1950–1960*. Trans. Alan Brown. Toronto: Methuen, 1984.

Romanow, Roy, John Whyte, and Howard Leeson. *Canada Notwithstanding: The Making of the Constitution, 1976–1982*. Toronto: Carswell/Methuen, 1984.

Rotstein, Abraham, ed. *Power Corrupted: The October Crisis and the Repression of Quebec*. Toronto: New Press, 1971.

Sheppard, Robert and Michael Valpy. *The National Deal: The Fight for a Canadian Constitution*. Toronto: Fleet, 1982.

Smith, Miriam. *Lesbian and Gay Rights in Canada: Social Movements and Equality Seeking, 1971–1995*. Toronto: University of Toronto Press, 1999.

Snider, Norman. *The Changing of the Guard: How the Liberals Fell from Grace and the Tories Rose to Power*. Toronto: Lester and Orpen Dennys, 1985.

Trofimenkoff, Susan Mann. *The Dream of Nation: A Social and Intellectual History of Quebec*. Toronto: Gage, 1983.

Wearing, Joseph. *The L-Shaped Party: The Liberal Party of Canada, 1958–1980*. Toronto: McGraw-Hill, 1981.

Contributors

Thomas S. Axworthy was Pierre Trudeau's principal secretary from 1981 to 1984, and is an Officer of the Order of Canada. He has written and edited several books, including *Our American Cousins*; *Towards a Just Society: The Trudeau Years*; and *Searching for the New Liberalism: Perspectives, Policies, Prospects*. He is executive director of the Historica Foundation of Canada, an adjunct lecturer at the John F. Kennedy School of Government at Harvard University, and chairman of the Asia Pacific Foundation of Canada.

Stephen Clarkson is a professor of political economy at the University of Toronto and co-author (with his wife, Christina McCall) of the award-winning two-volume biography *Trudeau and Our Times*. He has authored numerous other books and articles, including *Canada and the Reagan Challenge* and *Uncle Sam and Us*. His current research focuses on the impact of globalization and trade liberalization on the Canadian and continental states.

Bernard M. Daly is retired from thirty-three years of varied work with the Canadian Conference of Catholic Bishops, a career that began in 1958. He was editor and publisher of *The Catholic Register* from 1993 to 1996. He is the author of *Beyond Secrecy: The Untold Story of Canada and the Second Vatican Council* and *Remembering for Tomorrow: A History of the Canadian Conference of Catholic Bishops 1943–1993*; he co-authored (with Mae Daly and Bishop Remi De Roo) *Even Greater Things: Hope and Challenge after Vatican II*.

John English is a professor of history and political science at the University of Waterloo, and executive director of the Centre for International Governance Innovation in Waterloo. He has written the definitive biography of Lester B. Pearson, and is currently writing the official biography of Pierre Elliott Trudeau. Professor English was a member of parliament from 1993 to 1997 and served as parliamentary secretary for the minister of intergovernmental affairs and president of the privy council. His many publications have won numerous awards, and he is a Member of the Order of Canada and a fellow of the Royal Society of Canada.

John Godfrey has been a Liberal member of Parliament since 1993, and has chaired several committees and served as parliamentary secretary to a number of ministers. Prior to his parliamentary career, he was a professor of history for seventeen years at Dalhousie University, serving as president of the University of King's College, Halifax, for ten of those years. He was editor of *The Financial Post* from 1987 to 1991 and vice-president of the Canadian Institute for Advanced Research prior to his election.

Ron Graham is a political commentator, editor, and award-winning author who has written extensively for *Saturday Night, The Globe and Mail, The New York Times, Maclean's, Report on Business Magazine, Canadian Art* and *Toronto Life*. His books include *One-Eyed Kings; God's Dominion: A Sceptic's Quest; The French Quarter;* and *All The King's Horses: Politics Among the Ruins*. He hosted and narrated *God's Dominion,* a CBC documentary series, and conducted the English-language interviews for the television memoirs of Pierre Trudeau. Mr. Graham also edited *Straight from the Heart* by Jean Chretien and *The Essential Trudeau* by Pierre Trudeau.

Richard Gwyn has been an award-winning columnist with the *Toronto Star* since 1973, examining both national and international affairs. His books include *Northern Magus: Pierre Trudeau and Canadians; Smallwood: The Unlikely Revolutionary; Canada the 49th Paradox;* and *Nationalism Without Walls: The Unbearable Lightness of Being Canadian*. He appears weekly on TVO's *Studio Two* and *Diplomatic Immunity*, is a frequent commentator for the CBC, and serves as the chancellor of St. Jerome's University in the University of Waterloo. He was appointed to the Order of Canada in 2002.

Michael W. Higgins is president and vice-chancellor of St. Jerome's University. He has authored several books, including *The Jesuit Mystique; My Father's Business: A Biography of His Eminence Gerald Emmett Cardinal Carter; Power and Peril: The Catholic Church at the Crossroads;* and *The Muted Voice: Religion and the Media*. He is a columnist for several newspapers on the media, religious affairs, and Catholicism, and has written and narrated more than fifty scripts for the CBC's *Ideas* series.

P. Whitney Lackenbauer is assistant professor of history at St. Jerome's University. He is the editor of *An Inside Look at External Affairs During the Trudeau Years: The Memoirs of Mark MacGuigan* and co-editor (with John English and Kenneth McLaughlin) of *Mackenzie King: Citizenship and Community.*

The Honourable Otto Lang was a professor and dean of law at the University of Saskatchewan for twelve years before being elected to Parliament in 1968. He served in Pierre Trudeau's government as a minister for eleven years, including appointments as acting minister of energy, minister of manpower and immigration, minister of justice, and minister of transport, with responsibility for the Canadian Wheat Board. He is presently senior counsel for GPC International.

Solange Lefebvre is professor of theology and director, Centre d'étude des religions, at the Université de Montréal. She has published numerous books and articles on Quebec society and religion, including *Identités et religions dans l'école québécoise*; *Comment clarifier les enjeux*; *Sécularité et instituts séculiers*; and a multi-volume research project on generations in Quebec. She is currently exploring the relations between young adults and seniors and writing a book on Christianity and secularization.

The Honourable Allan MacEachen was first elected to Parliament in 1953, after teaching economics at St. Francis Xavier University. In a twenty-six-year parliamentary career, he served as minister of labour, minister of national health and welfare, government house leader, minister of manpower and immigration, president of the privy council, secretary of state for external affairs, minister of finance, and deputy prime minister. Mr. MacEachen served as leader of the government and leader of the opposition in the Senate from 1984 to 1996.

Jacques Monet, s.j., is director of the Canadian Institute of Jesuit Studies and co-director of the Jesuit Archives, Regis College, Toronto. He has taught at the Universities of Sherbrooke, Toronto, Ottawa, and Regina and has served as research director for the governor general of Canada and as special adviser on cultural policy to the secretary of state. His books include *The Union of the Canadas*; *The Last Cannon Shot: A Study of French Canadian Nationalism*; and *The Canadian Crown*. Fr. Monet was a commentator during the CBC's coverage of the funeral of Pierre Trudeau.

Marc Nadeau holds an M.A. in history from the University of Sherbrooke, where he also completed a certificate in pastoral theology. He works as an analyst with the Privy Council in Ottawa, and is a research assistant for John English on the official biography of Pierre Elliott Trudeau.

B.W. Powe, who teaches and lectures at York University and Humber College, has been called a visionary, an iconoclast, an inventor of new genres, and a literary entrepreneur. He is the author of the novel *Outage* and several non-fiction books. He coordinated The Trudeau Era conference at York University, and his writings on Pierre Trudeau have appeared in many places. He wrote the eulogies for *The Globe and Mail* and the *Ottawa Citizen* upon the former prime minister's death in 2000.

David Seljak is associate professor of religious studies at St. Jerome's University and the director of the St. Jerome's Centre for Catholic Experience. His doctoral studies in the sociology of religion at McGill University explored religion and nationalism in Quebec from 1960 to 1980, and he has published extensively in this field. His current research includes religion and ethnicity in Canada and the teaching of religious studies in Canadian public high schools. He is the editor of *The Ecumenist: A Journal of Theology, Culture, and Society.*

Nancy Southam, an author currently residing in Montreal, was a close friend and neighbour of Pierre Trudeau's. She recently completed a master's degree in divinity and has been a commentator for *The Globe and Mail.* She is the author of *Remembering Richard*, a profile of Richard Hatfield, and has recently edited a collection of essays on Trudeau entitled *Pierre: Colleagues and Friends Talk About the Trudeau They Knew.*

Andrew Thompson is a Ph.D. candidate in history at the University of Waterloo. His dissertation research is on the impact of human rights organizations' interventions at the Supreme Court of Canada. Prior to entering the doctoral program in the fall of 2000, he was the interim media officer for Amnesty International in Ottawa.

The Right Honourable John Napier Turner was first elected to the House of Commons in 1962, and he held several cabinet positions, including minister of justice, attorney general of Canada, and minister of finance, until his resignation from Parliament in 1976. The Liberal Party of Canada elected him as leader in June 1984 and he was sworn in as the seventeenth prime minister of Canada that month. From September 1984 to February 1990, Mr. Turner served as leader of the opposition before resigning to become a partner in the Toronto law firm of Miller Thomson. In 1995, he was appointed a Companion of the Order of Canada.

Michael Valpy writes about religion and ethics for *The Globe and Mail*, and has been a member of its editorial board, its national political columnist, Africa correspondent, deputy managing editor, and national columnist on social policy and urban issues. He is co-author of two books on the constitution: *The National Deal* and *To Match a Dream*. He has produced public affairs documentaries for CBC Radio, and has won three National Newspaper Awards.

Jean-Philippe Warren is professor at the department of sociology and anthropology at Concordia University in Montreal. He has published several books, including *Un Supplément d'âme: Les intentions primordiales de Fernand Dumont*; *L'Engagement sociologique: La tradition sociologique du Québec francophone*; *Les Visages de la foi: Figures marquantes du catholicisme québécois* (with Gilles Routhier); and *Sortir de la "Grande noirceur": L'horizon "Personaliste" de la Révolution tranquille* (with E.-Martin Meunier).